Revelation

What the Last Book of the Bible

Really Means

Michael W. Newman

CreateSpace Publishing (an Amazon.com company)
Seattle, Washington

Dedication

To Jim and the men's morning Bible class members who urged me (really, pestered me!) to write this book. I am grateful for your persistent encouragement.

To the Sunday ABC Class participants who let me teach on the book of Revelation and kept attending the class! Thank you for your faithfulness and desire to dig deeper into God's wonderful Word.

Contents

Preface

Preface

The Texas State History Museum is located in the heart of Austin, Texas. It is a towering structure—fairly new for a museum, built in the new millennium. The unique feature of the museum, in my opinion, is the layout. Visitors begin on the bottom floor and spiral around the displays until they reach the top floor. From Texas pre-history and relics on floor number one to Texas modern accomplishments and space travel on floor number three. From the bottom, through spiraling displays of history, movements, business, faith, and geography, up winding staircases to the top. From the earth to the stars. Then the journey is complete. Once you reach the pinnacle, you can look over the third floor railing into the museum entry area. The floor of the entry which appeared to be a swirl of randomly colored tiles is now revealed as a mosaic of Texas life and lore. The complete story is displayed before you.

So it is with the book of Revelation. It is a spiraling sojourn through the images of life's reality. From sin and sadness to grace and victory. From captivity and hopelessness to freedom and joy. From the woes of the corrupted earth to the splendor of the new creation. From death to life. From hell to heaven. And once the journey is complete, you look at the heavenly mural and see the whole story.

The book I've written doesn't have all the answers. It is not a comprehensive commentary. But it will, I pray, guide you as you take the incredible journey through the book of Revelation. While we will never fully understand everything in this final book of the Bible, God rejoices that His wild and wonderful vision keeps us engaged with and interested in His revealed Word. Revelation compels us to wrestle with God and with the deepest questions of life.

For your added information and growth, the verses of each chapter of Revelation are based on my translation of the original Greek language. I've tried to make the translation somewhat smooth for reading in English, but kept it a little raw so you can get a sense of the original flow and vocabulary. You'll notice run-on sentences that increase the intensity of the vision and recall Scriptural Hebrew narrative. This Hebrew style was familiar to the listeners of the book. It communicates truth, facts, the real deal. You can use another English translation for comparison and further clarity. I've used the New International Version when I make reference to verses within the chapters of this book.

Are you ready for the adventure? If you think you have God all figured out, if you are convinced that God's Word is boring or that you know it all, think again. When you follow Jesus, around every corner is something new—new insight, new understanding, new ideas, new challenges, new blessings. The book of Revelation captures that wild ride of life in Christ. Strap yourself in and enjoy your journey through the book of Revelation.

Michael W. Newman

Revelation
Chapter One

t

R evelation. Say the word and people tremble. Theologians scratch their heads. Pastors recoil in fear. Bible teachers mumble with confusion or spout frightening tales of global chaos. Mothers pull their small children off the streets. You may say, "I've always been interested in studying the book of Revelation, but it's too confusing and too scary. I've given up trying to understand it."

But hold on for just a minute. Did God make a mistake when He included the book of Revelation in the Bible? Was He having an "off day" when He decided to conclude the Scriptures with this visionary writing? Was this a heavenly quality control error?

The Bible says in 2 Timothy 3:16, *"All Scripture is God-breathed and is useful for teaching, rebuking, correcting and training in righteousness."* Is there an asterisk by that verse that points us to a note at the bottom of the page: "except for Revelation"?

You may feel that way at times, but the answer to all those questions is a resounding "NO!" Believe it or not, Revelation is one of the most practical, meaningful, and life-impacting books of the Bible. It was designed to be a believer's lifeline during the wait for Jesus' second coming. It arrived as the surprising grace of God in the midst of persecution and suffering. It was the cool drink of life-giving water in the middle of the desert of adversity, pain, and doubt. It was the trustworthy Word of God as the voices of the world broke the spirit of believers and cast a pall of doubt, depression, and despair over the hearts and minds of God's people.

In other words, it's good stuff—then and now.

The book of Revelation begins:

1The revelation of Jesus Christ, which God gave him to show his servants what is necessary to happen soon, and He made it known by sending his angel to his servant John, 2who bore witness to the word of God and the testimony of Jesus Christ, which he saw.

The word "Revelation" in the Greek language is a word you've probably heard before. It is "apocalypse." It means "to reveal" or "to uncover"—especially revealing or uncovering something about God. This word was used many times in the New Testament before the book of Revelation came on the scene. Christians who read the apostles' Biblical writings heard the term used often. For example, 1 Corinthians 1:7 says, *"Therefore you do not lack any spiritual gift as you eagerly wait for our Lord Jesus Christ to be **revealed**."* Believers were eager for the revelation to come. 2 Thessalonians 1:6-7 addresses the trouble of the world and how the revelation of Jesus will be the solution: *"God is just: He will pay back trouble to those who trouble* *you and give relief to you who are troubled, and to us as well. This will happen when the Lord Jesus is **revealed** from heaven in blazing fire with his powerful angels."*

In 1 Peter 1:7 we hear, *"These* (trials) *have come so that your faith—of greater worth than gold, which perishes even though refined by fire—may be proved genuine and may result in praise, glory and honor when Jesus Christ is **revealed**."* There it is again.

Did you notice the trend? The revelation of Jesus Christ is intimately connected with the answer to suffering. It is a word that describes the long-awaited return of Jesus, a return that brings relief and help to believers who are enduring trial. When first-century believers heard the word "apocalypse" they associated it with the helpful visible intervention of Jesus for sufferers.

WHAT WAS GOD DOING IN REVELATION?

At end of the first century, believers in Christ were experiencing trial, heartache, fear, and uncertainty. The Emperor Domitian ruled the Roman Empire. Domitian was a cruel and egocentric despot. Even the upper echelon of Roman citizens considered their emperor a tyrant. In addition to his forceful efforts to expand his presence in Asia Minor, Domitian insisted on being called "Master and God." Christians were trouble to this cruel ruler. He deprived them of resources and protection. He put them in prison. He even had some killed. Some believers in Christ were used as human torches at the emperor's parties. Life was at a low point for Christians during this time in history.

In addition to pressure and mistreatment from Rome, Christians were also being persecuted by the Jewish community. The pressure was on to inject the Jewish legal system back into Christian faith and practice. Believers in Jesus began to doubt the course they were on. Christians were hurting. They were confused and troubled. They were frightened and disoriented. Life was tough.

Does that sound familiar to you? How many times have you said to yourself, "If only Jesus would speak to me and show me the way;" "If only God would appear and let me know He cares;" "If only I could have a lightning bolt from heaven just to know that God is listening"?

In the book of Revelation God was responding to His people. He was stepping up, speaking up, showing Himself, and breaking into the lives of His loved ones. This wasn't unusual. Do you remember God's response to the enslaved people of Israel? God spoke compassionate words in Exodus 3:7-8: *"I have indeed seen the misery of my people in Egypt. I have heard them crying out because of their slave drivers, and I am concerned about their suffering. So I have come down to rescue them from the hand of the Egyptians."* God came down! He heard the cries of His people and He responded in a remarkable and miraculous way. At the end of the first century God did the same thing. He came down to His people to show them that their lives were more than just trial and tribulation. Jesus was alive. God was at work. The Lord was still on His throne.

This is a message you and I need every day. We need to know we're not alone. We need to know that our faith and our lives are not in vain. We need to be encouraged not to give up. We need to know that God is in control and that He hears our cries. He comes down to help.

That's why I think Revelation is one of the most practical and important books of the Bible. God was up to something special when He gave this vision to John.

KEY CHARACTERISTICS OF REVELATION

3Blessed is the one who reads in public worship and the ones who hear the words of the prophecy and keep the things written in it, for the time is near. 4John, to the seven churches in Asia: Grace to you and peace from the one who is and the one who was and the one who is coming, and from the seven spirits before his throne,

This Biblical writing is a prophecy. Prophecy looks to the future, but first it is an understandable message for the people of that period in time. This vision was not designed to be a twenty-first century puzzle meant to tell us the details of the rise and fall of the latest despot. The words of this vision were not meant to give us the latest scoop about UFO's, UPC symbols, or the development of the Internet and the European Union. This is a Biblical, prophetic message. Prophecies convey God's Word to the listeners of the day. They also bring all readers the message of salvation—ultimately connected to Christ and the cross. In addition, a prophetic message communicates the glory and hope of God's eternal kingdom—what is to come.

The book of Revelation was also communicated to a very distinctive person: the Apostle John. Just think about how wise God was to use John to bring this message to the churches. In an era of doubt, what living person would be most qualified to vouch for Jesus' identity? Someone who walked the earth with Him! Someone who spoke to Him and saw Him perform miracles. Someone who witnessed the transfiguration, crucifixion, resurrection and ascension! If anyone knew Jesus it was John. God picked a perfect messenger.

What key components were part of this Revelation message?

First, this revealed Word from God is filled with **symbolic numbers**. Verse four mentions the "seven spirits" before God's throne. Those seven spirits may refer to the perfect nature of the Holy Spirit who is present everywhere. What's important to understand is that this is a Hebrew book of the Bible. It is Eastern in thought and expression. Numbers were important to the Hebrews. Each number told a story of God's work in the world. Numbers were not random "good-luck" or "bad-luck" symbols. The numbers in Revelation point to God's action for and with His people in history.

For example, the number seven directs us to the most famous seven in the history of God's work: His complete creation of all things and His rest on the seventh day. The number seven always tells the story of completion and perfection—God's creation reflected His nature.

More number stories include:

2 – Two tablets of the Law
3 – The Holy God: Father, Son and Holy Spirit
3½ - Half of seven, not yet complete, in-between
4 – The earth (four corners), everything, YHWH
5 – The Law, books of Moses
6 – Short of perfection
8 – The day of circumcision and sacrifice, dedication back to God
10 – Wholeness, completeness (7 plus 3)
12 – God's people, 12 tribes and apostles, the church
40 – The time in the wilderness, the completion of a season of God's plan

Multiples of these numbers have significance. We'll encounter 10 x 10 x10 = 1000. We'll come across 12 x 12 x 1000 = 144,000. The story of each number crescendos as it is multiplied. But the story must be remembered. These numbers are not meant to be twisted into random numeric codes that are applied to whatever our imaginations might come up with. The numbers are rooted in the Word of God, in His miraculous and saving action for His people throughout history.

Second, this prophecy was **spoken to sufferers**. As I mentioned before, the Roman Empire and others were putting the pressure on believers in Christ. Verse five says:

5and from Jesus Christ, the faithful witness, the firstborn of the dead and the ruler of the kings of the earth. To the one who loves us and freed us from our sins by his blood,

The titles of Jesus in this verse are in direct opposition to Rome's emperor worship and multiple deities. Rome's pantheon of gods is "shot down" several times in the book of Revelation. The Roman goddess Fortuna was also called "the firstborn." Christians were being given a clear message: Jesus Christ is the true God! It was time for a reality check. Jesus paid the price. He won the victory. The kings of the earth must bow to Him. And, He loves us.

Not long ago I was listening to a Bible class leader describe the main point of the book of Revelation. This leader had no advanced academic degrees. He hadn't written any books. He was an ordinary guy who drove a Harley and wore cowboy boots. His summary of Revelation, however, was brilliant. What was Revelation all about? It tells believers in Christ that "Everything's going to be okay."

That's a message every sufferer needs to hear. Look at how verses six through eight describe the decisive rule, the certain coming, the complete justice, and the everlasting nature of the real king:

6and made us a kingdom, priests to God and his Father—to him glory and power into eternity! Amen. 7Look, he is coming with the clouds, and every eye will see him, even those who pierced him, and all the tribes of the earth will mourn because of him. Yes, amen. 8"I am the Alpha and the Omega," says the Lord God, "the one who is and the one who was and the one who is coming, the Almighty."

The word "Almighty" is one we'll run across several times in the book of Revelation. It is the Greek word "pantocrator," "ruler of all things." It is a word that the Bible uses only in the book of Revelation. It became a lifeline for the suffering church. When you ask the question, "Is God still in control?", the word "pantocrator" gives the answer. Yes, the Lord God reigns! Yes, He is on His throne! Everything around you and in you may appear to be crumbling, but God is still mighty to save.

This word became a key term in the Eastern Orthodox faith. Pantocrator became a hope-filled description of God. It was faith support for weary believers supplied by the beautiful book of Revelation.

A third characteristic of Revelation is that it is **Scripture saturated**. When I think of books of the Bible that quote other books of the Bible, I think of the Gospel of Matthew. Over and over again, the Gospel writer says, *"All this took place to fulfill what the Lord had said through the prophet…"* Then he goes on to quote a verse from the Old Testament. Throughout the Old and New Testaments you can find references to other portions of the Bible. It's a beautiful practice that reinforces the consistent message of the Bible. It also shows us how to interpret the Bible: by using the Bible itself. The principle is called "Scripture interprets Scripture."

The book of Revelation is not simply a book of the Bible that quotes other Scripture references. Revelation is a saturated Scripture sponge, dripping Bible phrases, verses and historical accounts. For the Scripture savvy listeners of the first century, Revelation sent hearers into the fullness, heart and meaning of God's revealed Word.

And why wouldn't it? Revelation is God's REVELATION to His people. The manner in which God revealed Himself throughout the ages naturally pops up everywhere in this grand finale book of the Bible.

A wonderful example happens in chapter 1:

**9**I, John, your brother and sharer in the trouble and kingdom and patient endurance in Jesus, was on the island called Patmos because of the word of God and the testimony of Jesus. **10**I was in the Spirit on the Lord's Day, and I heard behind me a loud voice like a trumpet **11**saying: "What you see write in a book and send to the seven churches, to Ephesus and to Smyrna and to Pergamum and to Thyatira and to Sardis and to Philadelphia and to Laodicea."

**12**I turned around to see the voice that was speaking with me; and after turning I saw seven golden lampstands, **13**and in the midst of the lampstands one like a son of man, wearing a long robe and wrapped around his chest a gold belt; **14**also his head and hair were white like shining wool, like snow, and his eyes were like flames of fire, **15**and his feet were like bronze refined in a furnace, and his voice like the noise of many waters, **16**and having in his right hand seven stars, and from his mouth is coming a sharp double-edged sword, and His face is like the sun shining in its power.

**17**When I saw him, I fell at his feet as dead; and he placed his right hand on me saying: "Do not be afraid; I am the first and the last,"

These verses give the details of the who, what, when, where, why, and how of Revelation. The Apostle John was in captivity on the island of Patmos off the coast of Asia Minor. Jesus appeared to him one Sunday to give him a message for the churches—suffering and battered communities of believers.

But did you catch the Scripture saturation? If you're thinking about the book of Daniel, you're right on target. Look at the next page to see what the verses above have in common with the book of Daniel (and a splash of Isaiah tossed in).

This is how the book of Revelation works. Scripture treasures are everywhere. When you least expect it, BAM! God throws a meaningful bit of His life-changing Word your way. In this section, the first-century Hebrew hearer would remember that Daniel was also given visions by God. Daniel was also in captivity. Daniel was also discouraged over his plight in Babylon. What did God do? In addition to His faithful and miraculous acts of deliverance, God gave Daniel visions to encourage him and to tell him that all was not lost. Everything was going to be okay.

Chapter one of Revelation brought the voices of Daniel and Isaiah to burdened believers. If they happened to forget that God had been and always will be faithful, all they had to remember was Daniel, Isaiah, and the servants of God throughout the ages.

John's Vision	Old Testament Description
Vs. 13 someone "like a son of man"	**Daniel 7:13** one like a son of man
dressed in a robe reaching down to his feet	**Daniel 10:5** dressed in linen
a golden sash around his chest	with a belt of the finest gold around his waist.
Vs. 14 His head and hair were white like wool, as white as snow	**Daniel 7:9** The hair of his head was white like wool.
His eyes were like blazing fire.	**Daniel 10:6** His eyes like flaming torches,
Vs. 15 His feet were like bronze glowing in a furnace	His arms and legs like the gleam of burnished bronze,
His voice was like the sound of rushing waters.	And his voice like the sound of a multitude.
Vs. 16 Out of his mouth came a sharp, double-edged sword.	**Isaiah 49:2** He made my mouth like a sharpened sword (a prophecy of Jesus)
His face was like the sun shining in all its brilliance.	**Daniel 10:6** His face like lightning
Vs. 17 He placed his right hand on me and said, "Do not be afraid."	**Daniel 10:10-12** A hand touched me…Then he continued, "Do not be afraid…"

In addition to the comforting nature of Daniel's message, the Scripture saturation reinforces the abiding truth of Revelation. This was not a new message. This was not a changed plan. God was not rethinking His saving action throughout history. He was still doing what He had always done: reaching out to His beloved people.

This brings us to a fourth characteristic of the book of Revelation: it is **salvation centered**. Look at verse 18:

18"and I am the living one, and I was dead, and behold I am living for ever and ever, and I have the keys of death and Hades."

As you read the book of Revelation you can easily get caught up in the mystery and intrigue of this symbolic and visionary book of the Bible. Some interpreters have woven complex schemes of meaning drawn from the book. They've pinpointed judgment day, identified the beasts, and singled out technological advances as the tools of the Harlot.

But they've missed the main point. The book of Revelation has Jesus as its focus. This vision is more about God reaching the lost and caring for the found than any end-times scenario or scheme. This gracious message from the lips of Christ tells us that the Living One is still alive and that death will not prevail, for He holds the keys. Salvation in Jesus is what this book of the Bible is about.

The fifth characteristic of Revelation is that it is **self-interpreting**. More accurately, it is Christ-interpreting.

You may have said to yourself, "There is no way I can understand the book of Revelation." So, when a Bible teacher weaves a mysterious and frightening interpretation that involves nuclear warfare, the Middle East, and the Internet, you may feel defenseless. You may say, "How can I argue with that?"

Jesus shows you how. Instead of relying on personal imagination to understand the vision of Revelation, Jesus sets the course for every listener. He said,

19*"Write, therefore, what you saw and what is and what is about to happen after these things. 20The mystery of the seven stars that you saw upon my right hand, and of the seven golden lampstands: The seven stars are the angels of the seven churches, and the seven lampstands are the seven churches."*

Right off the bat Jesus tells us how to hear, read, and understand this book. This is a vision. It is full of symbols. Stars represent angels. Lampstands represent churches. Jesus shows the way. If you get too far off course, the book of Revelation will correct and remind you how to treat this precious message.

DON'T GET DISTRACTED

Garrison Keillor penned an article in which he addressed the purpose of the church. He said the point of it all is to "drench us fugitive worshippers kneeling, naked, trembling, needy, in the knowledge of grace, and when we arise and go out into [the world], the blessing follows us"

("Moment of Sunday morning grace stirs memories in Baltimore," October, 21, 2007, San Antonio Express-News).

How easy it is to get distracted from the point of the book of Revelation! Complex and confusing explanations take the place of the beautiful presence of Christ, drenching us fugitive-sinners, naked, trembling, and needy with His life-saving and soul-replenishing grace. Surgical dissection of details replaces the call to go into this world with the message of the Almighty God who fights for us and is with us always.

My prayer is that this book will help change that.

If you're approaching the book of Revelation like an engineer poring over a schematic diagram of God's eternal plan, I want to urge you to reconsider your position. The book of Revelation is a vision. It is more comparable to a painting, a mural, than it is to a set of technical drawings.

During my high school years, as I planned for a career as an architect (a plan that God changed!), I drew house plans and engineering diagrams. With those drawings you could find exact measurements and specifications to construct complex machine parts or beautiful homes. The drawings were exact, detailed, and precise. Nothing was missing. They were blueprints for specific products.

The book of Revelation is NOT that! The book of Revelation is a creative, dynamic expression of God's miraculous and gracious movements among us. It is a dramatic description of the eternal truth that lies behind what we see. It is a vision filled with joy and pain, eternal bliss and eternal terror, the noblest of human aspirations and the most despicable darkness of the human heart.

You must read Revelation, not as an engineering schematic of the end times, but as an abstract painting that captures all the nuances of sin and grace, suffering and deliverance, Satan's opposition and God's victorious action.

Picasso's painting, Guernica, depicts the Nazi German bombing of Guernica, Spain, by twenty-four bombers, on April 26, 1937 during the Spanish Civil War. In this frightening battle, hundreds of people were killed and many more were injured. The painting is on the cover of this book. Take a look at it. Do you see a precise historical recounting of the attack? Do you see a fact sheet that summarizes the statistical data of the event? No, you see more than the simple facts. Look at the painting. Do you see the pain? Do you see the fear? Do you see the violence? Do you see the glimmer of hope and justice in the middle of unspeakable horror?

You may not be able to discover all the facts about the Guernica attack through this painting, but by looking at it carefully, you have a better understanding of what really happened than any historical account could ever give. The images in the painting show the personal struggle, the emotion, the gut-wrenching impact the attack made in the consciousness of every person who lived through it. The painting captures the true essence of the event—much more powerfully and graphically than any historical narration could ever do.

So it is with the book of Revelation. It portrays the essence of the Divine drama in which we are graciously involved. It paints the dark strokes of evil, the bright colors of hope, and the splashing colors of the Godhead involved intimately in creation—in humanity. In the book of Revelation God pulls the curtain back on the invisible world and shows us what is really happening in His eternal kingdom. While you may not be able to comprehend all the symbols, the message is powerful and meaningful—one to be discussed by believers throughout the ages.

As you continue this study of the book of Revelation and are tempted to treat it as God's diagram for uncovering the mystery of the end-times, remember what it really is. Remember that it portrays God's artistically revealing images of truth that will bring you more than a diagram could ever provide. Remember it is a great and marvelous mural of a God who cares so deeply about you that He comes down to help. Remember it is God's masterpiece message for us who need so desperately to hear from Him.

Are you ready?

Study Guide for Revelation Chapter 1

1. Read Revelation 1:1-4. Discuss what you know about the Apostle John (find key moments of his life in the Bible). Why was he a good choice to be the person receiving and delivering this revelation from God?

2. This book was meant to be read aloud. How might that have shaped the way Revelation was structured?

3. Why are the titles and descriptions of the Father and Son in verses 5-8 meaningful for you today?

4. Discuss what the details of the vision of Jesus in verses 9-18 communicate to believers and unbelievers.

5. Read Revelation 1:19-20. Why, in your opinion, did God communicate this message using a vision and symbols?

6. Talk about what is most confusing or frightening to you about the book of Revelation and why.

7. What new hopes might you have for Revelation after reading this chapter?

Revelation
Chapter Two

†

The second and third chapters of Revelation give a clear, practical, and non-threatening beginning to the vision. Jesus, the awesome, white-haired, fire-eyed, sword-tongued, trumpet-voiced, one "like a son of man," from chapter 1 simply sits down and has a personal talk with seven churches.

Some of the churches were well established and had a full menu of programs. Others were small churches that were barely surviving—experiencing a constant decline in membership and feeling lousy because of it.

And in this grand vision, Jesus pauses to converse, to talk, and to sit eyeball to eyeball with His bride, the Church. He stops to take her by the hand and to have a heart to heart conversation.

Let me remind you again, if you think the book of Revelation is all about the nuclear destruction of the earth that takes place under a despotic, demon-filled world leader, you haven't paid attention to how it begins. This is a personal message to the broken, suffering, and straying. This is a family intervention. This is love in action. In each message to each church, Jesus speaks firmly at times, tears up once in a while, raises His voice on an occasion or two, and pleads for His beloved to be true, faithful and strong.

With each message He gets a glimmer in His eye of better things to come. If only. If only His people will listen. If only we will pay attention.

Let's take a look at the moving and meaningful messages to each church. We'll examine facts, mysteries and personal meaning in the words of Jesus.

EPHESUS (Modern day Efes, Turkey)

1"To the angel of the church in Ephesus write: Thus says the one who holds the seven stars in his right hand, the one who walks in the midst of the seven golden lampstands:"

As you read each message from Jesus to the churches you'll notice that they share a common form. First, there is a significant description of Jesus. Second, Jesus recognizes each church personally by making the people aware that He knows exactly what is going on in their city and in their lives. Finally, Jesus offers encouragement to stay the course of faith by giving a wonderful promise.

2"I know your deeds, your hard work and your patient endurance, and that you are not able to bear evil ones, and you tested the ones calling themselves apostles but are not, and found them false; 3you have patient endurance, and you endured on account of my name, and have not grown weary. 4Nevertheless I have against you that you have let go of your first love. 5Remember therefore from where you have fallen, and repent and do the first deeds; but if not, I am coming to you and I will remove your lampstand from its place, if you do not repent. 6Nevertheless you have this: You hate the deeds of the Nicolaitans, which I also hate. 7He who has an ear, let him hear what the Spirit says to the churches. To the one overcoming I will give him to eat from the tree of life, which is in the paradise of God."

FACTS: Ephesus was a large city dedicated to the worship of Artemis (Diana), the goddess of wild beasts and fertility. You can check out the loyalty to this goddess in Acts 19. Acts 19:23 begins the description of the hubbub Paul started with his teaching. Economic and spiritual panic resulted in a near riot. During the first century, about 225,000 people lived in Ephesus. A great deal of building development took place during Domitian's reign—including the construction of pagan temples.

MYSTERIES: One of the mysteries of this first message from Jesus is the mention of the **Nicolaitans** (vs.6). We don't know who they were, but we do know they were an enemy within the church. This group was also mentioned to the church in Pergamum (vs.15). It could have been a group that tried to mingle the sexually immoral pagan rites with Christianity. It could have been a group that attempted to mix legalism with the Gospel. We don't know. What we do know is that a key danger for early Christians was the enemy of corruption and unfaithfulness from the inside!

The tree of life is mentioned to the church in Ephesus (vs.7) and reappears in Revelation 22:2, 14, and 19. The beautiful promise of heaven is given to believers who overcome. The word for "overcome" is used throughout these messages to the churches and throughout the book of Revelation. The Greek word is "nike" (yes, like the shoe company) meaning "victory." The word emphasizes the fact that this life is a battle for our lives and souls. Life is not simply a boring routine or a quest for money or a chase after popularity. A spiritual battle is raging!

The tree of life also shows God's plan for our lives. The first appearance of the tree of life is in Genesis 2:9, planted next to the tree of the knowledge of good and evil. God's plan for these trees was fouled up when Adam and Eve ate from the tree of knowledge of good and evil. The Lord had to banish Adam and Eve from the Garden of Eden so they wouldn't eat from the tree of life prematurely and live forever in a fallen state (Genesis 3:22). The tree's mention in Revelation brings a message packed with hope for believers. God's plan would prevail after all!

MEANING: At the end of the first century, life had become very complicated for believers. They experienced pressure in business, in social life, and in their religious practices. Christians were aberrations and outcasts. They were becoming enemies of both the Jewish and Roman cultures. Christians' heads were spinning.

In addition to the pressure from the outside, temptation to water down the message of the cross of Christ—the Gospel itself, was building from the inside. Jesus pleaded with the people of Ephesus to love the right things and hate the things that are wrong, the things outside His will. Jesus stood before His beloved and redeemed people in Ephesus and cast the vision for their lives in Him. They were designed to be a lampstand—a light, not put under a bowl, but on a stand so that many would see and

30

give glory to the Father in heaven (Matthew 5:15-16). Jesus called His precious people to remember their first love and get back to the basics—the first things (vss. 4-5).

I have encountered a person who knows his first love. He works in my neighborhood. He's a trash collector. In fact, he's the happiest garbage man I've ever seen. As the garbage truck speeds through the neighborhood, he hangs onto a handle on the back of the truck, smiles at passersby, waves, and shouts "good morning!" to all. Why is he happy while so many of the people who live in the neighborhood are not? Why does joy overflow from his life while people who have jobs that don't involve trash trudge through life with scowls and groans? He has a lock on his first love.

Remember what Jesus said, *"A man's life does not consist in the abundance of his possessions" (Luke 12:15).* Life will pull you away from what is truly important. The world will try to tell you how to measure your life: with stuff, with power, with fame. In our sin we want to believe those lies. They feel good at first. But then the emptiness sets in.

No doubt, the church in Ephesus was busy. It sounds like they had a lot going on. But only sixty years removed from the resurrection of Christ, the people were distracted and stagnant. Evangelistic passion and courage had deteriorated into efforts to keep the organization going. In the book of Ephesians, the Apostle Paul let the people of the church in Ephesus know that they were one in Christ. Now they were scattered and individualistic. People in Ephesus were missing out on Jesus' love because the

Christians there weren't showing love to each other. Their first love was being lost. The thrill and passion for the One who gave His life for them was fading into the background of their selfishness, busyness and pet projects.

Devotion to your first love will naturally fade during the course of your life. Remember, you are broken and fallen. My high school cross country coach used to say, "You can't run a race on emotion." No matter how fired up you are at the beginning of a race, the fatigue, the challenges of the course, and the rigors of the race conditions will leave you weak and ready to quit. This is true in marriage, family, personal purity, and faith life. In a race you need more than emotion. You need strength.

Jesus was calling the people of Ephesus back to the strength of the Word, back to the strength of an intimate walk with their Savior, back to devotion to Him—not devotion to projects and to-do lists. Jesus calls you to that first-love life, too. This message for Ephesus is a message that strikes at the heart of our modern culture and our present day church. How are you doing with your first love? Is it time to pause, turn away from the many "loves" you've been living for, and return to Jesus who always walks with you? Is it time to assess the level of passion and commitment in your service for Christ and renew your commitment to serve Him instead of the idols and distractions dominating your life? Is it time to see again that your real source of life is the Savior who breathes life into you, holds you in His hands, and has a place for you in eternity?

SMYRNA (Modern day Izmir, Turkey)

8"And to the angel of the church in Smyrna write: Thus says the first and the last, who became dead and came back to life."

Jesus' intimate knowledge of His listeners is profound. He knew which buttons to push when He addressed the Christians in each city. It is interesting to note that Smyrna was destroyed in 580 B.C. and was rebuilt in 290 B.C. This was a city that literally died and came back to life!

9"I know your trouble and poverty, nevertheless you are rich, and the blasphemy from ones saying themselves to be Jews, and are not, but are a synagogue of Satan."

Smyrna also had a large Jewish population. Unlike Christianity, Judaism was a sanctioned religion in the Roman world. The favored Jewish population was vehemently opposed to Christians.

10"Do not fear what you are about to suffer. Behold, the devil intends to throw some of you into prison in order to test you, and you will have trouble for ten days. Be faithful to the point of death, and I will give you the crown of life."

The Greek word used for "crown" in verse ten and through most of the book of Revelation is "stephanos." It is not a crown of royalty (diadem), but an athlete's wreath for winning a competition. This victor's wreath emphasizes the spiritual battle and the victory Jesus gives His people.

11*"He who has an ear, let him hear what the Spirit says to the churches. The one overcoming will most certainly not be wronged by the second death."*

FACTS: Smyrna was a harbor city that was thriving in the first century. People from around the world streamed in and out of the city. Influences from around the world permeated the culture. This meant that temptation was at a high pitch. The hustle, bustle, and confusion caused much distraction, straying, and persecution for believers.

Polycarp, the Apostle John's student, eventually became bishop of Smyrna. Persecution continued to grow in the second century. Ultimately Polycarp was martyred by the Jews in 156 A.D.

Smyrna was a loyal Roman city with the very first temple to the goddess of Rome in it. Opposition to Christianity was very strong. Smyrna was also famous for its sporting games. The ultimate victory wreath, however, was not connected with the athletes of Smyrna. It was given to believers in Christ who were faithful even to the point of death.

MYSTERIES: Synagogue of Satan (vs.9). Jewish opposition in Smyrna was powerful. Jesus' commentary on who really was a Jew, however, is quite interesting. Though many claimed to be Jews, Jesus said they are not. Who then, are true Jews? The Bible says: *"For not all who are descended from Israel are Israel. Nor because they are his descendants are they all Abraham's children" (Romans 9:6-7).* And, *"If you belong to Christ, then you are Abraham's* *seed, and heirs according to the promise" (Galatians 3:29).* Jesus made clear that blood was not the ultimate test of being a true Jew. Belief was. Belonging to Christ was. If first century Christians were being made to feel inferior, Jesus corrected their outlook. They were His people, true chosen children of God.

Ten Days (vs.10) – This is the first appearance of the number ten in Revelation. A ten day sentence doesn't seem so severe. What could it mean? Remember, numbers tell stories. They recall the work of God in history. Ten is the number of total completion. It combines the seven days of creation with the personhood of God, the Trinity, three in one. The message here is that God is in control. There will be an end to suffering and persecution. The cross that sufferers bear may be prevailing now, but the crown of victory would come!

Second Death (vs. 11) – Already in chapter 2 we encounter an example of the self-interpretation of the book of Revelation. In Revelation 20:14 and 21:8 "the second death" is explained. It is the lake of fire, the final destruction for death, Hades, and all who persist in rebellious acts against God. What a wonderful promise from the lips of Jesus that this second death will not hurt those who walk with Him!

MEANING: Verse eleven tells believers that they will not "suffer injustice" by the second death. For a group of people who were experiencing the unfairness of life, this was a word that refreshed their souls and gave them new hope. People with power were abusing that power to crush the weak and defenseless. Jesus would balance the scales and make things right.

Are you suffering injustice? How can the scoundrel boss or abusive husband get away with their wrongs? How can the lying girl at school be popular and the truth-teller with integrity be branded a nerd? How can you be forgotten? How can God seem as if He is doing nothing in a world where children suffer and the weak are oppressed?

As you join the citizens of Smyrna in these gut-wrenching questions, Jesus speaks to you. He says that justice will prevail. Unfairness will come to an end. It's a promise. God will make things right. You can count on it. You can rest your hope in that assuring word. Your course of action is in verse ten: Be faithful even to the point of death. You will receive the crown of life.

PERGAMUM (Modern day Bergama, Turkey)

12"And to the angel of the church in Pergamum write: Thus says the one having the sharp double-edged sword."

This was a statement of ultimate power in this Roman capital in Asia. Pergamum was a key city for emperor worship. Beneath the hoopla, grandeur, and allure of this pagan allegiance was truth revealed by Jesus. Verse thirteen exposes the reality:

13"I know where you live, where the throne of Satan is, but you are holding fast to my name, and did not deny faith in me even in the days of Antipas my faithful witness, who was put to death among you, where Satan lives."

We don't know who Antipas was or how he died, but the fact this execution took place shows the gravity of the situation. It also exposes Satan's aim: to destroy followers of Christ.

14*"Nevertheless I have a few things against you: You have there ones holding on to the teaching of Balaam, who taught Balak to throw a stumbling block in front of the sons of Israel, leading to eating idol food and to committing sexual immorality."*

This is a Scripture reference to Numbers chapters 22-24 and 31:16. This renowned Biblical account involved inducing people to worship idols and commit sexual immorality with the Moabites. Numbers 25:1-2 describes how the Israelites were conducting themselves: *"While Israel was staying in Shittim, the men began to indulge in sexual immorality with Moabite women who invited them to the sacrifices to their gods. The people ate and bowed down before these gods."* The history of God's people and the enduring truths of Scripture were being brought to modern listeners for the purpose of growth and life transformation.

15*"Likewise you also have ones holding to the teaching of the Nicolaitans.* **16***Repent therefore; If not, I am coming to you quickly, and I will fight against them with the sword of my mouth.* **17***He who has an ear, let him hear what the Spirit says to the churches. To the one who overcomes I will give the hidden manna, and I will give to him a white stone, and upon the stone a new name written which no one knows except the one receiving."*

FACTS: Pergamum was a capital city of the Roman province of Asia. The name "Pergamum" and the word "parchment" are related linguistically. Parchment was invented in Pergamum, the site of a library with over 200,000 works in it. This highly developed city also was a key medical center that honored the god of healing, Asclepius.

MYSTERIES: Throne of Satan (vs.13). God pulls back every earthly shroud and reveals the spiritual truth in Revelation. This is a wonderful example of how God strips away the veneer, clears up any doubts, and tells it like it is. The Roman rule was demonic.

Antipas (vs.13) Legend has it that Antipas was roasted in a bronze bull. The persecution under Domitian was vicious. Remember, this book of the Bible was directed to believers who were undergoing brutal suffering. They were wondering where Jesus was. To hear Jesus acknowledge the death of their friend, their family member, their neighbor, was life-changing. God was not far away. He knew the details of their lives. He knew their grief. He was close, attentive, and now He was speaking up. What comfort in persecution!

Balaam and Balak (vs. 14) See Numbers 22-24 and 31:16; Balaam taught Balak to put a stumbling block before the children of Israel, leading them to compromise their integrity.

Hidden Manna (vs.17) This could very well be a reference to the rabbinic idea that Jeremiah hid a jar of manna when the temple was destroyed. That manna would reappear when Christ returned. The mention of this end-time hope might reinforce the date of the writing of the book as post-temple destruction (70 A.D.) Some scholars claim that Revelation was not written in the late first century, but before the temple was destroyed in the mid-first century. The reference in verse seventeen might indicate that the temple was already destroyed and the reappearance of Christ was expected at any time. More indications that this vision was given in the late first century will surface later in Revelation.

White Stone The white stone—a pebble for voting—may mean acquittal from sin or it might relate to the rabbinic idea that precious stones fell with the manna from heaven. The hidden name indicates a new, personal relationship with God.

MEANING: These days, as was also the case in the late first century, clarity about what is right and wrong has become muddled. Criticism over life issues, sexual morality, a Biblical worldview, and the very existence of God comes rapid fire from academia, the media, and many broken and depleted souls. The loud shouts of protest, denial and criticism create confusion for a follower of Christ. What is really true? Jesus speaks up loudly and clearly, and, with the sword of His mouth, cuts through the din of godless chatter to make the truth clear. Satan is vying for power in this world. Immorality is serious and destructive. The world is being lulled into a "fatal attraction," seduced into following what seems beautiful and appealing, but stumbling into utter destruction and horror.

The spiritual battle is serious. It's a matter of life and death. But Jesus knows the names of those who pay the price—even the ultimate price. He knows your name, too.

Notice that Jesus brings up manna. This is one of many references to the wilderness journey of the people of Israel. While the wilderness was wild, God always worked provision and restoration in it. It became a place of life. This theme will recur in later chapters. There is no doubt; the Lord is truly fighting for you. In your wilderness, He will send His provision and abundant grace.

THYATIRA (Modern day Akhisar, Turkey)

18"And to the angel of the church in Thyatira write: Thus says the Son of God,"

This title for Jesus, "the Son of God," is used only once in Revelation. Jesus uses it of Himself—a powerful testimony to His true identity and an expression that offers complete clarity about who He is for every wavering and weakened listener.

"the one having his eyes as blazing fire, and his feet like burnished bronze. 19I know your works, and your love and faith, and service and patient endurance, and that your works are more than at first."

Love and faith, service and perseverance—what a wonderful summary of the Christian life!

20"Nevertheless, I have against you that you allow the woman Jezebel, the one calling herself a prophetess. She teaches—in error—my servants to be sexually immoral, to eat idol food. 21I have given her time to repent, but she does not wish to repent of her sexual immorality."

Repentance is a major theme in the book of Revelation. Jesus lets us know that God is working hard to bring the world to repentance. As Peter said in 2 Peter 3:9, *"The Lord is not slow in keeping his promise, as some understand slowness. He is patient with you, not wanting anyone to perish, but everyone to come to repentance."*

22*"Behold, I am throwing her onto a sickbed, and the ones committing adultery with her into great suffering unless they repent from her deeds. **23**And her children I will kill in death. And all the churches will know that I am the one who searches minds and hearts, and I will give to each of you according to your deeds."*

Satan did the throwing in Revelation 2:10. Jesus shows who has the last toss in verse 22. We don't know what "a bed of suffering" is, but the phrase "kill them with death" is a possible reference to a disease. Jesus is in control no matter how dominant evil might seem. Even the phrase "I am he" is another reference to being the true God. It is the same "I am" form used both in the Old Testament (*"I am who I am."* Exodus 3:14) and New Testament (*"'I tell you the truth,' Jesus answered, 'Before Abraham was, I am.'"* John 8:58) to indicate the identity and presence of the true God. Jesus is bringing the aggressive message to doubting and defeated believers that He is truly God and is most certainly in control.

24*"But to you I say, to the remaining in Thyatira who do not have this teaching, who have not known the deep things of Satan—as they say—I am not throwing upon you another burden."*

This may be a reference to the idea that false teachings were in-depth understanding of the faith. The Gnostic gospel craze of today is a similar trend.

25"*Only hold on to what you have until I come.* **26***The one overcoming and the one obeying my works until the end, I will give to him authority over the nations,* **27***'He will shepherd them with a staff made of iron; as the earthen vessel is shattered,'*"

Verse 27 is a quote from Psalm 2:9. The rabbinical method of teaching was to state a Scriptural phrase and allow the student to recall what was around it. Psalm 2 is a powerful Messianic Psalm that declares God's victory and calls all who hear to seek refuge in Him. Jesus knew where to direct His needy and hurting followers.

28"*Even as I have received from my Father, and I will give to him the morning star.*"

More self-interpretation happens here. In Revelation 22:16 Jesus says, *"I am the Root and the Offspring of David, and the bright Morning Star."* As this prophetic vision was read aloud to the churches, some of the meaning was made clear after the listeners heard certain phrases and had them swimming around in their heads for a while. The suspense built and then—BAM!—the meaning was revealed.

29"*The one having an ear, let him listen to what the Spirit says to the churches.*"

FACTS: Thyatira was the smallest of cities addressed in these chapters, yet it had the longest letter! God's economy is not like ours. Sometimes the smallest get the most care and attention. Thyatira had many businesses and trade guilds (Acts 16:14 introduces us to Lydia). Unfortunately, this led to a lot of idolatry and immorality.

MYSTERIES: Jezebel (vs.20). Ahab's wife—see 1 Kings 19ff. The "Jezebel" in chapter 2 was following in the footsteps of an evil and pagan leader. This trouble-causing woman was an evil person inside the church who opposed God's people and led them astray.

Bed of suffering (vs.22) This could be a sick bed, a funeral bed, or a couch where people reclined for meals (perhaps a play on the pagan feasts). We're not sure, but we do know it involves suffering.

The morning star (vs. 28) Revelation 22:16 identifies the morning star as Christ himself. This gift directs the believers in Thyatira to the presence of Jesus.

MEANING: The church in Thyatira faced the challenges of conformity and compromise. To the world, the church is "weird." As a believer it is difficult to be perceived as "weird" while the world watches. You pray when others plow forward in their own power. You take time to worship while others sleep or play. You sacrifice while others amass the trappings of the world's definition of success. You speak and act with purity and integrity while the world says you should cut loose and break the rules. You hold to age old values while the world blows in the wind. You reach out to those who are suffering while the world says to "look out for number one."

Walking with Jesus is no easy thing. In addition to feeling the pressure of the world, the path of Christ is truly the road less traveled. Faith in Jesus is difficult and challenging. It is body and soul testing. The solution? Jesus directed us to Psalm 2 in this message to Thyatira. Verse four of the Psalm says, *"The One enthroned in heaven laughs"* at those who scoff at Him. When it comes to the question of staying faithful to God, all you have to do is weigh the outcome. Psalm 2 sums it up well: *"Blessed are all who take refuge in him" (vs. 12).*

Study Guide for Revelation Chapter 2

1. Read Revelation 2:1-7 and discuss how Jesus' message to Ephesus applies to your life today.

2. Read Revelation 2:8-11. Discuss how Jesus' message to Smyrna applies to your life today.

3. How are you challenged to be faithful to Jesus in your life?

4. Read Revelation 2:12-17. Discuss how Jesus' message to Pergamum applies to your life today.

5. Read Revelation 2:18-29. Discuss how Jesus' message to Thyatira applies to your life today.

6. What overall concern did Jesus have with these four churches?

7. What seems to please Jesus, and what does He desire from His people?

Revelation
Chapter Three

✝

In Genesis chapter 16 the angel of the Lord appeared to Hagar, Abram's servant, as Hagar sat dejected in the wilderness. Sarai, Abram's wife, had already jealously berated and badgered Hagar until she couldn't take it any more. Hagar left. She felt like a nobody. Unwanted. Invisible. That's when the angel of the Lord stepped in with a message about the child Hagar would bear. The angel's words do not paint a bright picture about Ishmael, Hagar's son, but the fact that God cared enough to speak to Hagar was a surprise of grace to this downtrodden woman. She was in awe that God actually noticed her. She said, "You are the God who sees me."

The God who sees me. We're imperfect. We're corrupt. We're messed up. We hurt. This world can be a confusing place. There are times we wonder if God notices what is happening. Hagar met the God who sees us. So did the people who listened to the Revelation vision. In the swirl of persecution, weakness, doubt, and corruption on the one hand, along with faithfulness, perseverance, and sacrifice on the other, God noticed. He saw.

In chapter two God saw these things:

- A church that lost its first love

- False apostles and wicked people

- Persevering believers

- Pain caused by poverty

- Afflictions by Rome

- Imprisonment

- Jewish persecution

- Martyrdom – Antipas

- Sexual immorality

- Worship of idols

- Compromising, watering down the truth

- False teaching claims of a prophetess

God saw.

Sometimes we need to know that. We need to know that God is there, close by, seeing what's going on. It doesn't necessarily solve the problems, but it lets us know that a solution is close by, that Almighty God is breathing down the neck of evil and chaos.

When Job challenged God about the issue of evil, injustice, pain, and brokenness, God didn't give a point by point answer. He just spoke. And His very voice was enough for the broken Job. God saw. He was there. Life wasn't a meaningless void—even though it seemed like it was.

The book of Revelation is not something we can understand completely. It is not a flow chart that details God's plan. It isn't a corporate report that allows us to have the inside scoop about how the future is unfolding. First and foremost, it is God breaking the silence. He sees. He notices. He cares. He speaks. He is present.

This, of course, raises more questions. Is God *just* watching? Is He standing by, doing nothing? Not according to the messages to the churches. And not according to the rest of the book of Revelation. This is where the opening chapters are so strongly connected with every chapter of the book of Revelation. God sees, but God also acts— sometimes ferociously, sometimes gently.

Some readers of the book of Revelation say that the only sensible and useful portion of the book is in chapters two and three. After all, these are practical words of correction and encouragement. These are messages to churches. We get that.

But we cannot lose sight of the fact that the struggles, warnings, and promises of chapters 2 and 3 set the stage for the rest of the vision. We must remember the reality of what was happening to real people in real churches to fully appreciate the message of the book. Revelation brings us "down to earth" before it lifts us up to heaven. It makes Jesus' message a personal one, one that opens our hearts to His heartfelt word. Before we get too cosmic and otherworldly with interpretation, Jesus opens our eyes to see our own sins, our deep needs, our persistent struggles, and our very real lives lived between earth and heaven. Let's look at the final three cities.

SARDIS (Modern day Sartmahmut, Turkey)

1"To the angel of the church in Sardis write: Thus says the one having the seven spirits of God and the seven stars. I know your works, that you have a name which is 'you live,' but you are dead."

"Thus says the one" is a phrase that sounds very much like the Old Testament prophetic declaration, "Thus says the Lord." This is a prophetic message. The first-century listeners recognized it as such. It is used with each of the churches. As with every prophetic message, Jesus pulls no punches. He speaks the hard truth.

2"Wake up and strengthen what remains which is about to die, for I have not found your deeds complete before my God. 3Remember, therefore, how you received and heard; obey and repent. If, therefore, you do not wake up, I will come like a thief, and you will not know at what hour I will come upon you. 4Nevertheless, you have a few names in Sardis which have not soiled their garments, and they walk with me in white because they are worthy."

The verb for "soiled" is related to the name "Molech," the detestable god connected with child sacrifice in the Old Testament. Some serious sin was going on.

5"The one who overcomes will thus be dressed in white garments, and I will not wipe out his name from the book of life, and I will confess his name before my Father and before
50

his angels. 6The one having an ear, let him hear what the Spirit says to the churches."

FACTS: Sardis was built on a steep hill. It seemed impregnable, but was captured twice (549 and 218 B.C.) because no guard was posted. Troops scaled the hill at night and entered unopposed. This was truly a city that fell asleep! The art of dyeing wool may have been invented in this city. The mention of being dressed in white caught the people's attention. This region also had a history of earthquakes. An earthquake destroyed Sardis and many other cities in Asia Minor in 17 A.D.

MYSTERIES: Dressed in white (vs.4). God's restored people are dressed in white robes, a symbol of purity and new life—sharing in the glory of Jesus Christ. Chapter 7 will show us a vivid picture of the white-robed people of God.

The book of life (vs. 5) This is similar to Daniel 12:1, *"At that time your people--everyone whose name is found written in the book--will be delivered."* Salvation is not a forgotten fact. It has been recorded in God's book of life. The cross brought certain rescue!

MEANING: As I read the verses of Revelation chapter 3, I was struck with the harsh tone of Jesus. I asked myself, "If Jesus had to resort to this tone to get His own people to hear Him, what is He saying to ME in these verses—to all of us?" What might we not be hearing?

Verses one and two of chapter 3 were particularly attention-getting. Jesus told the people of Sardis that they had a name, "you live," but their deeds didn't back up the name. You and I cling to names. We're successful, friendly, efficient, hard-working, distinguished, devout, fun, laid back. Psychologists know something about us, however. We tend to overestimate ourselves. We exaggerate our own capabilities. A majority of people view themselves as above average. Think about that. We tend to believe that we're right most of the time, and that we're doing enough of God's will most of the time.

Jesus delivers a different assessment. He tells us to wake up. He tells us that we may be more wrong than we realize when it comes to what God wants. This is a sobering thought. It causes us to ask: "What if I'm wrong? What do I need to see that I'm not seeing—in others, in situations, and in judgments? How are we as individuals and as the Church falling short in obedience to God and in our witness to the world? What in God's will are we pushing aside and leaving incomplete?"

We live in a day and age in which the Church has grown weak in reaching the lost and suffering. In too many cases the Church has ceded the care of the poor and unwanted to other people or programs. Too often, the Church has developed an in-group mentality. Honestly, in too many situations, the Church has become lazy. Its leaders have focused more on money and success than service to God's people. Its shepherds, too often, have become distracted by personal preferences and long-held rituals. The harsh tone of Jesus in these verses rouses us from our sinful and selfish ways. It calls us from death to life.

Chapter Three

PHILADELPHIA (Modern day Alasehir, Turkey)

7"And to the angel of the church in Philadelphia write: Thus says the holy one, the true one, the one having the key of David, the one who opens and no one will shut, and who shuts and no one opens."

This is another great example of the Scripture saturation of Revelation—not merely quotes of verses, but deep meaning and connections that surprise us. This verse echoes Isaiah 22:22, *"I will place on his shoulder the key to the house of David; what he opens no one can shut, and what he shuts no one can open."* The "he" in this verse is Eliakim who was appointed as steward in charge of the king's palace in place of Shebna, an unfaithful assistant to the king. Eliakim, it turns out, was a subtle precursor of Christ and an indicator of God's total Lordship. What a powerful demonstration of the subtle messages God sends—some we don't even realize!

8"I know your deeds. Behold, I have given before you a door having been opened which no one is able to close because you have little strength and you kept my word and you did not deny my name. 9Behold, I am giving from the synagogue of Satan, who say they are Jews but are not, but lie—behold, I will make them come and bow before your feet and know that I loved you."

Faithful Philadelphia was suffering. Jesus wanted to get their attention. In verses eight and nine, Jesus says, "Behold!" It is as if Jesus was rousing a downtrodden and hopeless group of believers back to attention—eyes on Him instead of on their suffering and woe. The open door Jesus mentioned wasn't one that by chance happened to swing open for the people of the church in Philadelphia. The verb is passive—the door was opened by someone else, namely Jesus! This is a message of grace. For downtrodden sufferers, Jesus was working rescue.

Another Scripture image surfaces in verse nine. Do you remember who had enemies fall down at his feet, acknowledging that he was right all along? Verse nine recalls the Biblical account of Joseph and his brothers (Genesis 42:6). Jesus was making sure the believers in Philadelphia got the message: He would vindicate them. The truth would win out! It is interesting to note, once again, that Jesus was very clear about who His real chosen people were. The Jews in Philadelphia were fooling themselves about their identity and standing. Their genetic ties to Abraham meant nothing because of their disobedience and refusal to believe in Jesus as the Messiah. As the Christians in Philadelphia wondered about their own identity and about whether God really loved them, Jesus made the facts crystal clear. He loved them with His self-sacrificial and complete "agape" love. This is a powerful statement from Jesus for believers with hurting hearts and suffering souls: "I have loved you."

10*"Because you kept my word of perseverance, I will keep you from the hour of testing which is going to come upon the whole earth to test the ones who live upon the earth. **11***I am coming soon. Hold on to what you have, so that no one takes your crown. **12***The one overcoming, I will make a pillar* *in the temple of my God, and he will not go outside. I will also write on him the name of my God and the name of the city of my God, the new Jerusalem, which is coming down from heaven from my God, and my new name. 13The one having an ear, let him hear what the Spirit says to the churches."*

The message to the church in Philadelphia concludes with some great promises. The people would be protected from a coming time of testing. We don't know what Jesus was referring to, but the message was encouraging. If Jesus was making reference to the final days before His coming, the people in Philadelphia were definitely spared—we're still waiting for that day! They were able to enter heaven without experiencing that suffering. Jesus also promised that He was coming soon. If they "hold on," no one will take their crown. "Holding on" is a key theme in Revelation. It's a central message of Jesus to each of us. In the midst of suffering we're called to hold on to faith in our Savior. As we hold on, we can be sure that no one will take our crown. Once again, the Greek word "stephanos" is used for "crown." This prize for the winner of the contest is an ongoing reminder to fight the good fight of faith. Jesus is cheering us on.

For the ones who overcome, Jesus' promise is about becoming a pillar in the heavenly temple and about receiving a new name. The mention of the temple pillar may reinforce the fact that Revelation was written after the destruction of the Jerusalem temple in 70 A.D. There was hope! A new temple was coming. Believers would be an intimate part of it. The talk about a new name recalls the way God worked wonders with His servants in the Old Testament. God was including the Philadelphia believers in the same company as Abraham and Jacob!

FACTS: Philadelphia was founded in 189 B.C. by King Eumenes II of Pergamum (197-160 B.C.). He named the city because of his love for his brother ("Philadelphia" means "brotherly love"), Attalus II (159-138 BC). Attalus II would become his successor. Philadelphia was a city of many gods. It also prospered because of its good grape crop and the sale of wine. Philadelphia was damaged badly by the earthquake of 17 A.D. Subsequent earthquakes have left the city in ruins to this day.

MYSTERIES: The hour of testing (vs.10). Could it be an event or difficulty that would come to the region? It may be a reference to the even greater persecution and difficulty that will come before the Last Day. We're not sure, but God assured these believers that He would spare them from a difficult time.

A pillar (vs.12) Many pagan temples were in Philadelphia. Christians were outsiders when it came to pagan worship and social life. God gives good news that believers were not outsiders at all!

MEANING: A good question to ask when listening to the words of Jesus is, "What text is He using?" In other words, where in the Bible is the basis for what He is saying? In verse eight, Jesus mentioned an open door. The first occurrence of the word "door" in the Bible is in Genesis 4:7.

The Lord said to Cain, *"Sin is crouching at your door; it desires to have you, but you must master it."* This became a door of death as Cain killed his brother Abel.

In Exodus 12:22 God gave instructions about the Passover. The blood on the doorposts and over the door made it a door of life! In Hosea 2:14-23 we find a remarkable parallel to the promises Jesus made to the church in Philadelphia. New names were being given and there was mention of a very special door. God said He would *"make the Valley of Achor a door of hope."* "Achor" means trouble. God promised to transform trouble into an open door of hope!

For more "door" images we remember Jesus saying in Matthew 7:7, *"Ask and it will be given to you; seek and you will find; knock and the door will be opened to you."* In John 10:7 Jesus proclaimed, *"I am the door"* (Jesus used the Greek word "thura" in John 10:7 and in Revelation 3:8).

The question for you is: "Which door will prevail in your life?" There are too many doors of death and destruction open before you. Doors of depression and disobedience, of hopelessness, anger and fear, spring open every step of the way in our sinful and broken world. Jesus opens new doors before you. They are doors marked with His blood. They are doors of life and hope. They are doors of a listening Savior and a trustworthy Friend. More door talk is coming in Revelation as Jesus stands at the door and knocks in chapter 3, verse twenty. For now, the beautiful vision of Revelation opens a new and gracious door that changes outlooks and transforms lives.

LAODICEA (Modern day Eskihisar, Turkey)

14"And to the angel of the church in Laodicea write: Thus says the Amen, the faithful and true witness, the ruler of God's creation. 15I know your deeds, that you are neither cold nor hot. I wish you were cold or hot! 16So, because you are lukewarm and neither hot nor cold, I intend to vomit you from my mouth."

Jesus expresses a heartfelt yearning for His straying people in verse fifteen. His wish is expressed as an unattainable wish. If only the people could live as followers of His or as people who rejected Him! Instead, their lives were lukewarm, on the fence, indecisive, making no statement to anyone, simply blending in. They were lukewarm like the water that traveled to the city from the distant hot spring. People in Laodicea had a daily acquaintance with lukewarm water. Never a hot shower or a refreshingly cool drink. Always somewhere in between. Tiringly "blah." Like the many citizens who became fatigued with unexciting and ineffective water, Jesus was ready to spit the believers in Laodicea out of His mouth. He uses a forceful word that means "to vomit." This was no casual "ptooey" after a moderate morning workout. Jesus couldn't stand their presence anymore. He was repulsed by their flimsy so-called faith. This was a reality check for every believer.

17"Because you say, 'I am rich' and 'I am prospering and I have no need for anything,' and you do not know that you are miserable and pitiful and poor and blind and naked, 18I advise you to buy from me gold refined from fire, in order for you to prosper; and white garments to wear, so the shame of your nakedness is not revealed; and eye salve to rub your eyes in order that you can see."

The people in Laodicea were known for being financially self-sufficient. After an earthquake in 17 A.D., the city was rebuilt with its own wealth. Laodicea had bragging rights when it came to being rich. Jesus said the believers there did not realize their true standing. The word Jesus used is "to know"—"you do not know that you are wretched, pitiful, poor, blind and naked." The word "know" is the same verb Jesus uses with each of the churches. This strikes a contrast each of us needs to realize: Jesus knows all things; we know nothing in comparison.

Laodicea was also known for its "Phrygian powder" remedy for weak eyes and its black wool for clothing. With one sentence, Jesus destroyed their pride and exposed the reality of their impoverished faith. In verse eighteen Jesus emphasizes the invitation to come to Him—to Him alone for true wealth, lasting clothing, and spiritual medicine for restoration of their sight.

19"The ones I love, I show fault and I instruct. Therefore, be zealous and repent. 20Behold, I stand at the door and knock. If someone hears my voice and opens the door, I will come in and eat with him, and he with me. 21The one who overcomes, I will give to him to sit with me on my throne, as I have overcome and I sat with my Father on his throne. 22The one having an ear, let him hear what the Spirit says to the churches."

Verse nineteen recalls Proverbs 3:11-12 which is quoted in Hebrews 12:5-6:

> *"My son, do not despise the Lord's discipline and do not resent his rebuke, because the LORD disciplines those he loves, as a father the son he delights in."*

The word "discipline" involves showing faults and providing instruction. It contains the word "disciple." Jesus wants to save these lethargic Laodiceans! So, in one of the most memorable entreaties of Jesus in the New Testament, He begs the people: "Behold! Look! Attention! I've been standing outside your door and I continue to stand here, knocking." If you ever doubted the passionate heart of Jesus for your life, pay close attention to His words in verse twenty. Remember, these are words, not spoken as an appeal to unbelievers, but uttered to straying children of God.

FACTS: Epaphras brought the Gospel to Laodicea according to Colossians 4:12-13:

> *"Epaphras, who is one of you and a servant of Christ Jesus, sends greetings. He is always wrestling in prayer for you, that you may stand firm in all the will of God, mature and fully assured. I vouch for him that he is working hard for you and for those at Laodicea and Hierapolis."*

Even though the city produced many resources and rebuilt itself, another earthquake ultimately destroyed the city. It was never rebuilt.

MYSTERIES: Those whom I love I rebuke and discipline (vs.19) – Jesus references many Scriptural themes that reinforce the truth of both the Old and New Testament Scriptures. These references, as mentioned above, recall Scripture that was in circulation among the people (Proverbs 3:11-12 and Hebrews 12:5-6). Unlike earlier days in New Testament history, Christians had access to and were well versed in both the Old and New Testaments. These late first-century quotes underscored the truth of all of God's Word.

I stand at the door and knock (vs. 20) – While these words of Christ have been used by the modern church as the Lord's call to unbelievers, they are clearly Christ's appeal to those who have professed faith in Him. This verse is not one that asks unbelievers to simply "open the door of their lives" when Jesus knocks. We are dead in our sins and transgressions. It is only by grace we are saved (see Ephesians chapter 2). These words of Jesus call His redeemed people to return after straying and to enter into a deeper relationship with Him.

MEANING: Have you ever gone shopping the day after Thanksgiving? Some friends of mine are die-hard "Black Friday" shoppers. In the "old days" it meant getting to their favorite store as early as 5:00 a.m. These days it means camping out all night in front of the store. They even use a tent!

The post-holiday shopping frenzy has increased in its intensity year after year. Stores open at 3:00 or 4:00 a.m. Each tries to beat the other when it comes to luring eager customers. That's what our culture is like. Everyone has to be first—the first in line, the first to have the latest technology, the first to have the newest car. We are people who rush ahead to the next thing—whatever it may be. Sometimes, we rush ahead of God. In the process you may settle for less than He wants to provide for you, less than His plan for your life.

The people in Laodicea thought they had it all. With their own efforts they went far. They were rich. They had what everyone envied. But Jesus' perspective shook them to reality. They weren't really doing all that well. Their lives were empty and meaningless.

Living at God's pace is very challenging. Waiting on Him can test you to the very core of your being. Should you take things into your own hands? Should you jump at the latest opportunity? Should you chase after YOUR happiness, YOUR feelings of satisfaction, and YOUR desires? Or should you wait? In fact, how do you even know what God's pace is? It can be difficult to figure out.

Isaiah 5:18-19 says, *"Woe…to those who say, 'Let God hurry, let him hasten his work so we may see it. Let it approach, let the plan of the Holy One of Israel come, so we may know it.'"*

Sometimes what God is doing in your life and in the world is really none of your business! You are not called by Jesus to know everything. You are called to trust in Him, to listen to Him, to obey Him, and to love Him self-sacrificially.

Abraham and Sarah tried to rush ahead of God's plan as they waited to have a baby. Sarah recruited her servant Hagar. Abraham went along with the strategy (see Genesis chapter 16). What was the result? Trouble.

It's difficult NOT to want to rush ahead of God. When you're suffering, when you're waiting for an answer to prayer, when you're begging God for help, you crave resolution. You yearn for peace. You hunger for the complete plan. Sometimes, in your depleted and empty state, you try to make things happen. You may make an impulsive decision. You may try to mask your pain with destructive actions. You may retreat into anger or apathy.

But what does Jesus tell you in these verses? He calls you to go at God's pace. He appeals to you to remember His good and gracious plan. Jesus went through suffering and the cross before He could sit down in victory and rest at the right hand of the Father. Jesus calls you to follow in His steps, to go at His pace, to make sure restlessness does not send you into your own lukewarm, self-acquired life. The answer will come. Resolution will be realized. You will hear His voice and finally dine with Him. You need only trust that His resources and His plan will lead you home.

Study Guide for Revelation Chapter 3

1. Read Revelation 3:1-6. Discuss how Jesus' message to Sardis applies to your life.

2. Read Revelation 3:7-13. Discuss how Jesus' message to Philadelphia applies to your life.

3. Read Revelation 3:14-22. Discuss how Jesus' message to Laodicea applies to your life.

4. Jesus used a harsh tone in these verses. In what area of life might Jesus address you and the Church in the same way?

5. Discuss the questions in the first full paragraph on page 52. Apply them to recent experiences or current challenges in your life.

6. How has Jesus said, "Behold!"—gotten your attention recently?

7. How have you seen Jesus' faithfulness in your life after a time of waiting?

Revelation
Chapter Four

†

The messages to the seven churches have been completed. The sins and struggles, the joys and victories, the heartache and pain of the churches have been addressed thoroughly by Jesus. Each church was given the chance to look into the mirror of reality. All of the successes, all of the failures, and all of the challenges were part of the bigger picture of living during a time of suffering and persecution. Life was hard for these believers—really hard. It was ugly, scary, and painful. Yes, it was a blessing to know that Jesus held each church close and understood exactly where their hearts and souls were. But even as some held fast to the faith, life was being drained out of them.

This group of believers in the first century looked around and wondered, "There's got to be more than this."

How many times have you said the same thing? A few years ago I stood with a mom and dad as they looked into the casket of their 19-year-old son who died in a car accident. Their son, their only son, was gone. Now what? How would they cope? How would they face tomorrow? How would they live with aching hearts? How would they meet each day's new tears? There's got to be more than this.

It's what you say and feel when you experience tragedy, heartbreak, pain, and disillusionment. There's got to be more than this.

During a time of incredible pressure, persecution, and loss, it's what the people of the churches in Revelation were saying. That is why Jesus revealed Himself to John with the powerful message of the book of Revelation. Jesus cared so much about suffering believers that He parted the heavens and showed them a glimpse of His marvelous and faithful work behind the scenes.

He shows you, too. Let's look at where this vision takes us.

THERE'S GOT TO BE MORE THAN THIS

1After these things I looked, and behold, a door was opened in heaven, and the first voice I heard as a trumpet speaking with me said, "Come up here, and I will show you what is necessary to be after these things."

Now that you have become acquainted with the messages to the seven churches, it is important to see the consistent next steps of the book of Revelation. The remainder of the book is not disconnected from the practical and understandable beginning. The vision addresses the issues and needs of the churches. For example, chapter four begins with a reference to Jesus' message to the church in Philadelphia: the open door from Revelation 3:8. Jesus promised an open door. Here it is!

The time of help has come. No longer would suffering people look only at the hopelessness of their day to day lives. No longer would Christians with crushed spirits hear only the condemning noise of the world. Instead, they would see the rest of the story—the real story.

If you feel as if God's voice is being drowned out by the din of a cruel and anti-Christian world, the loud voice of chapter one proclaiming the message of God reappears in chapter four. Instead of the great sound of the voice being compared to rushing waters, the volume is now compared to a trumpet—another strong reinforcement of Biblical truth. The presence and voice of God in Exodus 19 were connected with a loud trumpet blast. The Lord's second coming was also connected with a sounding trumpet *("And in that day a great trumpet will sound."* Isaiah 27:13). For every sagging spirit and hopeless heart, God was drawing near. He was speaking up.

2Immediately I was in the Spirit, and behold, a throne there in heaven, and upon the throne one sitting,

This is an important transition in the book of Revelation. From earthly challenges, we are now whisked into heaven for a view of a second and refreshing reality. Each listener is invited to look closely at the mural of images meant to give hope and direction. It all begins with God's throne. God's throne appears in almost every chapter of Revelation—for a total of forty-seven times! The powerful message was that even in the midst of suffering and heartache, God was in charge. Even when all looks lost, THERE IS SOMETHING MORE!

I remember running up a mile-long hill in northern Michigan. The morning was beautiful. The air was crisp and clear. But the climb was punishing. As I moved forward, my legs ached and burned. My lungs strained. There seemed to be no end in sight. "Why am I doing this?" I thought. "There's got to be more than this." And then I crested the hill. The most beautiful vista was before me. I saw miles of lakeshore, sand dunes, and rocky cliffs stretching into the distance. The lake was a beautiful hue of bluish green, dotted with the bright white sails of sailboats. Church steeples pierced the tree-filled town below me. I realized that there was more to the climb than the pain. There was more to this journey. And it was beautiful! It was worth the struggle.

The book of Revelation will teach us much about heaven. For now, chapter 4 lets us know that heaven really exists, that God's throne is not compromised, and that beauty awaits us. Faith and life are worth the struggle when we are in the hands of our Savior.

THE STUFF OF HEAVEN

3And the one sitting there had the appearance of jasper and carnelian, and a rainbow surrounded the throne, in appearance like an emerald.

This vision of heaven resembles Ezekiel's vision in Ezekiel 1:26-28:

Above the expanse over their heads was what looked like a throne of sapphire, and high above on the throne was a figure like that of a man. I saw that from what appeared to be his waist up he looked like glowing metal, as if full of fire, and that from there down he looked like fire; and brilliant light surrounded him. Like the appearance of a rainbow in the clouds on a rainy day, so was the radiance around him. This was the appearance of the likeness of the glory of the LORD. When I saw it, I fell facedown, and I heard the voice of one speaking.

The gems mentioned in Revelation 4:3 are also reminiscent of the priestly garments described in the Old Testament. In Exodus 28:1-3, 15-21 God said to Moses:

"Have Aaron your brother brought to you from among the Israelites, along with his sons Nadab and Abihu, Eleazar and Ithamar, so they may serve me as priests. Make sacred garments for your brother Aaron, to give him dignity and honor. Tell all the skilled men to whom I have given wisdom in such matters that they are to make garments for Aaron, for his consecration, so he may serve me as priest. Fashion a breastpiece for making decisions--the work of a skilled craftsman. Make it like the ephod: of gold, and of blue, purple and scarlet yarn, and of finely twisted linen. It is to be square--a span long and a span wide--and folded double. Then mount four rows of precious stones on it. In the first row there shall be a ruby, a topaz and a beryl; in the second row a turquoise, a sapphire and an emerald; in the third row a jacinth, an agate and an amethyst;

in the fourth row a chrysolite, an onyx and a jasper. Mount them in gold filigree settings. There are to be twelve stones, one for each of the names of the sons of Israel, each engraved like a seal with the name of one of the twelve tribes."

These gems were also mentioned in Ezekiel 28:12-14—a prophecy about the king of Tyre and a description of the Cherub who went astray—possibly Satan.

Why the fancy clothing for the priests? Why are precious gems part of these Biblical visions? Because this is the stuff of heaven! The priest reflected the reality of God's dwelling place. The gems showed the otherworldly nature of paradise. In other words, there IS more to life than what you see. There is much more than the lost luster of a broken world. God has much more in store—and it's beautiful! It is worth the struggle.

CREATURES APPEAR

4Surrounding the throne were twenty-four thrones, and upon the thrones twenty-four elders, sitting clothed in white garments, and upon their heads gold crowns. 5From the throne came lightning and noise and thunder. And seven lamps were burning before the throne, which are the seven spirits of God. 6And before the throne there was what looked like a sea of glass like clear crystal. And in the middle of the throne and around the throne four living things covered with eyes in front and behind.

What was happening in heaven? First there was a complete representation of all believers. The number 24 is a number that tells a story. It recounts all of Old Testament history wrapped up in the 12 tribes of Israel. It adds New Testament believers represented by the 12 apostles. No one was left out. No one was forgotten. And not a single suffering believer would ever be left out of God's glorious presence. These crown-wearing, white-robed elders were a preview of what awaited those who walked with Jesus here on earth.

The images of victory crowns and white garments appeared in chapters two and three. They will appear again as persistent reminders that there is much more to life when it is life in Christ.

Once again, struggling believers receive encouragement from these words. The lightning and thunder bring listeners back to Mt. Sinai in Exodus 19:16-17: *"On the morning of the third day there was thunder and lightning, with a thick cloud over the mountain, and a very loud trumpet blast. Everyone in the camp trembled. Then Moses led the people out of the camp to meet with God, and they stood at the foot of the mountain."*

The people in the wilderness met with God! They were in His presence. He was close. Heaven was not as far away as they thought. In other words, there IS more than just this! God IS with us! Behind the scenes of life is God on His throne. We're not alone. Even the perfect presence of the Holy Spirit was fully with each church and was lighting the way as represented by the seven lamps.

In verse six, living things start to appear in the Revelation vision. Animals occupy key roles in the message of this book. The creatures are never ordinary. They are supernatural animals that bring messages as powerful as the animals in Picasso's "Guernica" on the cover of this book. The first living creatures introduced are powerful heavenly beasts under God's command. In other words, they're good guys. Let's take a closer look.

7The first living thing was like a lion, the second living thing like an ox, the third living thing had a face like a man, and the fourth living thing was like an eagle flying. 8And the four living things, each one of them, had six wings and was covered with eyes all around outside and inside. And they do not stop day and night saying: "Holy, holy, holy, Lord God Almighty, the one who was, and the one who is, and the one who is coming."

Ezekiel chapters 1 and 10 describe similar angelic beings called Cherubim. That's an important reference point as we listen to the description of this vision with New Testament believers. These are creatures of heaven. They are animals at God's command that show us how He is fighting for us. These are no ordinary creatures—and they're not wimpy!

A rabbinic saying from around 300 A.D. captures the message of the four living beings: "The mightiest among the birds is the eagle, the mightiest among the domestic animals is the bull, the mightiest among the wild beasts is the lion, and the mightiest among all is man" (Leon Morris, Revelation, Tyndale, p. 91). These creatures are all about the far-reaching strength of God. That strength serves Him and His redeemed people. It's good news for us—especially as we run into some of the threatening animals (called "beasts" in King James English) in the chapters ahead.

The creatures sing a familiar song. Isaiah 6:3 lets us in on the chorus of heavenly creatures: *"Holy, holy, holy is the LORD Almighty; the whole earth is full of his glory."* The connection of the book of Revelation to the rest of Scripture is significant. As believers get a glimpse of heaven, they can be assured that God was telling the truth all along. The Word of God is certain.

In addition to the appearance of animals in this heavenly vision, poetic verse—song—plays an important part in the revelatory message of God. At the end of chapter four, the songs of heaven swell in intensity.

THE NEW SONG OF HEAVEN

9And when the living things give glory and honor and thanks to the one seated on the throne, to the one who lives for ever and ever, 10the twenty-four elders fall down before the one seated on the throne and they worship the one who lives forever and ever, and they throw their crowns before the throne and say: 11"You are worthy, our Lord and God, to receive glory and honor and power, because you created all things, and through your will they were and they were created."

These are the songs of heaven that weave their way through the book of Revelation. They give us a picture of the enduring worship of the eternal God. In a world where the refrains of death, tragedy, war, and hatred seem to set the pace, God shows us that another song is, in reality, determining life's rhythm. In the first century when emperor worship, persecution, and secularism rang in the ears of believers, this song of heaven showed them that another powerful tune prevailed in the background. There was more to the story!

When my wife was pregnant with both of our children, the first few months were tough. There was morning sickness, sleeplessness, and plenty of discomfort. During our second daughter's pregnancy, my wife developed a high risk, life threatening condition. This was no easy trek. In fact, it was downright frightening and exhausting. It was one of those times when you feel like saying, THERE'S GOT TO BE MORE THAN THIS! But for each daughter, the bigger picture was revealed at the doctor's office. He let us listen to our children's heartbeats! It was music to our ears. We could only see part of the story, but there was more. It was beautiful. And it was worth the struggle.

That is the simple but desperately needed message of Revelation chapter 4 for every believer who waits for Jesus during these last days. Maybe it's the message you need to hear today.

Study Guide for Revelation Chapter 4

1. When do you find yourself saying, "There's got to be more than this?"

2. Read Revelation 4:1-3. How do these verses give you strength and encouragement during your times of fatigue?

3. Read Revelation 4:4-8. Talk about how this heavenly picture affects your outlook as one who lives on earth.

4. These living things appear to be angels. What new perspective about angels does their description give you?

5. Read Revelation 4:9-11. Discuss what comfort it is to know that God created everything.

6. How do these verses grow your understanding of worship?

7. What does this chapter tell you about God?

Revelation
Chapter Five

✝

    His name was Sisyphus. Have you heard of him? He tried to cheat death. It's a legend, of course, a Greek myth that showed the inevitability of what each of us is headed for: our demise, the end, dying. Sisyphus was the founder and king of ancient Corinth. According to the legend, he was also a wily trickster. When Hades, the god of the underworld, came to claim him for the kingdom of the dead, Hades brought handcuffs. Sisyphus convinced Hades to show him how these marvelous restraints worked. Hades ended up demonstrating on himself! Sisyphus proceeded to lock him in a closet. While Hades was locked away, Sisyphus wreaked havoc on earth with a population that couldn't die! Finally Hades freed himself and got the life-death cycle in the world back in gear. He also claimed Sisyphus for the underworld, but Sisyphus had more tricks up his sleeve. Using smooth talk and clever plots, he convinced Persephone, queen of the dead, to allow him to go back to the world of the living. His reappearance was short-lived, however, and his shenanigans caught up with him. Because of his trickery, Sisyphus was condemned to an eternity of hard labor in the underworld. His punishment was to roll a large boulder to the top of a hill. Each time he reached the top with the boulder, it rolled down the other side. Sisyphus had to start over and over and over again.

Sisyphus tried, but he couldn't conquer death. He could not maneuver his way out of his demise. In fact, the more he tried to avoid it, the heavier the weight of death became.

Throughout history human beings have tried to figure out what Sisyphus couldn't. They have developed rituals and sacrifices. They have invented anti-aging techniques, cosmetic surgery, and life-prolonging medical innovations. They have investigated genetic engineering. I read once that baseball great Ted Williams had himself cryogenically frozen after his death in hopes that one day the technology to bring him back to life would be invented. But the boulder of death is as heavy and relentless as ever. We do not have power over it. It is a fact of our broken lives.

With the boulder of death at one end of life's trouble spectrum, the other extreme of the human condition could be called "the pebble." The pebble represents pain and annoyance that remind us daily of our weakness. You know how the pebble works. Have you ever had one in your shoe?

When I go for my morning run on the rocky San Antonio soil, I frequently feel the sudden discomfort of a pebble in my shoe. I can't ignore it. Even though it is almost invisible, I have to stop and remove the pebble. I've run through snow and rain and sweltering heat. I've run in sub-zero temperatures and in high winds. I've waded through flooded pathways and climbed steep paths. I've run away from skunks and coyotes. I've forged ahead through injuries, illness, and lack of sleep. But put a pebble in my shoe and I can't go on. I have to stop. There's no option. I have to put on the brakes, untie my shoe, shake out the pebble, and go on. The pebble always wins.

Such little things can stop us in our tracks. We are so weak! It's hard to admit. We boast of our accomplishments, we dance in end zones, we flaunt our beauty. But, as Solomon said, it is all vanity. It all comes to an end. Let a microscopic virus invade your body; have a few muscle fibers decide to spasm in your lower back; or put a pebble in your shoe and suddenly you're laid low, out of commission, humbled, broken. Experience the heartbreak of a broken relationship; feel the oppressive shadow of depression's darkness; empty yourself as a caregiver for a loved one in need, and the limits of your own capabilities become very clear.

Both the boulder and the pebble show you that you can't make it through life on your own. You need help.

I'll never forget sitting with the family of a girl in her twenties as she lay dying. Both she and her family knew it was coming. They tried to deny it as her illness took its toll on her body. In her final moments I looked into their eyes and saw helplessness and desperation. They couldn't do anything.

If only we had help. If only someone was able to conquer the pebble and the boulder.

This is the power of Revelation 5. Someone appears who can do what no one else can. For people who are UNable, one appears who IS able. For Christians who were becoming confused and overwhelmed, inundated with the many gods of Rome, pressured by many factions to give up on Jesus, brought to tears of frustration and grief, came the One who was the Way and the Truth and the Life.

IT BEGINS WITH THE WORD

1And I saw in the right hand of the one seated upon the throne a book written inside and outside sealed with seven seals. 2And I saw a strong angel proclaiming in a loud voice, "Who is worthy to open the book and to break its seal?" 3But no one in heaven or on earth or under the earth was able to open the book or to look in it. 4I wept and wept because no one worthy was found to open the book or to look in it.

Suddenly, a book appears in the hand of the one seated on the throne. The Greek word for "book," "biblion," was used in 1:11 when Jesus commanded John to write this message to the churches. It was also used in 3:5 in the phrase "the book of life." It is used here in 5:1 as well. It is important to note recurring images in Revelation. This scroll (book) is God's message. The seven seals may communicate that it is for the seven churches or that it is the perfect plan of God revealed in the book of life (the number seven telling the story of completeness and perfection).

The question is asked, "Who can open the book?" Immediately we're sent back to 3:7—Jesus' message that He has the power to open and close. Was there another candidate with that kind of ability? Not "in heaven or on earth or under the earth." This all-encompassing summary brings to mind Philippians 2:10, *"At the name of Jesus every knee should bow in heaven and on earth and under the earth."* Remember that Revelation brings Old Testament and New Testament themes back to believers' minds. The powerful theme of Jesus Christ, the One and Only, is emphasized throughout Revelation.

The quest to open the scroll was not a quest for might, but for worthiness. A similar scroll situation developed in Isaiah 29:11-12:

> *For you this whole vision is nothing but words sealed in a scroll. And if you give the scroll to someone who can read, and say to him, "Read this, please," he will answer, "I can't; it is sealed." Or if you give the scroll to someone who cannot read, and say, "Read this, please," he will answer, "I don't know how to read."*

If you read the rest of Isaiah 29 you'll see that the ability to read and understand the message of God was not rooted in human strength and wisdom. It was rooted in worthiness before God, being declared righteous before Him, living as the work of His hands, receiving His grace and Spirit. John wept because he knew that human intelligence, might, and innovation did not provide what we really need. We need to hear from God. We need His Word of life and salvation. Our strength brings frustration and condemnation. Taking life into our own hands causes trouble, confusion, and heartache.

5And one of the elders said to me, "Do not cry! Behold, the Lion of the tribe of Judah, the Root of David, overcame to open the book and its seven seals."

The word "overcame" ("triumphed" in the NIV) is what Christ was urging the churches to do in chapters 2 and 3. It's the word "nike," the Greek word for victory. The Greek phrase says that the Lion of Judah (another animal image, by the way) triumphed IN ORDER TO OPEN the book and its seven seals. This tells us something important about the purpose of the book: it is to bring hope and salvation to the world. The central purpose of the One who is able was to overcome the boulder and the pebble!

This verse is another example of the Scripture saturation of Revelation along with the self-interpretation of the book. The Lion of the tribe of Judah is introduced in Genesis 49:8-10: *"Judah, your brothers will praise you; your hand will be on the neck of your enemies; your father's sons will bow down to you. You are a lion's cub, O Judah; you return from the prey, my son. Like a lion he crouches and lies down, like a lioness--who dares to rouse him? The scepter will not depart from Judah, nor the ruler's staff from between his feet, until he comes to whom it belongs and the obedience of the nations is his."*

Who knew that THE Lion would be the Savior of the world? The Root of David is introduced as the Root of Jesse (David's father) in Isaiah 11:10, *"In that day the Root of Jesse will stand as a banner for the peoples; the nations will rally to him, and his place of rest will be glorious."* If there is any question about the identity of this One who is able, take a sneak peak at Revelation 22:16. Jesus says, *"I, Jesus, have sent my angel to give you this testimony for the churches. I am the Root and the Offspring of David, and the bright Morning Star."* Mystery solved—compliments of Jesus speaking in the book of Revelation.

THE LAMB

6And I saw in the middle of the throne and the four living things, and in the middle of the elders, a Lamb standing, as one having been slaughtered, having seven horns and seven eyes which are the seven spirits of God sent to all the earth.

Notice how verse six tells us what the seven eyes are—the seven spirits of God sent out into all the earth. God helps us to remember that this is a symbolic vision bringing us important and beautiful truths about His work behind the scenes.

The Lamb is the first full-fledged animal image to appear in the vision. This is very important because all the other animals in Revelation ("beasts" in most Bible translations) submit to the Lamb. For the identity of the Lamb you can look at:

Isaiah 53:7, _"He was oppressed and afflicted, yet he did not open his mouth; he was led like a lamb to the slaughter, and as a sheep before her shearers is silent, so he did not open his mouth."_

John 1:29, _"The next day John saw Jesus coming toward him and said, 'Look, the Lamb of God, who takes away the sin of the world!'"_

1 Corinthians 5:7, _"Get rid of the old yeast that you may be a new batch without yeast--as you really are. For Christ, our Passover lamb, has been sacrificed."_

1 Peter 1:18-19, _"For you know that it was not with perishable things such as silver or gold that you were redeemed from the empty way of life handed down to you from your forefathers, but with the precious blood of Christ, a lamb without blemish or defect."_

Is there any question about the identity of the Lamb?

The word "Lamb" in Revelation 5:6 is the unique Greek word "arnion." Other New Testament verses that use the word "lamb" use the Greek word "amnos." "Arnion" is used throughout the book of Revelation. The word is also used in two key Old Testament sections. Psalm 114:4 and 6 use the word in the context of being freed from slavery in Egypt with miraculous acts of deliverance: _"When Israel came out of Egypt, the house of Jacob from a people of foreign tongue, Judah became God's sanctuary, Israel his dominion. The sea looked and fled, the Jordan_ *turned back; the mountains skipped like rams, the hills like* **lambs***. Why was it, O sea, that you fled, O Jordan, that you turned back, you mountains, that you skipped like rams, you hills, like* **lambs***? Tremble, O earth, at the presence of the Lord, at the presence of the God of Jacob, who turned the rock into a pool, the hard rock into springs of water."*

Jeremiah 11:19 uses the word to describe the prophet's persecution and God's victory: *"I had been like a gentle* **lamb** *led to the slaughter…But, O LORD Almighty, you who judge righteously and test the heart and mind, let me see your vengeance upon them, for to you I have committed my cause" (vss. 19a, 20).* Could it be that this unique word for "lamb" pointed listeners to the faithful deliverer and Savior who triumphed over Egypt in the wilderness and over sin at the cross?

Helping us to understand the Lamb's mission is the word "slain." The victorious Lamb, with perfect power and authority (seven horns and eyes), reigned because of His sacrificial death. The word "slain" is the terminology used for sacrificial slaughter of an animal in the religious sacrificial rite. Later in Revelation 6:9, this word is used for the slain martyrs—death that was not in vain, but was linked intimately with the work of God.

LIFE IN HEAVEN

7He came and took from the right hand of the one sitting on the throne. 8And when he took the book, the four living things and the twenty-four elders fell before the Lamb, each having a harp and gold bowl full of incense, which are the prayers of the saints.

Throughout the book of Revelation, the truth of God's existence and character is reinforced. Jesus calls Himself "the Son of God" in 2:18. We hear over and over again that God is the Almighty. In verse seven we see the unity of the Father and the Son as the Son takes the scroll from the Father's right hand.

Immediately the crowd around the throne falls down in worship. Then we see harps appear. This may be where our idea of harp-playing angels in heaven comes from. But the harps are far from cliché. They bring an important message to the listeners who are so familiar with the history of Israel. The harp was an instrument used for music that praised God. In 2 Chronicles 29:25-28 a scene is described where harps are used to worship God during the burnt offering sacrifices (*"He stationed the Levites in the temple of the LORD with cymbals, harps and lyres… As the offering began, singing to the LORD began also, accompanied by trumpets and the instruments of David king of Israel."*). But life changed for God's people. In their rebellion they were taken into captivity. Suddenly they were in exile and far from God. They mourned this life of separation and distance by hanging up their harps. Psalm 137:1-4 tells the story:

> *By the rivers of Babylon we sat and wept when we remembered Zion. There on the poplars we hung our harps, for there our captors asked us for songs, our tormentors demanded songs of joy; they said,*

"Sing us one of the songs of Zion!" How can we sing the songs of the LORD while in a foreign land?

The re-emergence of harps in Revelation showed the new hope of worshipping God. All was not lost. Suffering, distance, and exile were coming to an end.

Golden bowls full of incense were offered for the dedication of the tabernacle in Numbers 7:11-14. Suddenly we see the deeper meaning of this offering. Verse eight tells us that these are the prayers of God's people, treasured by God and cherished in His presence. What encouragement for first-century Christians and for all who cry out to God in prayer! Sometimes you wonder if God hears you. Verse eight brings assurance that no prayer is in vain.

9 *And they sing a new song: "You are worthy to take the book and to open its seals, because you were slaughtered, and with your blood you redeemed men for God from every tribe and tongue and people and nation. **10**And you have made them a kingdom and priests for our God, and they will reign on the earth."*

I love music. I'm so glad to get a preview of the music of heaven. It's a new song, a song of atonement and grace, a song that brings us back to the truth of the crucified and risen Christ. It is a melody of expansive redemption, salvation for the world. Jesus did what no one else could ever do. He also transformed our lives. Verse ten reinforces the truth of 1:6. Each of us has a purpose. Each of us is an irreplaceable part of God's plan. Over and over in the book of Revelation we hear that we have been created and redeemed to serve God. There will be no boredom in heaven—no sitting on clouds floating around with nothing to do. We will have exciting and stimulating work to do. We will also reign. For a frightened and outcast group of believers, this news brought hope and encouragement. If you feel like life is a dead-end, read verse ten one more time. It is God's plan and promise for you!

YOU ARE NOT ALONE

11I saw and heard the voice of many angels around the throne and the living things and the elders, and their number was ten thousand times ten thousand and thousands upon thousands, 12saying in a loud voice, "Worthy is the Lamb, the one slaughtered, to receive power and riches and wisdom and strength and honor and glory and blessing!" 13And all created things in heaven and on earth and under the earth and on the sea, and all the things in them, I heard saying: "To the one seated on the throne and to the Lamb be blessing and honor and glory and power, for ever and ever!" 14The four living things said, "Amen," and the elders fell and worshiped.

If you ever feel outnumbered in the world, Jesus intentionally parted the heavens to give you a glimpse of who is on your side. You are not alone! Thousands upon thousands, ten thousand times ten thousand, encircle the throne and worship Jesus. You're in good company with multitudes who follow the Truth. The seven qualities mentioned in verse twelve not only bring Old and New

Testament connections to God; they are a direct affront to emperor worship, as well. We'll encounter additional direct assaults on the false religion of Rome throughout the book of Revelation. People needed to know the truth. They were being saturated by the Roman lie. In Revelation, God weighed in.

The unity of the Father and the Son comes through again in verse thirteen. Both the Father on the throne and the Lamb are worshipped. For anyone in the first century or in the twenty-first century who doubts the true divine nature of Jesus, these words bring complete clarity. In John 10:30 Jesus said, *"I and the Father are one."* In these closing verses of chapter five, we see that truth in action!

This opening scene in the Revelation vision is so important and practical. Through the fog of the world's philosophies, religions, and ideologies we are shown Jesus, the Christ, the Redeemer, the Savior, the Victor, the Living King. For any person in doubt, for all who suffer pain, for all who face death, we are shown the way to receive help. We are shown the only One who is worthy and able to deliver us. We are shown the genuine article in the face of many counterfeits and false promises. We are shown Jesus. If you ever wished that God would open the heavens and show you a sign to prove He was active and working, you can't get any better than the powerful book of Revelation. We, too, say "Amen!" as the sight of this vision helps us walk by faith.

Study Guide for Revelation Chapter 5

1. Read Revelation 5:1-4. In what situations do you try to take life into your control?

2. What makes you realize that you are powerless and cannot control everything?

3. Read Revelation 5:5. How has Jesus' work helped you during times of tears?

4. How do the names of Jesus in verse 5 speak to your life today?

5. Read Revelation 5:6-8. What do you learn about Jesus from these verses?

6. Read Revelation 5:9-10. According to these verses, how did Jesus' sacrifice change your life?

7. Read Revelation 5:11-14. How do these verses give you confidence?

Revelation
Chapter Six

✝

Hidden in the middle of the Gospel of Matthew is a short parable that doesn't get a lot of attention. It's definitely not one of the "headline" stories of Jesus. Administer a most popular parable survey and you'll get answers like "The Good Samaritan," "The Prodigal Son," and "The Parable of the Sower." But immediately after the Parable of the Sower, Jesus told a story that answers one of the deepest questions of all humanity. Jesus told "The Parable of the Wheat and the Weeds." It's in Matthew 13:24-30:

> *"The kingdom of heaven is like a man who sowed good seed in his field. But while everyone was sleeping, his enemy came and sowed weeds among the wheat, and went away. When the wheat sprouted and formed heads, then the weeds also appeared. The owner's servants came to him and said, 'Sir, didn't you sow good seed in your field? Where then did the weeds come from?' 'An enemy did this,' he replied. The servants asked him, 'Do you want us to go and pull them up?' 'No,' he answered, 'because while you are pulling the weeds, you may root up the wheat with them. Let both grow together until the harvest. At that time I will tell the harvesters: First collect the weeds and*

tie them in bundles to be burned; then gather the wheat and bring it into my barn.'"

This parable offers the answer to the question, "Why?" Why is there evil and suffering in the world? Why does pain and brokenness continue as we wait for Jesus' return? Why does God allow sin to have its way among us?

Jesus answers, "There are weeds among the wheat." He interpreted the parable for His disciples in verses 37-43:

"The one who sowed the good seed is the Son of Man. The field is the world, and the good seed stands for the sons of the kingdom. The weeds are the sons of the evil one, and the enemy who sows them is the devil. The harvest is the end of the age, and the harvesters are angels. As the weeds are pulled up and burned in the fire, so it will be at the end of the age. The Son of Man will send out his angels, and they will weed out of his kingdom everything that causes sin and all who do evil. They will throw them into the fiery furnace, where there will be weeping and gnashing of teeth. Then the righteous will shine like the sun in the kingdom of their Father. He who has ears, let him hear."

Jesus does not want to lose any of his children, so both the weeds and the wheat must grow together until the harvest time, until His return. The parable reinforces the patience of God. As Peter said regarding the return of

Jesus and the restoration of all things, *"The Lord is not slow in keeping his promise, as some understand slowness. He is patient with you, not wanting anyone to perish, but everyone to come to repentance" (1 Peter 3:9).*

God is working out His plan. It's a good plan, and He is actively unfolding it every moment of every day. Though at times it seems as if we're abandoned, we're not. Though it seems that the wheat will be choked out of the field, the master is tending His crop and has the harvesters ready. This is the current reality of life as we await the coming of Jesus.

My grandfather fought in World War I. His job in the army was to drive a truck, transporting supplies, troops, and whatever was needed for battle. After the war was over, he was given a new task with his truck: battlefield clean-up. Imagine my twenty-four-year-old grandfather combing the trench warfare scarred landscape of France. He told a few stories—like the time he kicked a helmet that lay on the ground and saw a soldier's head roll out. This was a devastating war, a heartbreaking display of human violence, a time of tremendous loss and absolute destruction.

I wonder if my grandfather ever looked up to heaven and asked, "Why don't you put an end to this, God?" "Why don't you send your Son right now so we don't have to experience any more of this senselessness?"

I wouldn't be surprised if my grandfather asked those questions and wondered when Jesus would return.

But if God did decide to send His Son with hosts of angels, with the loud trumpet call, at that very moment, the plan would not have been complete. There were many in the decades ahead who still needed to hear the Gospel—you and I included! The story wasn't over yet. The weeds could not be pulled up because the wheat was still growing. It wasn't time for the harvest, so careful eyes kept close watch over the weeds among the wheat.

From a World War I battlefield, to the agonizing suffering and pain of today, to the hurt and despair of humanity throughout the ages, God doesn't want to lose any of His wheat. That's why the weeds keep growing. But the Master keeps watch over His field and the harvest will come at the right time.

That is what suffering believers needed to hear in the first century as they looked to the heavens and asked God where He was and why the agony kept going. And that is the powerful message of Revelation chapter 6.

The Father is on His throne. Now the Redeemer, the Lamb, Jesus, gives us a glimpse of His plan.

GOD IS CLOSE

1I looked when the Lamb opened one of the seven seals, and I heard one of the four living things speaking in a voice like thunder, "Come!" 2I looked, and behold, a white horse, and the one sitting on it having a bow. A crown was given to him and he went out conquering and in order to conquer.

Why did a horse appear when the seal was opened? The answer may be in two key sections of the book of Zechariah:

> *During the night I had a vision--and there before me was a man riding a red horse! He was standing among the myrtle trees in a ravine. Behind him were red, brown and white horses. I asked, "What are these, my lord?" The angel who was talking with me answered, "I will show you what they are." Then the man standing among the myrtle trees explained, "They are the ones the LORD has sent to go throughout the earth." (Zechariah 1:8-10)*

The best way to make sense of Biblical symbols is to check to see if other parts of the Bible shed light on them. Understanding Revelation doesn't mean that we assign meaning according to our imaginations. Our understanding is guided by Jesus Himself and made clear through the witness of the whole of Scripture. Remember, the people listening to this vision being read to them were familiar with the Old and New Testaments. The prophetic vision of Revelation alerted them to other prophetic visions of the Bible. These verses from Zechariah tell us that horses go throughout the earth. And there's more.

> *I looked up again--and there before me were four chariots coming out from between two mountains-- mountains of bronze! The first chariot had red horses, the second black, the third white, and the fourth dappled--all of them powerful. I asked the angel who was speaking to me, "What are these,*

my lord?" The angel answered me, "These are the four spirits of heaven, going out from standing in the presence of the Lord of the whole world. The one with the black horses is going toward the north country, the one with the white horses toward the west, and the one with the dappled horses toward the south." When the powerful horses went out, they were straining to go throughout the earth. And he said, "Go throughout the earth!" So they went throughout the earth. (Zechariah 6:1-7)

Horses represent the mighty spirits of heaven that stand in the presence of God. These spirits go throughout the earth. It appears that the opened seals in Revelation 6 reflect the truth communicated by the parable of the weeds and the wheat—the reality of the world at the time of this vision. In other words, God is not isolated up in heaven. He is not far removed from the reality of our suffering and pain—or the reality of those who do evil. God knows what is going on! He goes throughout the earth. More than that, He is in control and has a plan.

My daughter used to teach kindergarten and first grade students in an after school program. At first those little kiddos would try anything to convince her that they didn't have any school work to do. They wanted to play! My daughter learned that all she had to do was to keep her eyes open and walk around the room. She would see kids stashing assignments under their folders and in their backpacks. She spotted notes from teachers hidden beneath coloring sheets. She would hear students make up stories that fell apart with a few strategic questions. It wasn't difficult to see the truth and to make a plan.

As the seals are opened in chapter 6, we see that God has the enemy's number. All is not out of control— even when it seems to be. The Almighty Lord knows exactly what to do to make victory certain.

As you read the unfolding scenes in the chapters ahead, be sure to remember that this is not an engineering schematic for the end times. This is a mural, a vision. It is important that you appreciate the movement and flow of each part of the vision. The opening of the seven seals commences a flow of visionary scenes that tell important truths about life and about God. These truths are based in Scripture. The believers who were listening needed reinforcement of God's consistent message over time. They also were blessed with encouraging news about their particular situation.

Verse two begins the procession of horses with the white horse. Some scholars have said the horse rider represents Jesus. Others disagree. In the context of what the horses and riders represent, it appears that this horse and rider are about destruction and not salvation. The white horse and rider show us the tyranny of conquering kingdoms. Listeners during the first century would immediately relate to being under the domination and rule of a conquering empire. Rome opposed their faith and brought persecution to their lives. God showed that He knew what weeds existed among the wheat.

PAINFUL REALITY

3When he opened the second seal, I heard the second living thing say, "Come!" 4And another came out, a fiery horse, and to the one sitting on it, it was given to him to take the peace from the earth so they slaughter one another. And to him was given a large sword.

Notice that the Ruler of the heavens and Lord of all is in control as these destructive steeds make their way throughout the earth. It is only by invitation that they begin their quest. The power possessed by each one is given to him. They do not have the power in themselves. As the red horse and its rider bring persecution and conflict— forces very familiar to Christians in the late first century, the overriding theme is that God is still in control. Even when the worst of evil comes, life is not up for grabs.

5When he opened the third seal, I heard the third living thing say, "Come!" I looked, and behold, a black horse, and the one sitting on it having a balance in his hand. 6And I heard what sounded like a voice in the middle of the four living things, saying, "A quart of grain for a denarius, and three quarts of barley for a denarius, and let the oil and the wine not be harmed!"

These verses address the economic hardship of the late first century. People were suffering because of high prices and the lack of availability of food. A quart of grain for one day's pay (a denarius) was nearly unreachable for the average citizen. Three quarts of barley for a day's pay was an inflated price, but was not yet completely unreasonable during that time. The good news was that the oil and the wine would remain plentiful. The verb "damage" in verse 6 is the same verb used in 2:11—"do not treat unjustly"—referring to believers not harmed by the second death. The righteousness and justice of God still held sway in the midst of financial hardship.

Richard Duncan-Jones commented on the trend of inflation happening in the Roman Empire during this time period:

> "Average prices rose by roughly half between the first and second centuries. A typical level by the end of the second century seems to have been...approximately twice the normal level of the first century. Prices seem to have risen at least a further 50% by mid-century, and were roughly thirty times the first-century level by the 290s" (Richard Duncan-Jones, Structure and Scale in the Roman Economy, p. 150. 1990 Cambridge University Press).

Times were getting tougher and tougher. It is interesting to note that Emperor Domitian actually issued an edict to plant no new vineyards in Italy and to destroy half of the existing ones in order to produce more grain. There was such an outcry that this edict was repealed (Morris, p. 106). Yes, God was in control even as the Roman Empire experienced inflation and hardship. This message of Revelation also brings us encouragement as we face economic worries and woes.

7When he opened the fourth seal, I heard the voice of the fourth living thing say, "Come!" 8I looked, and behold, a pale-green horse, and the one sitting on it was named Death, and Hades was following him. They were given authority over a fourth of the earth to kill by sword, famine and plague, and by the wild beasts of the earth.

Hades and death always appear together in Revelation. Hades was considered the place of torment and judgment in first century culture. For first-century listeners, a familiar Biblical theme was used to summarize reality—the four modes of death mentioned in verse eight. Ezekiel 14:21 says, *"This is what the Sovereign LORD says: How much worse will it be when I send against Jerusalem my four dreadful judgments--sword and famine and wild beasts and plague--to kill its men and their animals!"*

This was reality for believers. It is familiar territory for us, too. Our broken world is riddled with tragedy and pain. But only one-fourth of the earth was affected. As the weeds grow among the wheat, the Master and His plan still prevail.

WAITING ON GOD

9When he opened the fifth seal, I saw under the altar the souls of the ones slaughtered because of the word of God and the witness they had. 10They cried out in a loud voice, "Until when, holy master and true, until you judge and avenge our blood from the inhabitants on the earth?" 11And a white robe was given to each of them, and they were told that they rest still a little time, until the number of their fellow servants and brothers who are to be killed as they had been was completed.

These verses contain a remarkable message for all who suffer for their faith—especially those who have been martyred around the world. The word "slain" in verse 9 is the same word used about the Lamb in 5:6 and 5:12. The believers who were killed followed in the footsteps of their Savior, Jesus. These verses also validate the suffering and fear of those who listened to this message. God knew their pain. He was aware of their trial.

Verse ten brings the cry reminiscent of Psalm 13, *"How long, O Lord?"* It is a cry that every believer knows. During pain and heartbreak, we cry out to the One who has promised to return. How long? How long will the hurt last? The answer brings comfort and confidence. Each slain saint was given a white robe. The language is similar to the horsemen—they received something from outside themselves. But this was a gracious gift from God, a white robe. Cleansing. Healing. New life. They would have to wait just a little longer as God unfolded His plan. Just a little longer living life among the weeds.

This is challenging news. More suffering would come. Our job is to wait. Why? We have a job to do. We are called to be the light of Christ in a dark world. We are called to make disciples. We are called to be God's holy people.

In an article by Gordon MacDonald called "Take Time to be What?" (Leadership Journal, Fall 2007, p.96), MacDonald brought up the subject of holiness. He asked, "Are we inadvertently losing interest in being holy and spending our energies on problem-solving, success, personal fulfillment, and avoiding anything that smacks of suffering?"

He went on to quote evangelist Samuel Brengle: "God does not make pets of His people, and especially of those whom He woos and wins into close fellowship with Himself, and fits and crowns for great and high service. His greatest servants have often been the greatest sufferers."

Why must we wait on the Lord? To grow in Him. To know Him. To bear witness to Him. When will justice finally happen?   How can you endure when extreme suffering exerts its crushing pressure? Look at the next seal:

12*I saw when he opened the sixth seal that a great earthquake happened, and the sun became black as a sackcloth made of goat hair, and the whole moon became as blood,*

If these events sound familiar to you, you're right. Luke 23:44-45a describes the scene: *"It was now about the sixth hour, and darkness came over the whole land until the ninth hour.*

How can you endure? When will justice happen? The answer is in Jesus. Jesus sustains you through the journey of life. Ultimate justice happened on the cross. In the midst of persecution and loss, God's people were directed to the cross. While pain, scarcity, Roman domination, and death were grim realities for believers, the ultimate reality was the atoning death of Jesus Christ. It was the reality that conquered the intrusions of sin and injustice. It was the reality that gave life and hope. "Remember Jesus!" is the cry of Revelation. "Remember your hope!"

13and the stars of the heavens fell to earth, as a fig tree throws its late figs from a fig tree by means of a strong wind. 14Heaven was split open as a scroll, rolling up, and every mountain and island was removed from its place. 15And the kings of the earth, the princes, the generals, the wealthy, the mighty, and every slave and every free man hid in caves and among the rocks of the mountains. 16They said to the mountains and the rocks, "Fall on us and hide us from the face of the one seated on the throne and from the wrath of the Lamb! 17For the great day of their wrath has come, and who is able to stand?"

The Scriptural truth of the end times is reinforced over and over again in the book of Revelation. Old and New Testament messages are brought again to the listeners' ears. Isaiah 34:4 says, *"All the stars of the heavens will be dissolved and the sky rolled up like a scroll; all the starry host will fall like withered leaves from the vine, like shriveled figs from the fig tree."* Jesus declared in Matthew 24:29-30, *"Immediately after the distress of those days 'the sun will be darkened, and the moon will not give its light; the stars will fall from the sky, and the heavenly bodies will be shaken.' At that time the sign of the Son of Man will appear in the sky, and all the nations of the earth will mourn. They will see the Son of Man coming on the clouds of the sky, with power and great glory."*

Revelation captures both the current state of affairs and the judgment to come. God's promises have not changed. Jesus spoke the words of verse sixteen in Luke 23:30: *"Then 'they will say to the mountains, "Fall on us!" and to the hills, "Cover us!"'"* The "great day of their wrath" is referred to in Joel 2:31: *"The sun will be turned to darkness and the moon to blood before the coming of the great and dreadful day of the LORD."*

Judgment is coming for all those who do evil. God has not forgotten His people. The book of Revelation seems to be God's way of shaking the cobwebs from the minds of believers. The Lord brings His Word back to them in a way that rekindles hope and reminds them of His active presence in the world—even in a world that seems to be falling apart.

God really does an amazing thing in the book of Revelation. Even for you, the reader of today, God compresses so much of His Word into the book that it sends you running into the Scriptures, searching for His promises and reviewing the context of those promises. Suddenly you remember God's attitude toward evil, His faithfulness to His people, His unwavering grace and love, and His undeniable track record throughout history. Suddenly, in a world full of grief, fear, and misery, you remember there is a reason to hope. God is in control. Everything is not as it seems. Evil will not win the day. In a world where everything seems so wrong, there is a multitude of faithful believers on earth and in heaven who bear witness to the truth of God's active, saving, and victorious presence.

As you feel the pressure and pain of weeds brushing up against you, you can take heart that the harvest will come. Until then, your Master will not forsake you. Even if life on this earth, with all its brutality, does you in, the blood of Jesus assures you that you will be brought safely into your Master's storehouse. And that's when life really begins.

Study Guide for Revelation Chapter 6

1. This chapter brings up the question of evil. Discuss why bad things happen and what God's role is in the midst of it all.

2. Read Revelation 6:1-4. How do you see this reality today?

3. Read Revelation 6:5-6. So far you've seen how the book of Revelation is filled with key messages for people living in the first century. What does this tell you about God?

4. Read Revelation 6:7-8. Only one-fourth of the earth was affected by the violence of verse 8. Talk about how the media might make you feel as if all is lost.

5. How does God correct your perspective?

6. Read Revelation 6:9-11. More Christians were martyred in the twentieth century that in all of history. What do these verses tell you about God's attitude toward them and care for them?

7. Read Revelation 6:12-17. How do these verses turn the priorities and values of our culture upside-down? What direction do they give to your life today?

Revelation
Chapter Seven

†

One book I have on my nightstand is <u>The Reagan Diaries</u>. These presidential journal entries are fascinating. You can read President Reagan's thoughts about everything from his assessment of international leaders to what movie he liked best in the White House theater. You can read how he missed his wife during extended trips and what he loved most about being the President of the United States. In some cases, Ronald Reagan seems like an ordinary guy. At other times it is simply overwhelming to read about the decisions and actions he had to handle. Who could have ever known what the president was really thinking about? The glimpse is remarkable!

The book of Revelation does something similar with the Almighty God. When you read this prophetic vision, you get a glimpse of what He is thinking. You gain insight into the mind of God!

THE MIND OF GOD

1After this I saw four angels standing on the four corners of the earth, holding the four winds of the earth in order that the wind would not blow on the earth or the sea or on any tree. 2And I saw another angel coming up from the east, having the seal of the living God, and he cried out in a loud voice to the four angels to whom it had been given to harm the earth and the sea: 3"Do not harm the earth or the sea or the trees until we seal the servants of our God on their foreheads."

In the book of Matthew, Jesus spoke of the four winds in the context of His second coming: *"At that time the sign of the Son of Man will appear in the sky, and all the nations of the earth will mourn. They will see the Son of Man coming on the clouds of the sky, with power and great glory. And he will send his angels with a loud trumpet call, and they will gather his elect from the four winds, from one end of the heavens to the other"* (Matthew 24:30-31). Judgment is on its way. What is God thinking as the great day approaches?

According to Revelation chapter 7, He is thinking about the people He loves and cares so deeply for. So, in order to make sure that no eternal harm comes to His children, He puts a hold on the entire judgment process! Why? To put a seal of ownership on the foreheads of the servants of God. Remember what Paul said in 2 Corinthians 1:21-22: *"Now it is God who makes both us and you stand firm in Christ. He anointed us, set his seal of ownership on us, and put his Spirit in our hearts as a deposit, guaranteeing what is to come."* Ezekiel 9:1-6 also contains a reference to marked foreheads of people who would be spared (*"Slaughter old men, young men and maidens, women and children, but do not touch anyone who has the mark."*).

Isn't it just like our Savior God to alter His plans in order to rescue and care for His people? His willingness to spare Sodom and Gomorrah for ten people (Genesis 18:32) shows that He will go to great lengths to reach out to His people. The effort of the shepherd in the parable of the lost sheep, the woman in the parable of the lost coin, and the father in the parable of the prodigal son (Luke 15) shows that God will stop at nothing to help us. The sacrifice of Jesus on the cross shows without a doubt that God will step in boldly when the lives of His loved ones are at stake. In Revelation 7 God puts the brakes on Judgment Day because He doesn't want to lose any of His servants.

THE 144,000

4And I heard the number of the ones sealed: 144,000 from all the tribes of the sons of Israel.

Verse four brings us one of the most intriguing questions in the book of Revelation. What does the 144,000 mean? Some claim it is the literal number of believers meant for heaven. But remember, numbers in the book of Revelation tell stories of God's action in the world and among His people. What God-story does 144,000 tell?

The story begins with the identity of the ones sealed. Verse three tells us that the number refers to "the servants of our God." Chapter 7 also tells us that the 144,000 are located on earth. These are living believers.

This 144,000 consists of followers of Christ who still suffer the challenges of life in a broken world.

The number 144,000 is also mentioned in Revelation chapter 14. It is used to refer to the multitudes of the redeemed in heaven. Are there two sets of 144,000? What story does this number tell?

We are offered clues in Revelation 21:9-17. In these verses the numbers 144 and 12,000 are used to describe the perfection, wholeness, and vast dimensions of heaven. We've already seen the number 12 used to symbolize the church, both Old and New Testament believers. The equation of 12 x 12 x 1000 tells the story of a large and complete group of God's people.

The number 144,000, therefore, tells the story of God's church, His people throughout the ages. It is a large number—a perfect number. The number 12 tells the story of the Old Testament Church—the twelve tribes of Israel, God's chosen people. The number 12 also tells the story of the New Testament Church—represented by the twelve disciples. In James 1:1, the writer even refers to New Testament believers as *"the twelve tribes scattered among the nations."* When the Old Testament and the New Testament are combined—multiplied, and again multiplied by perfection and wholeness (10 x 10 x 10), the vast and perfect number of believers is displayed. This is God's "rescue tally."

What a comfort for believers to hear that God sealed the perfect and complete number of His people—no one would be left out or forgotten. This is true of heaven as seen in Revelation 14. It is also true of earth. Chapter 7 emphasizes the fact that even though Christians on earth feel like persecution and corruption cut them off from God, they are not overlooked. They are seen, cared for, and sealed.

A few years ago the news of a cave-in at a South African mine hit the headlines. Three-thousand miners were trapped deep below the surface of the earth. Escape routes were blocked. The only way to reach the workers was through a supply elevator. Immediately, food and water were sent down to the trapped workers. Then, slowly and painstakingly, little huddles of miners were brought to the surface in the supply elevator. Each group was greeted with cheers. The name of each individual was checked against a master list of mine workers. The evacuation went on for days until the last worker was evacuated from the mine. Not one was lost. Every name on the list was accounted for.

The rescue list in Revelation 7 gave the powerful message to each individual believer that he or she would never be forgotten. Now matter how bad things looked, each precious child of God would be accounted for. In a world of turmoil and in a life that may be pushing you to your limits, the same message applies. You are not forgotten. You are not overlooked. Your name is on the rescue list. You are sealed for salvation.

The number 144,000 also showed that no believer in Christ is an afterthought. First-century believers could take heart that they were part of God's story of salvation throughout the ages. They were connected with God's saving work from the beginning of time, through the cross of Christ, all the way to the topsy-turvy and uncertain time in which they lived. The same is true of twenty-first century believers. God's plan of rescue includes you!

144,000 is a number that brings relief as well. The number told the story that the first-century followers of Jesus were not merely a few huddled groups of suffering believers isolated and alone in a culture of unbelief and persecution. There was a bigger picture. As Elijah was comforted with the news that God reserved *"seven thousand in Israel--all whose knees have not bowed down to Baal and all whose mouths have not kissed him"* (1 Kings 19:18), the suffering believers in the first century were encouraged and inspired by the 144,000 sealed for protection and care. The believers in the seven cities of Asia Minor weren't alone! This was God's Church, the body of Christ, the fellowship of the saints. There was more to it than met the eye, and nothing would separate them from His love! For every believer fighting the good fight of faith, the number 144,000 tells the story that we are not alone, we are not abandoned. God's church is not crumbling. His will is not being defeated. We press on in good company.

But there is more as the 144,000 is unpacked in verses 5-8:

5From the tribe of Judah 12,000 were sealed, from the tribe of Reuben 12,000, from the tribe of Gad 12,000,

6from the tribe of Asher 12,000, from the tribe of Naphtali 12,000, from the tribe of Manasseh 12,000, 7from the tribe of Simeon 12,000, from the tribe of Levi 12,000, from the tribe of Issachar 12,000, 8from the tribe of Zebulun 12,000, from the tribe of Joseph 12,000, from the tribe of Benjamin 12,000 sealed.

The Old Testament has at least eighteen different orders when it lists the twelve tribes of Israel. The order of the tribes in Revelation would immediately stand out to the listeners. Judah, though fourth born of the sons, is listed first. Revelation 5:5 introduced us to the Lion of the tribe of Judah, Jesus. He sets the pace.

Dan and Ephraim are missing from the list in Revelation. We hear in the Old Testament that these two tribes worshipped idols (For example, Judges 18:30-31: *"The Danites set up for themselves the idols, and Jonathan son of Gershom, the son of Moses, and his sons were priests for the tribe of Dan until the time of the captivity of the land. They continued to use the idols Micah had made, all the time the house of God was in Shiloh."* Also Hosea 5:11: *"Ephraim is oppressed, trampled in judgment, intent on pursuing idols."*). Joseph and Levi are included instead of the unfaithful tribes. Clearly, no unfaithful people would be allowed in God's company. For a culture in which Roman idolatry was a primary temptation, this was a meaningful message. Being faithful to God was worth it. Suffering for Him was not meaningless.

This message is underscored as the vision shifts from earth to heaven. Another multitude is introduced—

one that shows every earth-dwelling believer that heaven is real and wonderful.

A CROWD IN HEAVEN

9After this I looked and behold, a great crowd which no one was able to count. From every nation, tribe, people and tongue, standing before the throne and in before the Lamb, clothed in white robes, and palm branches in their hands.

This great multitude showed that God's people included a cross-section of all people. The Lord's reach of grace extends beyond what we can see or imagine. Salvation in Christ was not for one nation, tribe, people or language. It was meant for all nations and all people. First-century believers were being cast as "outsiders" by both Rome and the Jewish community. Verse nine shows that those who trusted in Christ were "insiders" in the salvation celebration by His grace.

10And they cried out in a loud voice: "Salvation belongs to our God, to the one who sits on the throne, and to the Lamb." 11And the angels were standing around the throne and around the elders and the four living things, and they fell before the throne on their faces and worshiped God 12saying: "Amen! Blessing and glory and wisdom and thanks and honor and power and strength be to our God for ever and ever. Amen!" 13And one of the elders asked me, "The ones clothed in white robes, who are they and from where did they come?" 14I answered, "My lord, you know." And he said to me, "These are the ones coming from the great tribulation; they have washed their robes and bleached them in the blood of the Lamb."

I love this heavenly scene. There is worship and praise in heaven for what really matters: salvation. As the throng bows before God, one of the elders asks John a question, "Who are these in white robes and where did they come from?" Why the question? John's response gives the answer, "Sir, you know." In other words, there's no mystery here. The answer is evident. Here is something we know for sure. The way to heaven, the way out of the broken, hurt-filled, life-crushing, faith-straining, sin-stained world is to be washed in the blood of the Lamb.

Hebrews 9:14 compares the blood of bulls and goats in sacrifices to the blood of Jesus shed on the cross: *"How much more, then, will the blood of Christ, who through the eternal Spirit offered himself unblemished to God, cleanse our consciences from acts that lead to death, so that we may serve the living God!"* How do you get to heaven? Through the blood of Christ. 1 Peter 1:18-19 gives the clear and straight truth: *"For you know that it was not with perishable things such as silver or gold that you were redeemed from the empty way of life handed down to you from your forefathers, but with the precious blood of Christ, a lamb without blemish or defect."* You know! That's what John said to the elder. You know! That's the way to heaven. That's the way to new life. That's the way to peace and protection in the presence of God. It's not a hidden mystery. The way has been made known!

THE GREAT TRIBULATION

We can't move past verse fourteen without asking the question, "What is the great tribulation?" Some teachers assert that it is a period of seven years of great suffering before a literal one-thousand year reign of Christ on earth. There have been popular books that make this claim as well. The "Left Behind" series of books uses this time progression in a fictional account of the end times and last days. The important question to ask is: What does the Bible say?

First, we notice that the people who are in heaven have already come out of the great tribulation. It's already happened to them. They've experienced it. It was suffering and persecution and sin they endured on earth. The Bible makes very clear that "tribulation" is all about this side of heaven—a broken and groaning world. The Greek word for "tribulation" is "thlipsis." This word is used four other times in Revelation:

1:9 – John is a companion in suffering (thlipsis).

2:9 – "I [Jesus] know your afflictions (thlipsis)."

2:10 – "You will have thlipsis ten days."

2:22 – "I am throwing the ones committing adultery with her into great thlipsis (great tribulation)."

Elsewhere in the Bible the word describes the pains of living on earth before Christ comes:

Matthew 24:21- "For then [the end times and fall of temple] there will be great tribulation (thlipsis), unequaled from the beginning of the world until now."

Matthew 24:29 - Immediately after the distress (thlipsis) of those days...(the coming of Christ in verses 29-30)."

1 Thessalonians 1:6 – "You became imitators of us and the Lord; in spite of severe suffering (thlipsis)."

Hebrews 10:32-33 – "Sometimes you were publicly exposed to insult and persecution (thlipsis)."

The Bible shows that tribulation is what is happening now as we wait for Jesus' final return. Jesus even mentions *great* tribulation as a current condition. The great tribulation is the groaning of creation as we await final redemption (Romans 8:23). Entering heaven means coming out of the great tribulation. These are not code words for a time yet to come. These are words that describe NOW. Believers in the first century knew it. So do we.

Jesus' mention of "great tribulation" in Matthew 24 was probably pointing to both the end of the world and to the coming destruction of the temple in 70 A.D. After Nero died in 68 A.D., Emperor Vespasian's troops advanced against rebellious Jerusalem. The siege caused horrible destruction and death. Thousands of Jews were slaughtered. Thousands were enslaved. Many more were sent to Rome's arenas to be butchered. Historian Josephus recorded the account of the slaughter in the temple. He said that blood ran out the doors due to the massive number of casualties.

The mention of ones who came out of the "great tribulation" in Revelation 7 may be a reference to Jesus' label for that deadly siege and the destruction of the temple in Jerusalem. In addition to offering comfort to scattered Jewish believers who remembered that day, the reference in chapter 7 reinforces a post-temple-destruction date of Revelation's writing.

We also know that "thlipsis," tribulation, will intensify as the end of the world draws closer. Chapter 8 will outline that difficult fact. In the meantime, the refuge and restoration of heaven brings comfort and strength for all who continue their journey through great "thlipsis."

WHAT IS HEAVEN LIKE?

15Because of this, "they are before the throne of God and serve him day and night in his temple; and the one sitting on the throne will spread his tent over them. 16They will not hunger anymore, nor will they thirst, nor will the sun beat upon them, nor any heat, 17because the Lamb who is at the center of the throne will tend them like a shepherd, and he will lead them to living springs of water, and God will wipe away every tear from their eyes."

Heaven has long been publicized as a place that is populated by harp-strumming angels floating on clouds.

As I grew up and heard heaven described this way, I thought it sounded pretty boring. Revelation 7 helps us understand that heaven is anything but boring.

The word for "serve" in verse fifteen ("latreuo" in Greek) is used to express the complete life-conduct of a believer in Christ. It communicates whole-life worship, just as Paul described in Romans 12:1, *"Therefore, I urge you, brothers, in view of God's mercy, to offer your bodies as living sacrifices, holy and pleasing to God--this is your spiritual act of worship."* The word also refers to using specific gifts and talents to the glory of God. Like the use of the word in Revelation 7, Revelation 22:3 also uses the word in the context of heaven. It reinforces the fact that we will not be floating on clouds in heaven. Life in the presence of the Lamb, our Shepherd, will not be boring. We will be using our specific gifts to glorify God. We will be engaged in activity that is stimulating, fulfilling, and helpful to the people of God. Life in heaven will be exciting! Every moment will be compelling. We will be complete, fulfilling the perfect purpose God has for our lives. Imagine getting out of bed in the morning, eager to face a new day of exactly what you love to do. That is the Biblical picture of heaven!

In addition to being engaged fully in what we are passionate about, obstacles of this world are removed forever in heaven. There is no more scarcity or suffering. There is no more sadness or pain. Tears are wiped away and life in all its fullness is what awaits us. Imagine the encouragement these words brought to the huddled masses of sufferers in the seven cities of Asia Minor. Do you see the encouragement this picture of heaven brings to you?

Heaven is our goal. It's where we're headed. Life this side of heaven is just a shadow of the glory that awaits us. Now is the warm-up for forever. And because God wants us to experience this precious gift, He waits. He stopped everything. He put judgment on pause.

As Peter said in his second letter when discussing the final coming of Jesus, *"The Lord is not slow in keeping his promise, as some understand slowness. He is patient with you, not wanting anyone to perish, but everyone to come to repentance" (3:9).* God loves you. He wants you to be with Him forever. So He waits.

Revelation chapter 7 lets every sufferer know what is on God's mind. You are.

Study Guide for Revelation Chapter 7

1. Read Revelation 7:1-3. How have you seen God's timing in your life?

2. Revelation 7:4-8 brings up the number 144,000. What have you heard about this number and how does this chapter shed light on it for you?

3. Read Revelation 7:9-14. How do these verses clarify what God has done and is doing to save people?

4. Discuss what you have heard about "the great tribulation." How does the discussion in this chapter help you understand what it means?

5. Read Revelation 7:15-17. This is one of the most comforting sections of the Bible. What comfort do these verses give you about your loved ones in heaven?

6. What comfort do they give you about your current journey of life?

7. How does this glimpse of heaven raise your hopes about the hereafter?

Revelation
Chapter Eight

✝

In Revelation chapter 8 the imagery of the seven seals flows into the imagery of seven trumpets. Trumpets were a big deal in the Bible and brought a set of power-packed messages to the listeners of Revelation. Adding trumpets to the mural of this vision deepened its meaning. These trumpets were "shofars." You may have seen pictures of these hollowed out ram's horns being blown by priestly figures. With just one mention of a shofar, first-century believers could recall the action of God throughout the centuries.

In Exodus 19:6 the shofar was sounded to show God's presence at Mount Sinai: *"On the morning of the third day there was thunder and lightning, with a thick cloud over the mountain, and a very loud trumpet blast. Everyone in the camp trembled."*

In Joshua 6:16 the shofar indicated the judgment and triumph of God as the walls of Jericho came tumbling down: *"The seventh time around, when the priests sounded the trumpet blast, Joshua commanded the people, 'Shout! For the LORD has given you the city!'"*

In Psalm 150:3 the shofar was used to give praise to God: *"Praise him with the sounding of the trumpet."*

In Nehemiah 4:20 the shofar summoned God's people to battle: *"Wherever you hear the sound of the trumpet, join us there. Our God will fight for us!"*

The trumpet was intimately connected with the presence of God and His action for His people. When first-century listeners heard the mention of the trumpet, they knew some powerful God-activity was in the works. And what activity stood out most? The return of the Lord!

Joel 2:1 says, *"Blow the trumpet in Zion; sound the alarm on my holy hill. Let all who live in the land tremble, for the day of the LORD is coming. It is close at hand."*

Zechariah 9:14 connected the trumpet to the coming of the Lord: *"Then the LORD will appear over them; his arrow will flash like lightning. The Sovereign LORD will sound the trumpet; he will march in the storms of the south."*

Jesus reinforced the Old Testament message of the trumpet when He spoke in Matthew 24:31, *"And he will send his angels with a loud trumpet call, and they will gather his elect from the four winds, from one end of the heavens to the other."*

Paul delivered the trumpet-call, coming-of-the-Lord message in 1 Corinthians 15:51-52, *"Listen, I tell you a mystery: We will not all sleep, but we will all be changed-- in a flash, in the twinkling of an eye, at the last trumpet. For the trumpet will sound, the dead will be raised imperishable, and we will be changed."*

The message was driven home in 1 Thessalonians 4:16, *"For the Lord himself will come down from heaven, with a loud command, with the voice of the archangel and with the trumpet call of God, and the dead in Christ will rise first."*

One mention of the shofar to a believer in the late first century brought the immediate hope and excited expectation of the return of Jesus. He was close! He is coming soon!

SOUNDS AND SILENCE

1When he opened the seventh seal, silence happened in heaven for one half hour. 2And I saw the seven angels who stand before God, and to them were given seven trumpets. 3Another angel came and stood on the altar, having a gold incense container, and much incense was given to him to give with the prayers of all the saints on the golden altar before the throne. 4The smoke of the incense with the prayers of the saints went up from the hand of the angel before God.

This book of the Bible is action packed, but chapter 8 directs us to realities of life with God that we may very well overlook. God isn't all about fast and frantic movement. If the Bible teaches anything, it seems to show us that God is very deliberate. He does everything in His time. He also urges us to savor living in His time. In Psalm 46:10 the Lord says, *"Be still and know that I am God."* 1 Thessalonians 4:11 tells us, *"Make it your ambition to lead a quiet life."* Not your hobby. Not your occasional activity. Your ambition!

In the context of constant worry, evasion, struggle, and scrimping, early believers saw that God was at peace. The silence of heaven and the careful offering of their very own prayers invited them into God's safe and restoring pace.

This brings up the question for today: what is life as a believer meant to be? Is it all about "getting it done"? Is it meant to mimic the relentless corporate rhythm of 24-7-365? Revelation chapter 8 introduces us to God's pace. Life is not meant to be frantic all the time. God desires and treasures quietness. Revelation shows us that prayer, time of solitude with God, and the small and quiet parts of our lives make a tremendous difference. They imitate His pace and unite us in His work.

While our gut reaction under pressure is to speed up, do more, and add to the schedule, God's reaction to the increasing pressure of a fallen world is to slow down and reach into the lives of His people. Our reaction to handling the problems of a broken world involves more programs, laws, and lists of things to do. God's reaction was a baby born in Bethlehem, a Son walking the earth, and a Savior nailed to a cross.

How do you respond when life gets complicated and demanding? Do you ramp up your activity level and exhaust yourself? Sure, you've got to meet responsibilities and get things done, but is there any space for what God wants to do in you and with you? Is there time for quiet and prayer? Will you let God accomplish His work in your life, or will all your activity drown Him out?

There was one half-hour of silence in heaven. What happened during that thirty-minute period? Was God thinking about you? Did He stop everything to marvel at the gift of salvation for you? Did He pause to ponder your fervent prayers and cries for help?

If the God of the universe quiets everything for a half-hour, shouldn't your life reflect His rhythm with some quietness, too?

THE ACTION BEGINS

5The angel took the incense container and filled it with fire from the altar, and he threw it to the earth; and thunder and noise and lightning and an earthquake happened. 6The seven angels having the seven trumpets prepared to sound them. 7The first sounded his trumpet, and it happened, hail and fire mixed with blood was thrown to the earth, and a third of the earth was consumed and a third of the trees were consumed and all the green grass was consumed.

Now the action begins. It is important to notice the pictures and themes that recall the Exodus of God's people from Egypt. This miraculous deliverance was the highpoint of God's saving activity before the coming of Christ. It was the reference point of God's people for centuries. The Exodus showed that even after a long time of suffering, God hears the cries of His people and responds with power to crush the enemy. The fire, thunder, lightning and earthquake of verse five recall the presence of God on Mount Sinai. The hail and the blood of verse seven bring to mind the plagues sent to Egypt. The message to God's first-century captive people was that He is near. He was responding to their cries. He has come down to save them!

This fearsome blast was directed to the persecutors of God's people. One-third of the earth, grass, and trees were burned up. God did not completely destroy the earth—there was still time for repentance. But God was at work to release His people from bondage.

What does this destruction and turmoil mean? First, it emphasizes the fact that God does address evil and wickedness with punishment and discomfort (in order to bring repentance—as we'll see). Second, it underscores the truth that the world is a battleground. Jesus reminded us about these challenging facts when He said in John 16:33, *"In this world you will have trouble. But take heart! I have overcome the world."*

The life of a believer is filled with struggle. Followers of Jesus are strangers in this foreign land of a world. A journey of faith doesn't mean that the world keeps getting nicer, that you experience less suffering as time goes by, or that pressure in life decreases. Yes, you enjoy blessings and provision and protection. But as we get closer to the end, God's people will face adversity and turmoil. As the Israelites in captivity were called to trust the Lord and be obedient to Him, you are also called to trust and obey. In these last days, how will you respond?

A NEW EGYPT INDICTED

8The second angel sounded his trumpet, and something like a large mountain of burning fire was thrown into the sea, and a third of the sea became blood, 9and a third of the living creatures in the sea died, and a third of the ships were destroyed. 10The third angel sounded his trumpet, and a great burning star like a torch fell from heaven, and it fell on a third of the rivers and on the springs of water, 11and the name of the star is Wormwood. A third of the waters became wormwood, and many people died from the waters that became bitter.

As the trumpets sound, all of creation begins to be affected by the devastation of judgment. There is no escaping God's pounding on the door of a rebellious world. The "Egypt" of the first century was the Roman Empire. Christians were suffering under persecution, deprivation, confiscation of goods, the inability to conduct business, rumors of being atheists (because they did not believe in the pantheon of Roman Gods), and even the accusations of cannibalism (because of misunderstanding about Holy Communion). Believers were being crushed by an arrogant empire that seemed to dominate every aspect of life.

Once again, the water that turns to blood in verse eight reminds us of the plagues in Egypt. What were God's people to do when the assault on evil began?

Psalm 46 gives guidance: *"We will not fear, though the earth give way and the mountains fall into the heart of the sea."* It was time to keep trusting in God.

The book of Revelation is filled with frightening images like the ones in these verses. Chaos and disaster rain upon the earth. What does it all mean? Are these prophecies of spaceships, nuclear warfare, or meteors? Do these verses give a secret look ahead to the technological warfare of modern times? You've heard that kind of teaching before. Is that the message of Revelation?

Before you get too far off course, you must remember to look at the big picture, the vision, the mural. Take a look again at the cover of this book. Look at the collection of images. Remember that Revelation is also a collection of images that offers a profound message— ultimately a message of truth that brings comfort and salvation. Chapter 8 gives us the unvarnished truth that what we live in and depend on will all come to ruin. The days are numbered for this earth and our resources. Faith in the true God is what lasts—nothing else! Not even the mighty empire of Rome.

That's where the mention of Wormwood in verse eleven comes into the picture.

Bitter water can be traced back to Jeremiah 9:15 and 23:15, *"Therefore, this is what the LORD Almighty says concerning the prophets: 'I will make them eat bitter food and drink poisoned water, because from the prophets of Jerusalem ungodliness has spread throughout the land.'"* Bitter, poisonous water is connected with ungodliness and false prophets. This is a strong message for the religion of Rome and for all false religions. They are deadly. Believers could take note and be warned not to give in to false teaching.

But the message runs even deeper. The scientific name for Wormwood is the genus "Artemisia." This name is taken from Artemis, the Greek name for the Roman goddess Diana. The ancient myth surrounding Diana says that she delivered the poisonous powers of Wormwood to Chiron the Centaur. He, in turn, named the plant after her (Botanical.com – "Wormwood").

Diana worship was central to the life of the Roman Empire (see Acts 19:28 and surrounding verses). With one clear reference, the Revelation vision shows that Diana (Artemis) is a poisonous curse who brings only death. This clarity about the corrupt and hollow Roman religion brought relief and courage to God's people who were being pressured to cave in and worship these false gods. More references to the gods of Rome will appear in Revelation. This assault on Diana served as a stirring apologetic for faith in the true God and Savior, Jesus Christ. The new "Egypt" was as corrupt as the old. Its destiny of destruction would be the same as well.

A WARNING TO THE UNFAITHFUL

12The fourth angel sounded his trumpet, and he struck a third of the sun, a third of the moon, and a third of the stars, so that a third of them would be darkened. A third of the day would not shine and the night likewise. 13And I looked and heard an eagle flying in midair saying with a loud voice: "Woe! Woe! Woe to the inhabitants of the earth, because of the trumpet blasts about to be sounded by the three angels!"

Once again we encounter Exodus plague imagery. Darkness begins to envelop the earth. God's work to free His people continued. Believers could let out a cheer. The Lord was not absent. He was not inactive. Just as He came through during the time of Moses, He was at work in the present day. He is at work for you—even now!

Then an eagle appears. The Scripture saturated nature of Revelation shows itself again as chapter 8 comes to a close. Reference points to the Old Testament prophets pop up over and over again in this grand vision. The Word of God was being brought to people who needed the truth. Verse thirteen brings images from the prophet Hosea. In Hosea 8:1 a trumpet and eagle appear together: *"Put the trumpet to your lips! An eagle is over the house of the LORD because the people have broken my covenant and rebelled against my law."*

The prophet goes on to pronounce judgment on faithless Israel. Hosea utters the famous line, *"They sow the wind and reap the whirlwind" (vs. 7).*

During these last days, as life seems to be coming apart, it is not time to be faithless. It is not time to walk away from the Savior. It is not time to deny Jesus.

Disaster is the only result of abandoning the faith. All who are venturing into or considering compromise are given fair warning. A life apart from Christ is a life of woe!

More noise is on its way in the next chapter of Revelation. Chapter 8 offers the silent peace of a listening God to suffering believers. It shows the destructive din of rebellious Rome. It also leads us to consider what this world offers compared to the promise of our Savior.

How are you being tempted to abandon Jesus and His ways? What poison is seeping into your life? How do you need to be still and know the true God in a new and life-restoring way? The book of Revelation seeks to keep these questions alive for each believer traveling through this challenging and broken world.

Study Guide for Revelation Chapter 8

1. Read Revelation 8:1-4. What do your prayers mean to God?

2. How does this affect your prayer life?

3. Think about how often you have quiet moments in life. What benefit do these times of solitude bring?

4. Read Revelation 8:5-7. Talk about how the punishment of evil is an encouraging message.

5. Revelation 8:8-11 provides insight into Roman religion. What false religions exist today, and how do these verses speak to them?

6. Discuss the questions in the final paragraph of this chapter on page 133.

7. Reflect on Revelation 8:12-13. What "woe" do you see in a life apart from Christ?

Revelation
Chapter Nine

†

Revelation chapter 8 highlighted the transitory nature of the world and exposed the deadly nature of Roman idolatry. In chapter 9, the direct assault against idolatry continues.

But why such a fuss over a few false gods? What harm could there be from a few idols on shelves here and there at home? What's the big deal?

The big deal is: idolatry will kill you. Idolatry means dedicating your life to that which will ultimately take life from you. In Roman times and in the centuries before the Roman Empire, allegiance to false gods involved making sacrifices (sometimes human sacrifices!), participating in sexual rites in order to appease the gods and ensure prosperity, seeking knowledge of the future through the gods, and becoming involved in other detestable and destructive acts. Dedication to false gods impacted life at home, life at work, spiritual life, and relationships with others. Idolatry was life-consuming. In Rome, citizens followed the crowd. They worshipped according to the emperor's direction. They dedicated themselves to the gods of the community. They blindly followed the whims of the day in order to stay in good standing with the political powers and with the local leaders. Some worshipped idols out of superstition. Others worshipped idols strategically—

they wanted a favorable position in business and desired to climb the ladder politically.

Unfortunately, those who became involved in idolatry were playing deadly games. Devotion to the Roman pantheon of gods and worship of the emperor led people into lies, corruption, drunkenness, sexual immorality, the destruction of family, and a self-centered life. It also led them further down the road to eternal death in hell. Satan loved the pressure toward and practice of idolatry.

In fact, he still does. Verses twenty and twenty-one of Revelation chapter 9 give a succinct summary of all idolatry, ancient and modern: *"The rest of mankind that were not killed by these plagues still did not repent of the work of their hands; they did not stop worshiping demons, and idols of gold, silver, bronze, stone and wood--idols that cannot see or hear or walk. Nor did they repent of their murders, their magic arts, their sexual immorality or their thefts."* Verse twenty addresses **the works of our hands**. Verse twenty-one points out **the desires of our hearts**.

We live in a time when we are infatuated with the works of our hands. Our attention is drawn to screens—cell phones, iPods, computers, televisions. We love gadgetry—the new things we create. We look for answers in science and revere the latest scientific findings. We seek fulfillment in our technology, in our knowledge, and in our innovations. We claim that if we put our minds to something, we can achieve it. We love the works of our hands! We worship ourselves. We look for wholeness in the next and latest development, in what is created rather than the Creator. But the quest is in vain. We end up with a room full of gadgets, but still have empty and unhappy hearts.

We also live in a time when we are completely taken in by the desires of our hearts. We put trust in our feelings. Our desires are used as the standard for steering our lives. The result is a society trapped in destructive addictions, confused morality, proliferating violence, rampant selfishness, growing unkindness, and decaying relationships.

This is modern idolatry. It all seems so innocent, but the price we pay is high. When our worship is directed away from God, away from truth, and away from life the way God created it and ordered it, everything crumbles. All the while, Satan laughs. He loves it when we destroy ourselves and each other. He loved it when Rome was crumbling under the curse of idolatry. And he wanted to drag every Christian into the destructive fray. This is why the ramped up message against idolatry in Revelation is so important—to believers then and now.

DEMONIC DECEPTION

1The fifth angel sounded his trumpet, and I saw a star that had fallen from heaven to the earth, and he was given the key to the shaft of the Abyss. 2He opened the shaft of the Abyss, and smoke went up from the shaft like the smoke from a great furnace. The sun and sky were darkened by the smoke of the shaft.

God puts His cards on the table right away in Revelation 9. He brings up the subject of hell—the Abyss. It is described as having a shaft that leads to the place of punishment. Shafts in the ground were commonplace in Biblical times—even in some places in the Middle East today. Many of these are wells dug by hand deep into the earth. They're not a place into which anyone wants to fall!

The star that fell to earth is a being. "He" opened the Abyss. Some say this being is Satan. We hear about the fall of Satan and his demons in Revelation 12:9. *"The great dragon was hurled down--that ancient serpent called the devil, or Satan, who leads the whole world astray. He was hurled to the earth, and his angels with him."* In verse four the demons may be portrayed as stars: *"His tail swept a third of the stars out of the sky and flung them to the earth."*

Isaiah 14:11-15 personifies the evil of the King of Babylon as that of Satan. In that description the devil is called a star—a morning star: *"All your pomp has been brought down to the grave, along with the noise of your harps; maggots are spread out beneath you and worms cover you. How you have fallen from heaven, O morning star, son of the dawn! You have been cast down to the earth, you who once laid low the nations! You said in your heart, 'I will ascend to heaven; I will raise my throne above the stars of God; I will sit enthroned on the mount of assembly, on the utmost heights of the sacred mountain. I will ascend above the tops of the clouds; I will make myself like the Most High.' But you are brought down to the grave, to the depths of the pit."*

The first-century listeners to chapter 9 were immediately made aware of the demonic danger they faced during these end times. They were also alerted to another dangerous connection with a prominent Roman god. The fallen star origin of verse one resembles the mythical birthplace of Apollo. Apollo and his twin sister Diana (Artemis) were born on the island of Asteria. The name of the island is very similar to the Greek word for "star": "astera." This is just the beginning of a clarifying assault on the god Apollo.

THE CALL TO REPENTANCE

3And out of the smoke came locusts to the earth, and authority was given to them as scorpions have authority of the earth. 4It was said to them not to harm the grass of the earth nor all the plants nor all the trees, except the men who do not have the seal of God on their foreheads. 5They were not given power to kill them, but only to torment them for five months. And their torment was like the torment of a scorpion when it stings a man. 6In those days men will seek death and they will not find it, and they will long to die and death will flee from them. 7The appearance of the locusts was like horses getting ready for war. On their heads they wore something like crowns of gold, and their faces were as faces of men. 8They had hair like women's hair, and their teeth were like lions' teeth. 9They had breastplates like breastplates of iron, and the sound of their wings was like the sound of many chariot horses running into battle.

The connections with God's plagues in the book of Exodus continue. Exodus chapter 10 recounts the plague of locusts against the Egyptians. For first-century listeners, the reference in Revelation 9 showed that God's judgment against evil had not fallen by the wayside. As He was at work with the patriarchs, He is still at work with His beloved people. But an additional Biblical connection to locusts existed. The prophetic book of Joel brought news of a locust plague. With a description similar to Revelation 9, Joel says,

> *"What the locust swarm has left the great locusts have eaten; what the great locusts have left the young locusts have eaten; what the young locusts have left other locusts have eaten. Wake up, you drunkards, and weep! Wail, all you drinkers of wine; wail because of the new wine, for it has been snatched from your lips. A nation has invaded my land, powerful and without number; it has the teeth of a lion, the fangs of a lioness" (1:4-6).*

The locusts in Joel are also portrayed as horses:

> *"They have the appearance of horses; they gallop along like cavalry. With a noise like that of chariots they leap over the mountaintops, like a crackling fire consuming stubble, like a mighty army drawn up for battle" (2:4-5).*

Most important is the purpose of this locust plague. Joel describes it in 2:12-13:

> *"'Even now,' declares the LORD, 'return to me with all your heart, with fasting and weeping and mourning.' Rend your heart and not your garments. Return to the LORD your God, for he is gracious and compassionate, slow to anger and abounding in love, and he relents from sending calamity."*

The desired outcome of the locust onslaught was repentance, returning to the Lord for life and salvation. The same result was the point of the fifth trumpet. God desired the salvation of His people. He strained to call them back. He went to great lengths to rescue them. The first-century listeners were reminded that even turmoil in the world is used by God to bring people back to Himself. Revelation 9:20 reinforces this point: *"The rest of mankind that were not killed by these plagues still did not repent of the work of their hands."* The goal was repentance.

How important it is to realize that turmoil on earth and in life does not mean God has ceased to be in control. On the contrary, sometimes He is working through the worst of circumstances to bring us to the best outcomes. This is a difficult truth. It requires total dependence on God and unwavering faith and trust in Him. This trust is fueled by His Word—His track record through history. As Scriptural connections surface in Revelation, listeners are reminded that God is faithful. He does come through. He keeps His promises. He wins the day.

While God uses these awful events for His goals and purposes, there is no question about the source of these afflictions. The locusts came from the Abyss. They originated in hell's dark smoke. God lets believers know that disobedience has demonic roots. Evil's tentacles reach to hell. Toying with that which opposes God is dangerous business. St. Paul highlighted the real nature of this earthly battle in Ephesians 6:11-12:

> *"Put on the full armor of God so that you can take your stand against the devil's schemes. For our struggle is not against flesh and blood, but against the rulers, against the authorities, against the powers of this dark world and against the spiritual forces of evil in the heavenly realms."*

The good news in this stinging plague of locusts is that Christians would be spared. Those who had the seal of God on their foreheads could not be harmed. God was in control. The locusts' power could only go as far as God determined. What a relief to know that God is guarding His redeemed from the full onslaught of the world's turmoil. What a wake-up call to realize that dabbling in the demonic and allying oneself with evil will lead to terrible suffering!

Revelation 9:5 indicates that this suffering would happen for five months. The number five may tell two stories in this verse. First, the lifespan of a locust is about five months. The suffering from this trumpet was not final. It was temporary in nature for the purpose of bringing people to repentance. Second, the number five tells the story of the Pentateuch, the first five books of the Old

Testament. The message may be that these locusts will bring people through the course of God's law. He has a complete will and plan for His people. God's precepts will hold sway, not the dominance of Rome, false religion, or selfish human wills.

The locusts in this section recall the fearsome look of the locusts that would plague disobedient Judah. They also unmask the evil of the god Apollo. Revelation 9:7 describes the locusts as wearing *"something like crowns of gold."* The word for "crown" is "stephanos." The god Apollo was always pictured wearing this type of laurel leaf victory crown. This is also the crown Jesus gives to believers and that He himself wears as the Lord over all the earth. The mention of this crown in the context of Apollo (whose presence will be articulated even more clearly in verse eleven) brings up a theme in Revelation that will grow stronger throughout the vision: the devil's attempt to mimic Jesus in order to deceive the people of the earth. Apollo's crown was a cheap imitation. He wasn't the real deal. He was nothing but trouble!

APOLLO UNMASKED

10They have tails and stings like scorpions, and in their tails they had power to harm men for five months. 11They had as king over them the angel of the Abyss, whose name in Hebrew is Abaddon, and in Greek, Apollyon. 12The first woe is past; behold, still two woes come with these things.

Who is king of these destructive forces? Abaddon. The word means "destroyer" in Hebrew. We hear mention of Abaddon in Proverbs 15:11, *"Death and Destruction lie open before the LORD—how much more the hearts of men!"* The word for "death" is "Sheol." The word "destruction" is "Abaddon." Names are important in the Bible. They display character and communicate a person's purpose and destiny. Abaddon sends a strong message to listeners. Everything about the Abyss and everything connected with false gods adds up to destruction.

In the Greek language the name of the angel of the Abyss is Apollyon. It's no coincidence that the name points directly to the god Apollo. In Revelation chapter 8 Apollo's twin sister was highlighted. Now another dominant personality of false worship was being unmasked.

The Greek god Apollo became a chief god for Rome under Caesar Augustus (27 B.C.-14 A.D.). Augustus claimed to be a son of Apollo. Apollo, along with Diana (Artemis), became two of the twelve main gods in the Roman pantheon. Revelation chapter 9 shows that worship of Apollo was deadly and dangerous. He was the god who supposedly could control plagues. He was also connected to the grasshopper and locust. Apollo was the god who punished the wicked and overbearing. One of his surnames was "shining" or "brilliant"—like a star. One of his titles was "savior." Bringing up his name in the context of this destruction unmasked him as a pawn of the devil. Apollo was nothing but a destructive demonic sham.

Following him meant sure destruction, not salvation. Roman idolatry was, once more, exposed as false and harmful.

The Revelation John received was direct, truthful, and unapologetic to a world cowering under Roman oppression and ready to cave in to the worship of false gods. The message was: don't go there! The battle raging was deeper and darker than they could imagine. God was fighting for His people. They needed to stay faithful.

This book of the Bible brings us the same message. It's a wake-up call to realize that what appears innocent and trendy may actually be crippling and destructive. What feels good may really be that which tears our souls apart and hurts us more deeply than we could ever fathom. Spiritual danger is out there. God calls us to be aware and to take refuge in Him.

BRUTAL HONESTY

13The sixth angel sounded his trumpet, and I heard one voice from the horns of the golden altar that is before God, 14saying to the sixth angel who had the trumpet, "Release the four angels who are bound at the great river Euphrates." 15And the four angels who had been prepared for this hour and day and month and year were released to kill a third of mankind.

Verse fourteen revisits the angels we met in Revelation 7:1-3. They are released for a deadly mission. The river Euphrates directs us to a theme that will recur in the book of Revelation: the city of Babylon. Babylon, the pagan city that took God's people captive, is used as a symbol of evil and rebellion. Babylon is the enemy. It is everything evil and counter to God's will. The destructive kingdom from the north would be used to destroy evil once and for all.

The specific time indicated in verse fifteen underscores God's Lordship, perfect purpose, and plan. Life was not following a random course. God's help and intervention was not an afterthought. His careful preparation was resulting in an intentional plan. For every frightened heart, this news brings a dose of peace and confidence.

16And the number of the cavalry troops was two hundred million. I heard their number. 17Thus I saw the horses and the ones sitting on them in my vision: having breastplates fiery red, dark blue, and sulfur-yellow. The heads of the horses were like heads of lions, and from their mouths came fire, smoke and sulfur. 18From these plagues a third of men were killed—from the fire, smoke and sulfur coming from their mouths. 19For the power of the horses was in their mouths and in their tails; for their tails were like snakes—they have heads and with them they do harm. 20The rest of men who were not killed by these plagues, did not repent from the work of their hands in order not to worship the demons and the idols of gold, silver, bronze, stone and wood—which are not able to see or hear or walk. 21And they did not repent of their murders, nor of their witchcraft, nor of their sexual immorality or their thefts.

Suddenly the mural images shift from locusts to troops with horses. The images are frightening. The numbers boggle the mind. God is pulling back the curtain to show the scope and ferocity of the spiritual battle raging behind the scenes. The demonic troops make us shudder—and they should. God is giving an honest glimpse of the destruction evil brings. The Lord is exposing the real nature of idolatry and the tragic result of rejecting the true Savior.

It is all for the goal of repentance, however. God yearns for his children. He wants all to be saved and come to the knowledge of the truth (1 Timothy 2:4). He wants to rescue us from the deadly trap of idolatry.

This is a disturbing chapter of Revelation. It could definitely cause a few bad dreams! But, in these last days, God knows that this is no time to pull punches or sugarcoat the truth. Satan is behind all idolatry, and all idolatry will lead to death.

If you've seen the movie "Fatal Attraction," you have an idea of what the trap of idolatry can do. The story is about a man who has an extra-marital affair. The woman with whom he has the affair becomes obsessed with him, violent, and scary! She goes off the deep end as this "innocent" affair becomes a horrible nightmare. What once looked so attractive resulted in devastation and horror. That's what God is trying to communicate in Revelation chapter 9. Because of our sinful nature, we are drawn to idolatry. We romanticize the fatal attraction to the works of our hands and the desires of our hearts. We think these idols will bring us happiness, contentment, and pleasure. But after the pleasant veneer wears off, guilt, emptiness, hurt, and destruction are left. In Revelation 9 God is honest about all idolatry. He tells Christians, "It will kill you!"

But God also calls believers to seek refuge in Him, to trust Him, and to walk safely with Him. Chapter 9 reveals that God is still in control. He still cares about us. He wants our eyes to be open to the truth. He eagerly desires our eternal salvation. He gives us His life-giving Word and shepherds us faithfully.

Will you be on guard against idolatry in your life? Can you see more clearly which works of your hands and desires of your heart may lead you astray? Will the trumpet calls of chapter 9 awaken you to a renewed faith and a renewed determination to follow in the footsteps of Jesus?

Study Guide for Revelation Chapter 9

1. What modern idolatry stands out to you most?

2. Read Revelation 9:1-2. Why was it so important for this book of the Bible to make specific reference to Roman false gods?

3. Read Revelation 9:3-12. Knowing what you do about locusts in the Bible, how did these verses inform and motivate early believers?

4. What message do these verses bring you today?

5. Read Revelation 9:13-15. Think of a time you doubted God's timing but saw Him come through. How did that experience affect your relationship with Him?

6. Read Revelation 9:16-21. How does the world try to lull you into complacency toward an awareness of the devil's schemes and temptations?

7. Discuss how you stay alert and aware of God's will and truth.

Revelation
Chapter Ten

✝

We leave the frightening images of Revelation chapter 9 ready to catch our breath and take a break from the fierce spiritual battle raging in the heavens. God obliges and gives us chapter 10. While chapter 9 reveals the deception of idolatry and its tragic impact, chapter 10 calls believers to the sweetness of God's Word and the high calling of reaching the lost.

These are important messages in Revelation. Evil is unmasked and the spiritual battle is seen with full force. At the same time, the Christian's calling to be a prophetic voice of truth in the corrupt world is lifted up. God works to turn hearts to repentance through calamities, but He also works to turn hearts to repentance through His living Word. The Lord has a message of truth to share with the world. He prepares and calls His people to bring this message to the ends of the earth.

THE MESSAGE IS TRUE

1And I saw another strong angel coming down from heaven dressed in a cloud, with a rainbow above his head, his face like the sun, and his feet like pillars of fire.

As you've noticed, Revelation is full of angels. The vision shows how active God's servants are in His work for us. Multitudes of these invisible warriors and helpers surround us and fill the heavens. Revelation 10 opens with a strong angel similar to the one we met in Revelation 5:2. The characteristics of this angel show us that the message of God is the truth.

The mighty angel was wearing cloud clothes. Psalm 18:11 says, *"[The Lord] made darkness his covering, his canopy around him—the dark rain clouds of the sky."* Psalm 97:2 tells us, *"Clouds and thick darkness surround him; righteousness and justice are the foundation of his throne."* Who wears cloud clothes? God does! He alone is robed with heavenly raiments.

The angel had a rainbow above his head. Jesus was described with a rainbow in his vicinity in Revelation 4:3, *"And the one who sat there had the appearance of jasper and carnelian. A rainbow, resembling an emerald, encircled the throne."*

The face of this mighty messenger was like the sun. We see the same characteristic displayed by Jesus in Revelation 1:16, *"In his right hand he held seven stars, and out of his mouth came a sharp double-edged sword. His face was like the sun shining in all its brilliance."*

The angel's legs were like fiery pillars. God's presence was displayed in a fiery pillar in Exodus chapter 13: *"By day the LORD went ahead of them in a pillar of cloud to guide them on their way and by night in a pillar of fire to give them light, so that they could travel by day or night" (vs.21).*

This angel wasn't Jesus. He wasn't the Almighty God. But he bore the characteristics of God. He reflected the truth of who God is. He showed that the message he carried was truthful and authoritative. He delivered the Word of God!

God's imprint was all over this angel. Have you ever met someone like that? I knew a precious lady who shined with the character of God. She taught Sunday School for years. But her passion was to welcome people to worship. For every worship service, she was there at the door. She greeted, she smiled, she shook hands, and she hugged. She helped people in need. Rain or shine, hot or cold weather, she was there. Talking with her meant that you would hear grateful and humble testimony to the grace of God in her life. She lived out the words of Psalm 84:10, *"I would rather be a doorkeeper in the house of my God than dwell in the tents of the wicked."* She glorified and served her Savior Jesus. God's imprint was all over her.

Can the same be said of you? At first, you might say, "No way!" But think again. Jesus died to put His imprint on you. He rose from the dead so you could walk in the newness of life (Romans 6:4). He sealed you with the Spirit in your baptism—you're a new creation in Him (2 Corinthians 5:17)! It is no longer you who lives, but Christ who lives in you (Galatians 2:20). By grace you are saved (Ephesians 2:8-9). By God's grace in Jesus Christ you've been imprinted with the character of God. Like Moses whose face shone brightly after being in the presence of

God, you shine with the character of God (Exodus 34:29). It's a gift. It's given so all can see and know the beauty and wonder of our Savior.

While God gives you a glossy finish, the devil wants your life to have a flat finish. He doesn't want you to reflect God. He wants you to be isolated, alone, and miserable. But God's character is meant to be shared. It is meant to inspire and encourage. God wants you to be encouraged by your fellow believers. He places a cloud of witnesses around you to cheer you on in your course of faith (Hebrews 12:1). Your Savior wants you to finish well, showing that His Word is alive and well in you, and that His message is true.

In addition to being a shining testimony to the character of God, the mighty angel of Revelation chapter 10 serves as another assault against Roman idol worship. The Greek word "iris" is used for "rainbow" in verse one. Iris was the goddess of the rainbow, the messenger of Juno, wife of Jupiter. She was the messenger of the gods, the bringer of cleansing rain. She wore a robe, had wings, and resembled the traditional portrayal of an angel! Romans were very familiar with Iris. Ovid, Virgil, and Cicero lauded her in their writings. Chapter 10 offers a course correction for erring souls. It shows who the real messenger is and whom the real messenger serves. Once again, Roman idolatry is shown to be a poor and mythical imitation of the true and faithful messengers of the Almighty God. His glorious message of life is true!

Chapter Ten

THE MESSAGE IS ALL ABOUT THE WORD OF GOD

2*In his hand was an opened little scroll. He put his right foot on the sea and his left foot on the earth,* **3***and he cried out in a loud voice like a lion roars. And when he cried out, the voices of the seven thunders spoke.* **4***And when the seven thunders spoke, I intended to write; but I heard a voice from heaven saying, "Seal up what the seven thunders spoke and do not write it down."*

How big is an angel? The raw power of God is displayed as the angel is described further. This is not the first time a giant angel appeared in the Scriptures. 1 Chronicles 21:16 says, *"David looked up and saw the angel of the LORD standing between heaven and earth, with a drawn sword in his hand extended over Jerusalem. Then David and the elders, clothed in sackcloth, fell facedown."*

David's response to this massive angel was humility and repentance. Dr. Louis Brighton, author of the commentary Revelation, said, "The angel dominates everything on earth. As he stands astride the earth, no power, human or demonic, can push him aside or overthrow him. That is to say, the mission which the angel represents will rule everything on earth, so much so that not even the 'gates of hell' (Matthew 16:18) can oppose and overcome it" (Revelation, Louis Brighton, p. 265, CPH).

The Word of God, that little scroll in the angel's hand, would prevail—no matter what. This was an important message to Christians as they were called to speak God's Word of truth in a corrupt and high-pressure environment. Believers could trust God's Word.

After the angel let out a lion-like shout (once again reflecting the character of Jesus—the lion of Judah), the voices of the seven thunders spoke. This mysterious phrase may be a reference to Psalm 29. In the Psalm thunder is linked with seven mentions of "the voice of the Lord." God's voice is also compared to thunder several times in the Scriptures.

Louis Brighton comments on an interesting Rabbinic tradition that may have been brought to mind when this portion of Revelation was read aloud: "According to a rabbinic tradition, God gave the Law at Sinai to Moses through his thunderous voice, which divided itself into seven voices, which in turn were divided into seventy languages, thus demonstrating that the Law was to be spoken to all nations" (Revelation, Louis Brighton, p. 267, CPH).

Whether or not this tradition was brought to their minds, the believers of the first century were being called to speak up and to speak out with the message of God's Word. They were to be shining lights in a dark world. They were to be the voice of truth in a culture of lies. Their voices were to be prophetic voices, reflecting the glory and truth of Jesus. The source of their message rested in God's Word and in His Word alone.

John was told that he should not write down what he heard from the seven thunders. Paul had a similar experience. He mentioned it in 2 Corinthians 12:1-4:

"I must go on boasting. Although there is nothing to be gained, I will go on to visions and revelations from the Lord. I know a man in Christ who fourteen years ago was caught up to the third heaven. Whether it was in the body or out of the body I do not know--God knows. And I know that this man-- whether in the body or apart from the body I do not know, but God knows—was caught up to paradise. He heard inexpressible things, things that man is not permitted to tell."

There are some things we do not need to know. God's Word gives us what we do need to know, but the whole plan of God isn't meant to be charted out for us. This is difficult for us at times. We want to know the whole story. No doubt you've heard plenty of Revelation teachings that map out the schedule of God's actions through the time of Jesus' return. Throughout history people have predicted the exact time the end would come. But that's not the point of the Bible or the book of Revelation. The purpose of the Word of God is not to give us the scoop about dates and times. It's not to show that we have a corner on the God-market when it comes to His plan. The purpose of the Bible is to bring the Good News of salvation through Jesus Christ to each of us. That is the message we're called to be all about. That is the mission God calls us to.

5And the angel who I saw standing on the sea and on the earth raised his right hand to heaven. 6And he swore by the one who lives for ever and ever, who created the heavens and all that is in them, the earth and all that is in it, and the sea and all that is in it: "There will be no more delay! 7But in the days of the voice of the seventh angel who intends to sound his trumpet, the mystery of God will be completed, just as he announced to his servants the prophets."

No more delay. These words of encouragement reach the heart of every suffering believer. These words bring hope to each person who is waiting on the Lord. The passing of time is no longer what prevails. God's moment has come. He is at work.

When did God announce this news to his servants the prophets? Amos 3:7 says, *"Surely the Sovereign LORD does nothing without revealing his plan to his servants the prophets."* We may not know every detail, but God doesn't keep us in the dark. The message to the listeners of Revelation is: pay attention to the Word of God! Listen to the prophetic voices God has sent through the ages. They bring the news we need to hear. It is the good news of a Savior. It is the mystery of God with us.

The word "announced" in verse seven underscores this message. It is the Greek word "evangelize," meaning: "to bring good news." Think about that: God evangelized His servants the prophets. He evangelized all of us! The beautiful mystery of salvation was revealed in the past. Today this mystery is unfolded before us in Jesus.

158

THE MESSAGE IS TO BE SHARED WITH THE WORLD

8And the voice that I had heard from heaven spoke to me again: "Go, take the opened scroll in the hand of the angel who is standing on the sea and on the earth." 9So I went to the angel saying to him to give me the little scroll. He said to me, "Take and eat it. It will make your stomach bitter, however in your mouth it will be as sweet as honey." 10I took the little scroll from the angel's hand and ate it. It was sweet as honey in my mouth, but when I had eaten it, it made my stomach bitter. 11And they said to me, "It is necessary for you to prophesy again about many peoples, nations, tongues and kings."

As we get deeper into the book of Revelation, you will notice growing references to the validity and urgency of the mission of God's people, the church. Believers are being called from a cowering stance under persecution and the crush of the culture to a bold, prophetic ministry. In verse eleven the angel says, "It is necessary for you to prophesy again" to everyone! Just when everyone thought the church was dying, God responds: "There is no delay! Now is the time!"

Having a prophetic voice means speaking God's Word to the world. It means living out God's ways when others are flowing with the culture. It means standing out as a follower of Christ. It means holding out the Word of life. Some people think prophets simply told the future. That was part of their ministry, but their primary task was to represent God to the people, to speak His Word.

As God's people, the church, we are called to this urgent task. In a sense we can tell the future: "The Lord is coming back! The time is short! It's time to repent!" But the big picture is that we are called to bring the Word of God and ways of God to a distracted and dying world. The sufferers of Revelation were not just being encouraged to hang in there. They were being stirred to action—the holy and bold action of speaking up for the true God.

John was told to eat the scroll. A similar episode took place in the book of Ezekiel. The prophet Ezekiel was given a mission to speak to rebellious Israel. God encouraged him in this difficult and challenging mission. He urged him to be faithful and courageous as he brought a difficult message of judgment to a stubborn people. Then God said to him: *"Son of man, eat what is before you, eat this scroll; then go and speak to the house of Israel."* The episode continued in Ezekiel 3:2-4:

> *"So I opened my mouth, and he gave me the scroll to eat. Then he said to me, 'Son of man, eat this scroll I am giving you and fill your stomach with it.' So I ate it, and it tasted as sweet as honey in my mouth. He then said to me: 'Son of man, go now to the house of Israel and speak my words to them.'"*

It was time to speak up. God wanted His Word to get into the lives of the people. This is a powerful calling for each one of us in these last days. Who will speak God's Word if we don't? Who will tell the truth if we don't take a stand for it? Who will lead people to a life that really works if we don't introduce them to the Shepherd of their souls? It is time for prophetic action!

Eating the Word of God is a powerful image of internalizing God's Word in order to share it. The Book of Common Prayer, later quoted in the 1941 edition of The Lutheran Hymnal, calls us to "read, mark, learn, and inwardly digest" the Word of God.

Unlike Ezekiel, John tasted the sweetness of God's Word, but experienced a bitter feeling in his stomach. This serves as an accurate description of the paradox of being a believer. Psalm 119:103 says, *"How sweet are your words to my taste, sweeter than honey to my mouth!"* But the difficult challenge and heavy burden of being concerned for the lives of others, for their eternal well-being, can be overwhelming. A believer in Jesus experiences great joy, but bears very real pain. The Christian sees clearly. We live in a world of right and wrong, light and darkness, good and evil. The mantle of being a prophetic voice in this confused world can be heavy and bitter.

But that is the mantle we bear. The book of Revelation calls us back to our mission. We are here to share God's message with the world. We are here to announce God's Good News before the final trumpet sounds.

Study Guide for Revelation Chapter 10

1. What shining examples of God's grace do you have in your life? Talk about one person, say a prayer of thanks for him or her, and write a note of thanks to this person if you can.

2. Read Revelation 10:1-4. With this additional information about angels, discuss how these heavenly servants give you help and encouragement.

3. What do you think the seven thunders said, and why couldn't John share the message?

4. Read Revelation 10:5-7. What mystery of God has been completed already?

5. For what do we wait to be completed?

6. Read Revelation 10:8-11. How is God's Word bitter and sweet to you personally?

7. Think and talk about your calling to be a prophetic voice for God. What are the bitter and sweet implications for the way you are called to live and reach out to others?

Revelation
Chapter Eleven

✝

Revelation 10 concluded with God's command to prophesy, to speak His Word to the world. It was a bitter-sweet proposition, but one that was essential for a lost and perishing people. Even in the midst of suffering we have a mission. Sometimes suffering is the entry point for the accomplishment of God's precious mission in our lives.

I'll never forget a friend of mine who had to undergo kidney dialysis. He never would have asked for failing kidneys. His illness caused him pain and great discomfort. There were times when he thought he wouldn't survive. But in the dialysis facility he met people who needed the news of Jesus. He started bringing sermon tapes to play for everyone in the room as they sat for hours in dialysis. They talked about their need for a Savior and the blessing of Jesus' death and resurrection for them. People who would have never known the love of God learned of their salvation in that treatment facility. For my friend, unwanted illness opened the door to meaningful mission. And there was only one way to enter that mission field: through the doorway of suffering.

The fragile first-century church in the book of Revelation needed to hear that suffering did not mean God was defeated or that His Word was fading away. Suffering was an entry point for meaningful proclamation. They had a mission! God spoke up to remind them of that high calling. He also made sure to give them everything they needed to accomplish that mission.

AUTHORITY IS GIVEN

1And a reed was given to me like a staff, saying, "Get up and measure the temple of God and the altar and the worshipers in it. 2But exclude the courtyard which is outside the temple; do not measure it, because it has been given to the Gentiles. They will trample on the holy city for 42 months."

A few years ago I remodeled two bathrooms at my home. It was a big job. In addition to the detailed work of replacing floors and fixtures, I had to update some very old and very slapped together bathroom construction. One key part of my remodeling project was measurements. In order to blend the new into the old I had to know exactly how everything would fit together. I had to know those bathrooms inside and out.

Throughout the Bible, measuring takes place to show that there is a deep knowledge and thorough understanding of what is happening. It is a prophetic action, calling to mind what the prophets of God did long ago. Zechariah 2:1-2 gives an example: *"Then I looked up--and there before me was a man with a measuring line in his hand! I asked, 'Where are you going?' He answered me, 'To measure Jerusalem, to find out how wide and how long it is.'"*

Ezekiel 40:1-5 shows us another episode of God preparing His prophet to bring a thorough message to His people:

> *In the twenty-fifth year of our exile, at the beginning of the year, on the tenth of the month, in the fourteenth year after the fall of the city--on that very day the hand of the LORD was upon me and he took me there. In visions of God he took me to the land of Israel and set me on a very high mountain, on whose south side were some buildings that looked like a city. He took me there, and I saw a man whose appearance was like bronze; he was standing in the gateway with a linen cord and a measuring rod in his hand. The man said to me, "Son of man, look with your eyes and hear with your ears and pay attention to everything I am going to show you, for that is why you have been brought here. Tell the house of Israel everything you see." I saw a wall completely surrounding the temple area. The length of the measuring rod in the man's hand was six long cubits, each of which was a cubit and a handbreadth. He measured the wall; it was one measuring rod thick and one rod high.*

Revelation 11 begins by showing that God was doing what He always did when He dealt with His people. He measured. He demonstrated that he knew them inside-out. He was not a distant God who was disconnected with reality. He knew the scoop. His remodeling plan was thorough and on target. The measuring action we encounter later in Revelation 21:15 reinforces this point: *"The angel who talked with me had a measuring rod of gold to measure the city, its gates and its walls."* Heaven is measured. God is preparing a place for us in a meticulous and caring way.

The measuring in chapter 11 also shows that God's people have the authority and role of the prophets of old. Even the "reed like a staff" emphasizes this prophetic point. Who comes to mind when you hear about a staff? Moses! Moses' shepherd's staff became a tool of God. Exodus 4:20 tells us, *"So Moses took his wife and sons, put them on a donkey and started back to Egypt. And he took the staff of God in his hand."*

Chapter 11 points to the prophetic role of the Christian in the world—following in the train of the greatest prophets ever. More Moses reminders are in store in the verses ahead.

The reference to the "outer courts" referred to the area of the temple complex that was for the Gentiles. The temple served as a picture of how God's Kingdom unfolded. Unbelievers had a degree of access, but God reserved holy space for His people. Through their witness, God would open the Kingdom to all people.

The reference to 42 months is another number that tells an important story. Similar numbers appear in verse three—1,260 days, and in verses nine and eleven—three and a half. 1,260 days equal 42 lunar months. Each number is equivalent to 3½. What story does 3½ tell?

God's people wandered in the wilderness for 42 years (two years traveling to Mt. Sinai and 40 years in the desert—see Numbers 1:1). Elijah shut the heavens for 3½ years (James 5:17). The Greek conqueror Antiochus Epiphanes terrorized the Jewish people for 3½ years around 168 B.C. The Jewish War from 67-70 A.D. was another 3½ year experience. This war ended with the destruction of Jerusalem.

Each of these periods of time consisted of both the reality of suffering and the prevailing and helping presence of God. These were "in-between" times, times of waiting on God during difficult wilderness journeys. These were times of great uncertainty, but also seasons of trust in God's restoring power. In other words, they were times just like the first century. They were seasons of life just like the season of waiting we're in as we await the coming of Christ today. We live in-between Christ's resurrection and second coming. We rejoice in the presence of God with us, but we await the culmination of His return. 3½ tells the story of living as ones who wait and trust, as ones who suffer, but suffer with hope. The number tells the story of the last days, our story as we await Christ's return. The number assures us that we are smack-dab in the middle of God's unfolding plan.

What does Revelation say about the events during this in-between time?

3"And I will give to my two witnesses, and they will prophesy for 1,260 days, dressed in sackcloth." 4These are the two olive trees and the two lampstands that stand _before the Lord of the earth._ **5**_If anyone wishes to harm them, fire comes from their mouths and consumes their enemies. And if someone might wish to harm them, it is necessary for them thus to be killed._ **6**_These men have the authority to close the heavens so that it will not rain during the time they are prophesying; and they have authority over the waters to turn them to blood and to strike the earth with every plague as often as they wish._

As you read verses from Revelation, remember to try to picture the scene. You're looking at a mural, a Picasso, not an engineering schematic. Chapter 11 reveals the power of God's witnesses during this in-between time. In the Greek text, the word "power" isn't mentioned in verse three. It is added in English translations. When God gives, however, power and authority are received. The witnesses show us that even downtrodden believers have a powerful role this side of heaven.

Notice the fire in verse five. It recalls one of the greatest prophets ever: Elijah. 1 Kings 18:36-40 tells of the great victory:

At the time of sacrifice, the prophet Elijah stepped forward and prayed: "O LORD, God of Abraham, Isaac and Israel, let it be known today that you are God in Israel and that I am your servant and have done all these things at your command. Answer me, O LORD, answer me, so these people will know that you, O LORD, are God, and that you are turning their hearts back again." Then the fire of *the LORD fell and burned up the sacrifice, the wood, the stones and the soil, and also licked up the water in the trench. When all the people saw this, they fell prostrate and cried, "The LORD--he is God! The LORD--he is God!" Then Elijah commanded them, "Seize the prophets of Baal. Don't let anyone get away!" They seized them, and Elijah had them brought down to the Kishon Valley and slaughtered there.*

Can you hear the message to trembling, afraid, and doubting first-century believers? The Lord is God! The Lord is God!

Verse six also references the withholding of rain. Once again, we're brought face to face with Elijah. The book of James tells us: *"Elijah was a man just like us. He prayed earnestly that it would not rain, and it did not rain on the land for three and a half years" (James 5:17).* This is all-out prophetic power from God's servants!

Verse six continues by saying that God's witnesses, his lampstands, have the power to turn water into blood and strike the earth with plagues. Moses is placed before us again. Exodus chapters 7-11 recount what God worked through Moses of whom it is said: *"No one has ever shown the mighty power or performed the awesome deeds that Moses did in the sight of all Israel" (Deuteronomy 34:12).* Revelation reminds us that God gives His people prophetic authority and a prophetic mandate. Like the prophets of old, we are here to be the voice of truth. And that truth has power!

Remember that Moses and Elijah appeared with Jesus at His transfiguration. These living servants were revered by believers. Is the message of this chapter, therefore, that Moses and Elijah would come back to life as some have claimed? No. The text says that these witnesses are olive trees and lampstands.

Zechariah 4:1-6 tells us what that means:

Then the angel who talked with me returned and wakened me, as a man is wakened from his sleep. He asked me, "What do you see?" I answered, "I see a solid gold lampstand with a bowl at the top and seven lights on it, with seven channels to the lights. Also there are two olive trees by it, one on the right of the bowl and the other on its left." I asked the angel who talked with me, "What are these, my lord?" He answered, "Do you not know what these are?" "No, my lord," I replied. So he said to me, "This is the word of the LORD to Zerubbabel: 'Not by might nor by power, but by my Spirit,' says the LORD Almighty.

Jesus told us about lampstands in Revelation 1:20 as well: *"The mystery of the seven stars that you saw in my right hand and of the seven golden lampstands is this: The seven stars are the angels of the seven churches, and the seven lampstands are the seven churches."*

The two witnesses of Revelation 11 are olive trees and lampstands. They are the Church, the Spirit-filled Word of God going out from Him to the world. They are

God's people with His prophetic message. They bring God's say to a secular and rebellious culture. Revelation 11 isn't talking about the reappearance of Moses and Elijah. It isn't referring to two mysterious strangers who prophesy for 3½ years of literal time. It is talking about the prophetic calling of God's Church during this in-between time of suffering and straying. The testimony of believers has the same power that dwelt in the greatest prophets ever. In other words, today's believers are not second class wimps who can't compare to the great servants of the past. God's Spirit and power are alive and well in His Church today!

I served at a summer youth camp for several years. When we trained the college-age counselors we had to remind them that they had authority. Even though they were only a few years older than the campers, the counselors were not there to be buddies or peers. They were present to lead, guide, teach, and nurture. True, they *felt* like peers. But we needed to remind them of their authority. We had to bestow authority upon them. They needed that.

The same is true for us as God's people. We need to be reminded that we carry the authority of God when we bear His Word. We need to know that God bestows His authority on us as we serve Him. Jesus reminded the disciples in Matthew 28: *"All authority in heaven and on earth has been given to me. Therefore go and make disciples of all nations, baptizing them in the name of the Father and of the Son and of the Holy Spirit, and teaching* them to obey everything I have commanded you. And surely I am with you always, to the very end of the age" (vss.18-20). Those common fishermen and workers had the authority Jesus earned through His death and resurrection. We share that authority from the risen Christ. The Word we proclaim will not return empty. It is living and active. We can be confident as we share His Spirit-filled Word in the world.

OPPOSITION IS CERTAIN

7And when they have finished their testimony, the animal (beast) that comes up from the Abyss will make war with them, and conquer them and kill them. **8**Their bodies will lie on the street of the great city, which is spiritually called Sodom and Egypt, where also their Lord was crucified. **9**And men from every people, tribe, tongue and nation look at their bodies for three and a half days and did not permit them burial. **10**The inhabitants of the earth rejoice over them and celebrate and send gifts to each other because the two prophets tormented the inhabitants of the earth.

Unfortunately, suffering is a fact of the believer's life. It's good to know this up front. God is honest about the price we pay. The cross comes before the crown, and there will be plenty of crosses to bear as we walk in faith. Verse seven breaks the bad news that the beast from the Abyss attacks and kills the witnesses as part of the dramatic action of chapter 11.

The beasts that appear in Revelation have caused much fear and misunderstanding. "Beast" is a word from the King James Version of the Bible. It is Old English for "animal." Today, however, when we read the word "beast," we don't think of the wild beasts of the jungle. We think of aliens and scary movies. It doesn't help that the beasts of chapter 13 are described in ways that rival our horror movies. The word "beast," however, is better translated as "animal." Animals appear throughout the book of Revelation. We've already run into the lion and lamb. The use of animals in this prophetic vision communicated clear and powerful messages.

The animal in chapter 11 is no exception. It is from the Abyss—the devil's lair. It kills the prophets. Jesus even used animal language when He exposed the nature of church leaders who were trying to destroy God's plan— and who killed the prophets! He said in Matthew 23:33, *"You snakes! You brood of vipers! How will you escape being condemned to hell?"*

Jesus labeled them as animals. It is interesting to note that one of the words for "snake" in Greek is the word used in Revelation for "beast." It is the Greek word "thārion." Jesus used different words for "snake" and "viper" in Matthew 23, but "thārion" is used in Acts 28:4 after Paul found himself bitten by a snake that was driven from the fire on the island of Malta. The verse says, *"When the islanders saw the snake hanging from his hand..."* This snake is a "beast," an animal, a "thārion." It may not be a coincidence that Jesus described kingdom killers as snakes and that Revelation 11 uses a snake-category animal to reveal the satanic nature of opposition to Jesus and His Word. All attacks against all witnesses of the Gospel have the same devilish roots. Once again, Revelation reveals the real origin of warfare.

Verse eight brings us an interpretation clue, a reminder of Revelation's self-interpreting quality. The bodies of the witnesses lie in the streets of the great city. English translations of the verse say the city is "figuratively" known as Sodom and Egypt. The actual Greek word used in verse eight is "spiritually." This portion of the vision is bringing us spiritual meaning and wisdom. This is not about two prophets from the Old Testament who come back to life and roam the streets of 21st century Jerusalem. This is a vision, a symbol, an expression of a spiritual truth.

What is Sodom, Egypt, and the place where Jesus was crucified? It is a sinful and rebellious earth. That is where witnesses for the Gospel are being assaulted. Right here on earth. The earth is Satan's domain. Chapter 12 will tell of his being hurled to the earth and his rage-filled battle with those who hold to the testimony of Jesus. This broken and sinful earth is where Jesus was killed and where we struggle.

Verse nine mentions 3½ days. For the duration of these in-between times, God's people will suffer. The warfare will be brutal. The opposition to God will be strong. Following Jesus during these days before His return may knock the wind out of you. It may test you to your limits. Tragedy may discourage you. Humiliation may dishearten you. The gloating and the sending of gifts mentioned in verse ten show that spiritual warfare attacks the integrity and public standing of God's people. Evil is a bullying force that humiliates. It digs deeply into the heart and spirit of the Lord's servants. It hurts.

The sending of gifts was also an indication of idolatry. Gifts and idols went together. We hear in Ezekiel 20:39, *"As for you, O house of Israel, this is what the Sovereign LORD says: Go and serve your idols, every one of you! But afterward you will surely listen to me and no longer profane my holy name with your gifts and idols."* The problem in ancient Israel was also the problem in the Roman Empire and its provinces. Gift-giving idol worship was rampant. This arrogance would also be part of the humiliation of persecuted believers during the last days.

This kind of opposition may take you by surprise. Josef Tson, a Romanian pastor who was persecuted under the anti-Christian regime in his country, commented on the surprising and torturous nature of being persecuted for Christ:

> "Josef, let me tell you how you imagined your martyrdom: going to your cross to be crucified but passing among two rows of Christians applauding. 'Bravo, Josef!' But what if I make those brothers and sisters of yours as you pass with your cross stoop down, take mud, and throw it on you and your cross? Will you accept a cross with mud on it?" (Quoted from Charles Colson's <u>The Body</u>)

Tson expected suffering. He was willing to suffer for Christ in a heroic way. But he never anticipated total humiliation—a character smear in front of his friends, family, and parishioners. Revelation 11 reveals the true and cruel nature of opposition witnesses for the Lord Jesus would face.

VICTORY IS ASSURED

11But after the three and a half days a breath of life from God entered them, and they stood on their feet, and great fear fell upon the ones watching. 12And they heard a loud voice from heaven saying to them, "Come up here." And they went up to heaven in a cloud, and their enemies looked at them. 13In that hour a great earthquake happened, and a tenth of the city fell, and seven thousand men were killed in the earthquake, and the remaining became afraid and gave glory to the God of heaven. 14The second woe has passed; behold, the third woe is coming quickly. 15The seventh angel sounded his trumpet, and there were loud voices in heaven, saying: "The kingdom of the world has become the kingdom of our Lord and of his Christ, and he reigns for ever and ever." 16And the twenty-four elders, who are before God sitting on their thrones, fell on their faces and worshiped God, 17saying: "We give thanks to you, Lord God the Almighty, the One who is and who was, for you have taken your great power and you reign."

What was happening here? God was completing the story! This in-between time is not just all about suffering, persecution, opposition, sin, and the devil's destructive work. It is about the resurrection and ascension too! Can this possibly happen to witnesses for

Christ? Will they hear the words, "Come up here"? In Christ they will. We will! The resurrection of Jesus is a fact. The Bible declares that *"in Christ all will be made alive" (1 Corinthians 15:22).* This is the promise we rely on. Revelation 11 tells every believer in Jesus that this promise is certain.

The scene in Revelation 11 changes quickly from evil's celebration to God's victory. The gloaters and gift-givers are suddenly shaken to reality by a severe earthquake. Devastating earthquakes were common in Asia Minor. As you read previously, several cities experienced total loss due to terrible earthquakes. This chapter of Revelation reminds people that the Lord of all creation is the One sending them a message. The survivors bow before the God of heaven. And every believer cheers!

Even in these last days, worship in the heavens continues. No matter how bad things look, Jesus reigns. As we suffer, as we give bold witness, as we press on, Jesus reigns. Victory is assured in Christ our risen Lord.

18"The nations were angry; and your wrath has come. And the time has come for the dead to be judged, and to give the reward to your servants the prophets and to the saints and to the ones who fear your name, the small and the great, and to destroy the destroyers of the earth." 19And God's temple in heaven was opened, and his ark of the covenant was seen in his temple. And lightning and noise and thunder and an earthquake and great hail happened.

Revelation 11 makes a powerful statement to those who feel like giving up. It calls every Christian to keep going, to press on. God's judgment and reward would come. His righteousness would prevail. His victory was certain.

The presence of the ark of the covenant underscored this victory. The writer of the book of Hebrews described the ark in this way:

> *Now the first covenant had regulations for worship and also an earthly sanctuary. A tabernacle was set up. In its first room were the lampstand, the table and the consecrated bread; this was called the Holy Place. Behind the second curtain was a room called the Most Holy Place, which had the golden altar of incense and the gold-covered ark of the covenant. This ark contained the gold jar of manna, Aaron's staff that had budded, and the stone tablets of the covenant. Above the ark were the cherubim of the Glory, overshadowing the atonement cover...(Hebrews 9:1-5).*

The ark brought the presence of God among His people. It was lost when the temple was destroyed in 586 B.C. We hear nothing about it after King Josiah's reforms in 2 Chronicles 35:3. Its reappearance in Revelation 11 shows that victory in Christ is assured. God is present! If people thought He was gone, He was back with full force and complete grace. With the victory assured, each believer was called to press on with hope, with trust in

God, and with the important mission of bringing His Word of life to the world.

Former Super-Bowl winning football coach Tony Dungy, who has experienced his share of tragedy and triumph, expressed the calling well in his book Quiet Strength:

> And so we press on. We press on with our memories, our hearts buoyed by a God who loves us and wants us to know Him deeply. We press on with our sense that life's not always fair. And we press on with the knowledge—and assurance—that even though we can't see all of God's plan, He is there, at work and in charge, loving us. We press on with the conviction that even though we don't deserve the gifts and blessings we've been given, He gives them anyway. We press on into an abundant life on earth, followed by an eternity with God (Tony Dungy, Quiet Strength, p.297).

Study Guide for Revelation Chapter 11

1. Read Revelation 11:1-2. What does it mean to you that God knows you inside-out?

2. Read Revelation 11:3-6. What particular challenges for the Christian faith do you see during these "in-between" times?

3. Why were the witnesses dressed in sackcloth?

4. How do the symbols of olive trees and lampstands help describe your role as God's servant in the world?

5. What stands in the way of giving a confident and bold witness for Christ?

6. Read Revelation 11:7-10. What humiliation did God's witnesses endure, and how might you experience some of that as you witness for Christ?

7. Read Revelation 11:11-19. What specific phrases and ideas in these verses encourage you to press on?

Revelation
Chapter Twelve

✝

As you reviewed Revelation 11 you may have noticed the delicate balance of this book of the Bible. On one hand, suffering believers are encouraged with news of hope in Jesus. People who are persecuted and struggling are given the certain word that God is still on His throne; the story isn't over; in fact, God is working harder than ever to fight for His people. On the other hand, Christians are also given a big dose of boldness. They are called away from timidity and fear, and roused to a vibrant and confident witness to the world. Followers of Jesus may think they are sitting on the bench as the world takes control of the game. God shows His children that they are key players. He sends them onto the playing field of the world to influence the outcome with the mighty and living Word of truth.

When times are difficult we need this balance. We need both encouragement and mission. Helmut Thielicke, a German pastor and author who lived through World War II, reflected on what it was like to experience such a time:

"I did not merely live through and suffer this hour and its meaninglessness in a creaturely way, but rather asked the question whether God was not thinking his higher thoughts about its meaninglessness, whether and in what way even it was a chapter in the story of salvation and therefore was not excluded from God's great compendium of history" (<u>The Trouble with the Church</u>, p.8).

These are two issues we must struggle with in our lives—especially when times are difficult. We must ask two questions: "Where is God's presence?" and "What is God's mission?" I've had to wrestle with balancing those issues when death took a person in an untimely way, when tragedy struck part of our world, and even when meaninglessness and hopelessness gripped my own soul.

The book of Revelation brings us out of mere speculation when it comes to answering those crucial questions. As Dr. Louis Brighton said in his commentary on Revelation, "These chapters visually explain to John why the events on earth are occurring" (p.325). Revelation gives serious answers to big questions. God doesn't leave us hanging. He assures us that He is with us. He also lets us know that He has a plan.

CHRISTMAS!

1A great sign was seen in heaven: a woman clothed with the sun, and the moon under her feet, and upon her head a crown of twelve stars. 2She was pregnant and cried out having birth pains, being tormented to give birth.

Revelation chapter 12 begins with Christmas. This is the fourth account of Jesus' birth in the Bible. Matthew presents us Joseph's perspective and shows that Jesus' birth is a miraculous and redemptive fulfillment of Old Testament prophecy (Matthew 1:18-25). Luke gives us a detailed look at that wonderful day in its historical setting (Luke 2:1-20). John shows us that the birth of Christ is a deep and miraculous mystery as the Creator of the world became flesh and made His dwelling among us (John 1:1-14). Revelation lets us see the invisible and powerful spiritual advance caused by Jesus' presence on earth.

Verse one appears to be a symbolic representation of the Virgin Mary, reflecting the glory of God as a special servant of His church. Rick Larsen of the Bethlehem Star Project (see bethlehemstar.net) has a unique theory. According to his calculations, the constellation Virgo ("virgin" in Latin) may have been prominent in the sky at the time of the conception of Jesus—the annunciation of His birth to Mary. Charts of the sky around that time show that the moon was in position to be at the feet of the Virgin and the sun was located in the middle of the constellation! Could the very heavens have declared the gift of the Savior through a humble virgin? Is that what John saw as a sign in the skies? It's an intriguing theory. One thing we know for sure: the baby to be born would change eternity!

THE BATTLE BEHIND ALL BATTLES

3And another sign was seen in heaven: behold, a great fiery dragon with seven heads and ten horns and seven crowns on his heads. 4His tail dragged away one-third of the stars of heaven and he threw them to the earth. And the dragon stood before the woman who was about to give birth, so that when she would give birth to her child, he would devour. 5She gave birth to a son, a male, who will rule (shepherd) all the nations with a staff made of iron. And her child was snatched up to God and to his throne. 6The woman fled into the wilderness where she has a place prepared for her by God, where she might be sustained for 1,260 days. 7And a war happened in heaven. Michael and his angels fought against the dragon, and the dragon and his angels fought. 8But he was not strong enough, and their place was no longer found in heaven. 9The great dragon was thrown down, the ancient serpent called the devil and Satan, who leads the whole world astray. He was thrown down to the earth, and his angels with him were thrown down.

Chapter 12 gives us another example of the way God guides us in the understanding of the book of Revelation. We're not left to our own imaginations. Jesus leads the way. Verse nine reveals the identity of the enormous red dragon: "*The great dragon was hurled down--that ancient serpent called the devil, or Satan, who leads the whole world astray.*"

In addition to his identity, the devil's character is revealed in this chapter. The devil appears to be holy and complete. Seven heads, ten horns, and seven crowns show that he is a counterfeit of the true God. He is deceptive—like the false gods of every era of history, but his schemes are evident. He wears crowns that belong on a king—diadems. These kingly crowns also appear on the beast in Revelation 13:1 and finally on Jesus in 19:12.

The devil strives for power. He strains to gain the upper hand. He deludes himself into believing that he is in charge. But it is a sham. His final defeat is only a matter of time. The devil is also destructive. He creates havoc with the stars in the heavens—perhaps a symbol of the fallen angels that followed him. He also stands ready to devour the child. The devil is a cosmic troublemaker, thrown down to the earth and filled with fury because he cannot have his destructive way (Revelation 12:17). Even his names betray his character. "Devil" means "slanderer." "Satan" means "adversary."

The male child born to the woman has a clear and wonderful identity. Revelation 12:5 directs us to Psalm 2:7-9, *"You are my Son; today I have become your Father. Ask of me, and I will make the nations your inheritance, the ends of the earth your possession. You will rule them with an iron scepter."* The symbolism in Revelation 12 is not overly mysterious. The message from the Scriptures is clear. This is all about Jesus.

Once the child was born, he was taken up to God and his throne. This may be a reference to the Ascension of Jesus. It could be reference to the protection given him by the Father. The woman was also protected. At this point in the vision, the woman becomes a symbol for all believers, the Church. She would be taken care of for 1,260 days.

Chapter 12 leads us to another encounter with the number 1,260. We'll also come across another synonym for 3½ in verse fourteen: "a time, times and ½ a time" (one year, two years, and half a year). During the in-between time of waiting for Christ to return, His people would be cared for. Evil did not have a corner on the market when it came to the 3½ season of life. God was at work protecting and delivering.

A special perspective about God's help comes through the word "desert" in verse six. The woman was brought to the desert to be taken care of. Normally a desert would not be a place to be taken care of! The wilderness was full of danger. The desert lacked shelter, food and water. But God's people knew something special about the wilderness. It was where God did some of His best work.

Remember the people of Israel in the book of Exodus. God brought His people to the desert to teach them His ways and to show them that He is a caring and faithful God: *"Then Moses led Israel from the Red Sea and they went into the Desert of Shur"* *(Exodus 15:22)*. Elijah found refuge and provision in the desert: *"Then the word of the LORD came to Elijah: 'Leave here, turn eastward and hide in the Kerith Ravine, east of the Jordan. You will drink from the brook, and I have ordered the ravens to feed you there.'"* The preparing message of the arrival of the Messiah happened in the desert: *"In those days John the Baptist came, preaching in the Desert of Judea and saying, 'Repent, for the kingdom of heaven is near'"* *(Matthew 3:1-2)*. Jesus beat back the devil's temptations and stayed the course for our salvation in the desert: *"Then*

Jesus was led by the Spirit into the desert to be tempted by the devil" (Matthew 4:1).

God did remarkable work in the desert. Where no resources were available, He came through. Where it was impossible for people to live, He provided a home. Where danger lurked from every direction, He brought protection. Where the elements struck fear in people's hearts, He brought peace. For Christians, the wilderness became a place to get excited about. It became God's place. So when the woman in Revelation 12 was brought into the wilderness, every listener knew that this was all about miraculous and God-given survival. Even greater than that, it was about thriving!

What a wonderful pattern for believers today. If you find yourself in the wilderness, in a desert season of life, you have the track record of God who does His best work in those situations! If you feel hopeless, weak, battered, or without resources, that is when God comes through best. He is at work in your wilderness! He will refresh you and grow you during your desert times. He will be faithful. Even when life appears to be at its worst, you can wait upon Him in hope. He is working for you. He is fighting for you.

We see the fight in verses seven through nine. Michael is the only named angel in Revelation. The name is Hebrew for "who is like God." Michael is the leader of God's troops as they fight against the dragon and his angels. The significance of Michael's name will become clearer in chapter 13.

The victory over the devil and his angels is decisive. Great emphasis is placed on the fact that the dragon, the devil, the slanderer, the adversary, the accuser (see Job 1:6-11, 2:1-5; and Zechariah 3:1-7 for more references to the devil as the accuser) the deceiver, was "thrown down." This verb is used five times in Revelation chapter 12: three times in verse nine, once in verse ten, and once in verse twelve. Do you get the picture? Do you see the real reality? If there's any doubt about the devil's defeat, if you ever think he has the upper hand, if you ever feel like he's the winner and God is the loser, just take a look at Revelation 12! The devil has been thrown down! Jesus reinforced the fact in John 16:11, *"The prince of this world now stands condemned."*

THE BLOOD OF THE LAMB

10And I heard a loud voice in heaven saying: "Now have come the salvation and the power and the kingdom of our God, and the authority of his Christ, because the accuser of our brothers has been thrown down, the one accusing them before our God day and night. 11They overcame him because of the blood of the Lamb and because of the word of their testimony; they did not love their lives—even to the point of death."

Smack-dab in the middle of the vision are the blood of the Lamb and the Word-saturated testimony of the saints. Salvation has come. God's kingdom prevails. It's all because of Jesus. Even the "word of their testimony" points to Jesus. The Greek term for "word" is "logos," the reference to Jesus in John chapter 1: *"In the beginning was the Word, and the Word was with God, and the Word was God"* (vs.1).

Revelation is about the Gospel. It is salvation centered. It is a vision that dramatically shows the Way and the Truth and the Life. It is the Word of truth that reveals how people can overcome the torturous temptations and trials of life in a broken world. You may remember the word "overcome" being used in the messages to the seven churches of Asia Minor. Jesus said that overcoming was what the churches had to do. As mentioned previously, the word is rooted in the Greek word for "victory." How does a church overcome the assault of Satan? How do God's people overcome persecution? How does an individual overcome personal failure? How can anyone overcome the heaviness of a broken heart or spirit? Not by personal might or power. Overcoming takes place by the blood of the Lamb. Overcoming happens when the living Word breathes life and forgiveness and hope and strength into frail, failing, and falling sinners. Overcoming flows from the cross of Jesus Christ, in the life-giving waters of baptism, and in the living presence of Jesus in communion. Overcoming is God's work, His victory. It is by grace—a gift for us. Carried by God's servants through the ages, this gift is passed along to each new generation.

A HELPLESS ENEMY

12"Because of this, rejoice, heavens and the ones living in them! Woe to the earth and the sea, because the devil went down to you with great anger, knowing he has little time."

The reality of life this side of heaven is that the devil is ticked off. He is angry because his time is short. We may think the wait is too long, but in God's scheme of things, the devil will only be allowed to rage for a short time. He will not win. He cannot win. He can only lash out in a limited way until God completes His redemptive plans. This truth is revisited in Revelation chapter 20. It is important to remember where Satan stands because of the cross.

13When the dragon saw that he was thrown down to the earth, he pursued the woman who gave birth to the male child. 14The woman was given the two wings of a great eagle in order to fly to the wilderness, to her place where she was sustained for a time, times and half a time, in front of the serpent. 15And the serpent threw from his mouth behind the woman water like a river, in order that she might be swept away by a river. 16But the earth helped the woman and the earth opened her mouth and swallowed the river that the dragon threw from his mouth. 17And the dragon was angry at the woman and went away to make war with her remaining seeds, the ones obeying God's commandments and having the testimony of Jesus.

Now the unfolding drama continues. Mary, the mother of our Savior, becomes a woman who gives birth to all *"who obey God's commandments and hold to the testimony of Jesus."* She becomes the church, the body of Christ, giving birth to new creations born of water and the

190

Spirit (John 3:5). How can the images change so quickly? Remember, this is a vision. It's a moving mural that communicates important Christ-given truths. The swirling activity in the heavenly realms is being revealed as God pulls back the curtain of heaven to give us a glimpse of what He is doing behind the scenes.

These verses give all believers a wake-up call. The devil is after all those who confess Christ. That is Satan's ultimate goal. He wants to drag as many people to hell as he can. He wants to destroy and devour the church. That is the real battle. It wasn't about Rome. It isn't about political empires. Our straying, our sinful actions, and our destructive ways are sinister means to an awful end. Life this side of heaven is all about eternal life and death. The stakes are high.

But God is at work. No punches are pulled as God reveals the real enemy, but God also gives a heaping helping of the truth of His deliverance and care. If any believer doubts God's help in time of need, these verses bring back His track record through the ages. The church is given wings of an eagle:

> *"You yourselves have seen what I did to Egypt, and how I carried you on eagles' wings and brought you to myself" (Exodus 19:4).*

> *"Those who hope in the LORD will renew their strength. They will soar on wings like eagles; they will run and not grow weary, they will walk and not be faint" (Isaiah 40:31).*

God's people are protected from the flash flood of evil in the wilderness:

> *"If the LORD had not been on our side when men attacked us, when their anger flared against us, they would have swallowed us alive; the flood would have engulfed us, the torrent would have swept over us, the raging waters would have swept us away" (Psalm 124:2-5).*

> *"But now, this is what the LORD says—he who created you, O Jacob, he who formed you, O Israel: 'Fear not, for I have redeemed you; I have summoned you by name; you are mine. When you pass through the waters, I will be with you; and when you pass through the rivers, they will not sweep over you. When you walk through the fire, you will not be burned; the flames will not set you ablaze. For I am the LORD, your God, the Holy One of Israel, your Savior'" (Isaiah 43:1-3a).*

> *"The rain came down, the streams rose, and the winds blew and beat against that house; yet it did not fall, because it had its foundation on the rock" (Matthew 7:25).*

The devil rages. God wins. His people are protected and delivered. They praise Him for His faithfulness and love. Even the earth helped the woman by swallowing the raging river of the dragon. You might think this is a strange little reference, but it may be another indication of the complete Scripture saturation of the book of Revelation. In Numbers 16:30-32 Moses had the earth's help in swallowing up rebellious evil: *"'But if the LORD brings about something totally new, and the earth opens its mouth and swallows them, with everything that belongs to them, and they go down alive into the grave, then you will know that these men have treated the LORD with contempt.' As soon as [Moses] finished saying all this, the ground under them split apart and the earth opened its mouth and swallowed them."* God's enemies were destroyed. His people never forgot this miraculous act of judgment.

Verse seventeen brings us back to the raging spiritual battle. This fight was prophesied in the book of Genesis. The word for "offspring" (seed) used in verse seventeen was also used in Genesis 3:15. God said, *"And I will put enmity between you and the woman, and between your offspring and hers; he will crush your head, and you will strike his heel."* Genesis 3:15 is the first Gospel, the "protevangelion." Enmity will exist between those born of the woman and the devil. It is a spiritual battle, not just a physical one. The devil wants to destroy. God wants to give life. But there is no doubt about the victory. The offspring of the woman—referred to as "he" in Genesis 3:15—will crush Satan's head. Jesus is the victor. In Him we have victory.

Allow me to offer two final notes about the assault of Satan mentioned in Revelation 12. First, the spiritual battle takes a variety of forms throughout the course of history. During our era it seems that ridicule of faith in

Jesus is on the increase. Mean-spirited criticism is coming from bold, culture-empowered atheists. The latest strategy against Christianity is to laugh at it and call its adherents foolish. An "ad hominem" argument is taking hold (an argument against the man instead of against the subject matter). Intellectual and historical objections seem to be less frequent than outright ridicule and denial. But it's no surprise. The devil has lost his temper. His fury boils over at times. Calm and rational debates give way to senseless and humiliating discrediting of Christians and the teachings of Scripture. It's the same old strategy of the devil. It shows his hateful hand. We must be ready.

Second, in the midst of spiritual struggle, we have a "place." We are rooted and at home. The word "place" is mentioned in verses six, eight, and fourteen. It is the Greek word "topos"—where we get the term "topography." It directs us to a real physical location. Verse six tells us of a place prepared for the woman. Verse eight lets us know that the devil and his angels lost their place. Verse fourteen reassures us that the woman has a place prepared for her.

In John 14:3 Jesus said, *"I will prepare a place for you."* Jesus gives you a place. The devil lost his. But you have one. In the middle of the spiritual battle, the devil tries to make you feel "placeless." He tries to get you to believe that you don't belong, that you have no certain foundation, no unconditional love, no solid place in God's heart or in anyone else's for that matter. The devil will even try to make you believe that you have no home in heaven. You know how the warfare is waged. Inner and outer voices of inferiority and criticism tell you that you don't have what it takes, that you don't measure up, that you don't belong. You may even find yourself saying, "Who am I? I'm nothing. I don't fit. I'm no good." But God responds with emphasis in Revelation 12: "You have a place." It is a place in His heart and mind. You are precious and valuable to Him. You are an indispensible part of His plan. You are part of His saving effort in the world.

It is also a place in heaven. God prepared this place for you through His Son. It is real, tangible, beautiful, life-giving, and eternal. It is prepared and reserved for you, not because of your successes, good qualities, and possessions. It is made possible through the blood of Jesus. You fit. You are precious. You belong to God.

Be ready for the battle. Know you have a place. It's the balance of mission and encouragement we need.

Study Guide for Revelation Chapter 12

1. Read Revelation 12:1-9. What insights into Christmas do these verses give you?

2. Discuss how the description of Satan in these verses helps you understand his true character, goals, and limitations.

3. Read Revelation 12:10-11. How did the blood of Jesus overcome the devil's accusations and power?

4. How does God's Word do the same thing?

5. Read Revelation 12:12-17. The book of Revelation lifts up the importance of the Church. What challenges does the Church face today—from the inside and outside?

6. How is God sustaining the Church during these last days?

7. What mission have you discovered in times of suffering?

Revelation
Chapter Thirteen

✝

We left the devil enraged in chapter 12. Chapter 13 picks up the action as the devil's ugliness is further exposed. God wants each of us to be aware of Satan's true colors and destructive schemes. First-century believers were being enticed to walk away from the true God. They were being lured by the desire to belong, to be "insiders." They were being pressured to become the "haves" instead of the "have-nots." They were being invited to experience the "fulfillment" of idol worship during parties and feasts that involved sexual immorality and drunkenness. They were being told that faith in God and in His grace wasn't enough. Instead, the job of pleasing God was on their shoulders. It was their works that would save them. They could be in control of their lives. All they had to do was forsake Jesus.

Compared to their persecuted, ridiculed, and lonely lives, these invitations began to look appealing. You may feel the same way at times. It can be lonely and difficult to do the right thing, to follow Jesus and trust Him with your life. Sacrifice, patience, and self-control can be painful. When it looks like everyone else is so happy and having so much fun, the motivation to resist the enticement of the world can disappear. That's why God spoke up in Revelation, and that's why He revealed what He did in chapter 13. He wanted to save you from destroying your life.

This chapter shows the story behind the story. It reveals the absolute ugliness of all that would entice you to give up on Jesus and His ways. It also shows that the devil is a master deceiver. He will always attempt to make you believe that bad is really good and that his ways are just about the same as Jesus' ways.

Chapter 13 captures the essence of the Evil One by using the imagery of animals. The animals' characteristics reveal the devil's nature and method of operation.

THE BEAST FROM THE SEA

1And the dragon stood on the shore of the sea. And I saw a beast coming from the sea, having ten horns and seven heads, and ten crowns on his horns, and on each head a blasphemous name. 2The beast I saw was like a leopard, and his feet like a bear and his mouth like the mouth of a lion. The dragon gave him his power and his throne and great authority. 3One of the heads seemed fatally slaughtered, but his fatal wound was healed. The whole world marveled after the beast 4and they worshiped the dragon because he had given authority to the beast, and they also worshiped the beast saying, "Who is like the beast? Who is able to make war against him?"

In Revelation 10:1-2, the mighty angel stood on the sea and on the land. This was not an accidental location. The rule of Jesus and His Word was established on land

and sea—the whole world. In chapter 13, the dragon stood on the shore as a counterfeit, intruding upon God's territory.

The deep, fearsome sea was regarded by people of the first century as the Abyss. When the first animal of this chapter emerges from the sea, his "home" is made clear to every listener. This is an evil animal from hell.

The fact that an animal arrived to do Satan's dirty work showed that the devil operates a web of deceit. The devil always tries to have the appearance of being interesting and intriguing. He tries to persuade people that his ways are normal and natural—even innocent and good. He attempts to convince us that there is something deeper and wiser and more fulfilling in what he offers. He mixes lies with the truth. He sounds pious. He encourages "spirituality" as he pushes Christianity away. He's glad to let people hold onto belief in "a god" or the supernatural, as long as they don't become "narrow minded" by limiting themselves to Jesus.

Revelation exposes this "spiritual openness" as a deadly sham. It's all smoke and mirrors. The holy and complete numbers of ten and seven and the symbols of power and wisdom in the crowns, horns, and heads appear to be godly, but are, in reality, covered with blasphemy. The devil is trying to mimic the Holy God, but his imitation is a thin disguise. This is an important lesson for each of us. We're called to be alert and on guard. It's important to take a second look at the course we're on, to evaluate it in light of God's Word of truth, and to return to Him by His grace and Spirit.

The animal out of the sea has features that resemble other fierce animals: a leopard, bear, and lion. Daniel 7:3-7 uses this imagery to describe the destructive kingdoms of history:

> *Four great beasts, each different from the others, came up out of the sea. The first was like a lion, and it had the wings of an eagle. I watched until its wings were torn off and it was lifted from the ground so that it stood on two feet like a man, and the heart of a man was given to it. And there before me was a second beast, which looked like a bear. It was raised up on one of its sides, and it had three ribs in its mouth between its teeth. It was told, "Get up and eat your fill of flesh!" After that, I looked, and there before me was another beast, one that looked like a leopard. And on its back it had four wings like those of a bird. This beast had four heads, and it was given authority to rule. After that, in my vision at night I looked, and there before me was a fourth beast--terrifying and frightening and very powerful. It had large iron teeth; it crushed and devoured its victims and trampled underfoot whatever was left. It was different from all the former beasts, and it had ten horns.*

The similarities are not coincidental. The animal in Revelation is a combination of all these terrible reigns. This beast shows Rome's true colors as well as the devil's sinister methods. The devil uses other entities to accomplish his dark and sinister tasks.

The animal out of the sea also brings a strong prophetic message. Destruction will come to those who ally themselves with evil. Hosea 13:7-8 proclaims judgment on Israel: *"So I will come upon them like a lion, like a leopard I will lurk by the path. Like a bear robbed of her cubs, I will attack them and rip them open. Like a lion I will devour them; a wild animal will tear them apart."* The people of the first century recognized the animals and remembered what they meant in God's Word.

These initial verses of chapter 13 are loaded with Messiah mimicry. Verse two shows the dragon giving power to his vassals on earth, but the Lord is the only one with authority to give power. The head of the animal seemed to have a fatal wound. The verb used here is the same verb as Revelation 5:6—the Lamb that appeared to be slain. This is a counterfeit Christ! Even the question "Who is like the beast?" is a cheap imitation of the meaning of the angel Michael's name, "Who is like God?" It is also an attempt to supplant the true and familiar Scriptural praises of God:

> *"Who among the gods is like you, O LORD? Who is like you-- majestic in holiness, awesome in glory, working wonders?" (Exodus 15:11)*

> *My whole being will exclaim, "Who is like you, O LORD? You rescue the poor from those too strong*

for them, the poor and needy from those who rob them" (Psalm 35:10).

Unfortunately, the unbelieving world worshipped this animal and trusted in his strength. First-century dwellers could point to the Roman temple on the corner to demonstrate the truth of this prophecy. We point to "gods" like power, money, sex, and self. These false gods, chapter 13 reveals, are deadly and ugly tools of the devil that will devour us.

5The beast was given a mouth speaking great things and blasphemies, and authority was given to him to be active for forty-two months. 6He opened his mouth for blasphemies toward God, and to blaspheme his name and his dwelling place and those dwelling in heaven. 7He was given power to make war against the saints and to conquer them. And he was given authority over every tribe, people, tongue and nation. 8And they will worship him, all the inhabitants of the earth on the earth whose name is not written in the book of life of the Lamb that was slain from the creation of the world. 9If someone has an ear, let him hear. 10If anyone is to go into captivity, into captivity he will go. If anyone is to be killed with the sword, with the sword he will be killed. Thus is the patient endurance and faith of the saints.

Verse five begins a series of uses of the phrase "it was given to him." The phrase happens six times from verse five through verse fifteen (one time in verse 5, twice in verse 7, once in verse 14, and once in verse 15). Though the beast is frightening and powerful, he can only act within the parameters God allows. Even in the middle of the dark ugliness of Satan's work, God is still in control.

We also encounter the 42-month time frame in verse five. As mentioned earlier, this is a number that tells the story of "in-between" times. It's half of seven—three and a half years. We are waiting for perfection and completion—as in the 7 days of creation and God's rest, but it's not here yet. We're still in the middle of the journey. What's happening during our days of waiting—this 3½ period of time? Revelation has told us so far:

- The unbelieving world opposes believers in Christ (11:2)

- God's Word of truth is proclaimed (11:3)

- The church will appear to be defeated (11:9)

- God's people will be protected (12:6)

- God cares for His church (12:14)

- Evil is allowed to exercise its power (13:5)

Life in the in-between time will be difficult. Jesus pulls no punches. He is brutally honest about the battle believers are in and about the price they will pay. He also lets every believer know that each person whose name is written in the book of life, each person bought by the blood of the Lamb, doesn't have to cave in and worship the devil's puppets. Listen, Jesus says. Hear that a faithful Christian does not have to give up and go along just because the winds of the world are blowing the way of compromise. Times will be hard. But notice how Revelation prepares believers for those hard times. Verse nine serves as a pause, a way of setting the next verse apart from the others. Verse ten quotes Jeremiah 15:1-2:

> *Then the LORD said to me: "Even if Moses and Samuel were to stand before me, my heart would not go out to this people. Send them away from my presence! Let them go! And if they ask you, 'Where shall we go?' tell them, 'This is what the LORD says: "Those destined for death, to death; those for the sword, to the sword; those for starvation, to starvation; those for captivity, to captivity."""*

These verses from Jeremiah are in the context of God's judgment. God is letting us know that His judgment is happening. His eternal plan is moving forward. He is working His righteousness. We may not see it or understand it, but He is at work. What's required during times like these is not our knowledge or control. We are called to patient endurance and faithfulness.

God lets us know that patient endurance and faith are not fair weather qualities. This spiritual fruit is required in the furnace of real suffering. Patient endurance and faith are called for in the midst of captivity and death. They are summoned when everything has gone wrong. They are about selflessness that trusts the plan of God even when it seems as if there is no plan. Listen carefully, God says in 13:9-10. This is the real challenge. Are you ready? Are you up to it?

THE BEAST FROM THE EARTH

11And I saw another beast coming up from the earth. He had two horns like a lamb, but he spoke like a dragon. 12He exercised all the authority of the first beast on his behalf, and he made the earth and the ones dwelling in it to worship the first beast, whose fatal wound had been healed. 13And he does great signs, so that fire may come down from heaven to earth before men. 14And he leads astray ones dwelling on the earth because of the signs given to him to do on behalf of the first beast, telling people of the earth to make an image to the beast who has the fatal wound but lived. 15He was given power to give breath to the image of the beast, so that the image of the beast might speak, and he caused to be put to death all who will not worship the image of the beast. 16He makes everyone, small and great, rich and poor, free and slave, to receive a mark on his right hand or on his forehead, 17so that no one could buy or sell unless he had the mark, which is the name of the beast or the number of his name. 18Thus is wisdom. The one having reason, let him figure out the number of the beast, for it is a number of man; and his number is 666.

A second animal now appears in this portion of the vision. Honestly, reading chapter 13 has caused more than a few people to become extremely distressed and fearful about the book of Revelation.

Not long ago, the town of Reeves, Louisiana had phone numbers that started with the numbers 666. People were a little startled when Reeves residents gave out their phone numbers. Something had to be done. Finally, after 40 years of having the number of the beast as the opening digits of their phone numbers, businesses and individuals were given the option of changing them to 749. A sigh of relief was breathed by all.

The mark of the beast has caused other panics. I remember when some Christians opposed the use of UPC symbols on products, claiming it was the beginning of everyone carrying the mark of the beast. There are plenty of rumors about what this mark might be. Those rumors, however, are off the mark.

The second animal demonstrates that the whole of creation is impacted by evil—both sea and land. It is also a satanic counterfeit of Christ as it looks like a lamb but speaks like a dragon. This animal is about worship. It is referred to as "the false prophet" in Revelation 16:13, 19:20, and 20:10. The first animal showed how the secular nations are deceived. This second beast shows that spiritual life the world over will be attacked and corrupted. Forced false religion will be a fact of life—as the sufferers under Roman rule knew very well. The forced worship of the first animal whose fatal wound was healed may be a reference to the Nero Redivivus legend that claimed Nero came back to life after his death in 68 A.D. Several imposters appeared on the scene over the years. Even Domitian, who ruled during the time of

Revelation, was thought to be Nero come back to life. Having a mark on the hand or forehead was a common indication of slavery. A "mark" and a "seal" were two different indicators. To be sealed by the king's authority was good news. To be marked as a slave was devastating.

Perhaps the most important eye-opening contrast this section of chapter 13 provides is that of true worship versus false worship. We've come across several worship sections in the book of Revelation. In chapters 4, 5, 7, 11, and 12, elders fall on their faces to worship along with throngs of the heavenly host. It is willing and spontaneous praise for the One who has conquered death, for the gracious and victorious God and King. The worship of the dragon and beasts is quite different. It is forced worship. It is coerced. People are baited into it through trickery. Verses 12-16 show the stark difference between the worship of the true God and the worship of the devil's cheap imitations. In these five verses of chapter 13, the same verb is used seven times to describe the worship of the beast. It is the Greek verb "poieo." The verb means "to make, to do, to cause." How does evil entice people to worship? The words in bold represent the verb "poieo":

*He **exercised** all the authority of the first beast on his behalf, and **made** the earth and its inhabitants worship the first beast (verse 12)...And he **performed** great and miraculous signs, even **causing** fire to come down from heaven (verse 13)...He ordered them **to set up** an image in honor of the beast (verse 14)......so that it could speak and **cause** all who refused to worship the image to be* *killed (verse 15)…He also **forced** everyone, small and great, rich and poor, free and slave, to receive a mark (verse 16).*

True worship is willing and authentic. It is done in spirit and in truth (John 4:23-24). Worship is about freedom and gratitude. Worship of the beast was about deception, coercion, threats and control. Worship was a big part of the lives of first-century citizens. It impacted their relationships, business, family, and social life. Christians needed to know what true worship was all about. The same is true today. Worship of material things caused by slick advertising and flashy products is not true worship. Worship of sports or hobbies or self isn't the worship God desires. Worship that focuses on personal preferences or legalistic forms isn't real worship. That worship is self-made or coerced. True worship means humbly and gratefully praising the God who enters our lives by His grace and gives His gifts of life and salvation. All believers need to know the characteristics of true worship versus false worship. Chapter 13 shows the way.

Another contrast chapter 13 provides is that of true prophetic authority verses false teachers. Verse 13 states that the second beast caused fire to come down from heaven. This is reminiscent of Elijah (1 Kings 18, 2 Kings 1). It also was an attempt to imitate the "signs," the miracles, of Jesus. But this was just for show. The goal was to impress men with deceptive trickery. Verse 15 refers to a talking idol. This was a common "magic" practice during the Apostle John's time. The verse shows

Christians that idol trickery could be expected. It also reinforces Jesus' words to every believer: *"Watch out for false prophets. They come to you in sheep's clothing, but inwardly they are ferocious wolves" (Matthew 7:15).*

As I mentioned, the mark of the beast in verse seventeen may refer to the way slaves were marked on the hand or forehead. The message may be that evil will enslave you. It also shows that not going along with the crowd will bring trial and challenge into your life. Not being able to buy or sell without the mark would bring about difficulty and suffering. This was happening already as Christians in the first century were being excluded from the trade guilds that would allow them to conduct business.

The mark of the beast was also about Satan's ongoing deception and attempted mimicry of Jesus. When Revelation is read aloud in Greek, the phrase "mark of the beast" (karagma tou thayriou) sounds very similar to the phrase "grace of God" (kariti tou theou). The same is true of the phrases "image of the beast" (eikona thayriou) and "image of God" (eikona theou). Chapter 13 exposes the ugliness of evil by showing its "beastly" nature. It also shows how deceptive and slick the devil can be as he tries to counterfeit what is good, right, and Christ-like—all to grab power and destroy people.

Verse eighteen mentions the number of the animal, 666. Remember, numbers tell stories in Revelation. Some have called this number "the unholy trinity," referring to the dragon and the two beasts, each falling short of perfection (six is one less than seven). The verse says "it is man's

209

number, six-hundred, sixty-six." The number may tell the story of the creation of humans on the sixth day—the beloved creatures of God who became self-centered, disobedient, and sinful. It may signify all who are in need of redemption—the story and number of humanity.

Ultimately, we don't know. We can't understand everything in the mural of Revelation. While we don't know all the details, we do know the general sense of it all—even the number 666. It calls for wisdom and insight to see that the real character of the devil is corrupt and no good.

The details of chapter 13 are important. However, asking "Who are the beasts?" may be the wrong approach. The overall message of the chapter may be what is most important. Chapter 13 describes the strategies of the dragon. He will be on the attack in both the earthly and spiritual realms. He will infiltrate the secular and the sacred. He will be about deception—even copying Christ and mimicking the grace of God. His enticing temptations will look attractive, but, in reality, life with the dragon is ugly and deadly.

This is an important message in our day and age when God's will and ways are being pushed aside. God sounds the alarm in chapter 13. It's time to see the real story. The way of faith and trust in God erodes slowly and subtly. Against this deceptive and destructive flow, believers are called to faith and perseverance. But even in the face of evil's ugliness, God assures us: There's no need to fear. He is still in control.

Study Guide for Revelation Chapter 13

1. Read Revelation 13:1-4. Picture this image in your mind. What characteristics of the devil and his evil ways stand out to you?

2. How does this help you to be on guard against Satan's sneaky ways?

3. Read Revelation 13:5-10. What must the saints (God's redeemed people) patiently endure?

4. Describe what it means to have patient endurance and faith in the midst of suffering?

5. Read Revelation 13:11-18. What specific truths does Revelation bring to your understanding of worship?

6. What are some genuine improvements needed in our Christian worship life today?

7. What counterfeit teachings and temptations are strong and prominent during our time? Why are they so tempting?

Revelation
Chapter Fourteen

✝

While the animals of chapter 13 get a lot of attention, the animal that follows quickly in Revelation chapter 14 doesn't get mentioned as much. The mark of the beast also gets a lot of press, but the name of God the Father written on the foreheads of believers in chapter 14 isn't discussed as often. This underscores why it is so important to look at the whole book of Revelation, the flow of the vision, not simply a few hot spots or points of curiosity. Chapters 13 and 14 bring believers a remarkable message. In the face of the strong, hideous, deceptive and destructive powers of the devil, the Lamb of God, victorious on Mount Zion, steps forward to vanquish the foe. The introduction of the beasts in chapter 13 serves not as much to frighten, but to display how great the victory of the Lamb really is. Chapter 14 is a chapter of sweet victory. Even though the end of the story hasn't arrived for suffering believers in the first-century Church, they're given a grand preview in this chapter.

NO SUSPENSE

1And I looked, and behold, the Lamb standing on Mount Zion, and with him 144,000 having his name and his Father's name written on their foreheads. 2And I heard a noise from heaven like the noise of many waters and like noise of a great thunder. The noise I heard was like harpists playing harp on their harps. 3And they sing a new song before the throne and before the four living things and the elders. No one is able to learn the song except the 144,000, the ones redeemed from the earth. 4These are the ones who did not defile themselves with women, for they are virgins. These are the ones following the Lamb wherever he may go. These were redeemed from men as first-fruits for God and the Lamb. 5And in their mouth a lie was not found; they are faultless.

The devil and his animals couldn't make a dent in the plan of the Lamb of God. His complete church, symbolized by the 144,000 marked with the Father's name, stood victorious on Mount Zion. Mount Zion has long been a symbol of heaven. The victory of Mount Zion is described in Isaiah 25:

> *On this mountain he will destroy the shroud that enfolds all peoples, the sheet that covers all nations; he will swallow up death forever. The Sovereign LORD will wipe away the tears from all faces; he will remove the disgrace of his people from all the earth. The LORD has spoken. In that day they will say, "Surely this is our God; we trusted in him, and he saved us. This is the LORD, we trusted in him; let us rejoice and be glad in his salvation" (vss.7-9).*

God did it! He came through! He kept His word. He was faithful. Trusting in Him was worth it. He accomplished His gracious salvation. The harps hung on trees during exile in Babylon (Psalm 137:1-2) were now being played. The Greek phrase "harpists playing harp on their harps" emphasizes the victory and new freedom. The heavenly host sang the new song mentioned in Revelation 5:9-14 and celebrated in Psalm 40:

> *I waited patiently for the LORD; he turned to me and heard my cry. He lifted me out of the slimy pit, out of the mud and mire; he set my feet on a rock and gave me a firm place to stand. He put a new song in my mouth, a hymn of praise to our God. Many will see and fear and put their trust in the LORD (vss. 1-3).*

In addition to the perfect number of saints in heaven mentioned in Revelation chapter 7, we find that not one of God's redeemed on earth is left out of His heavenly Kingdom. No one is forgotten. The number 144,000 is used again and is explained for us. These are the ones *"who had been redeemed from the earth."* Listeners could be assured that their Savior would never forget them. The 144,000 of the vision were the firstfruits—just the beginning.

Revelation 14 goes even further to tell us about how these purchased children of God lived. They were faithful, obedient, and truthful. Our gracious Savior was teaching distressed and persecuted people how to live, what to do, and how to give him glory. There was no suspense. The victory belonged to Jesus. The Way and the Truth and the Life was the One to follow.

THE FINAL WORD

6*And I saw another angel flying in midair, having the eternal gospel to evangelize to those who live on the earth and to every nation, tribe, tongue and people.* **7***He said in a loud voice, "Fear God and give him glory, because the hour of his judgment has come. Worship the one who made the heavens and the earth, the sea and the springs of water."*

What can change hearts? What can turn people from godlessness to faith? What can lead people to repentance? Not our determination. Not laws. Not anything within ourselves or created by us. What changes hearts? The Word of God. His eternal Gospel changes people, saves people, makes them new creations.

If anyone ever wonders if God is fair, whether He is truly righteous, or if He condemns people without giving them a chance, verses six and seven give an encouraging and clarifying answer. The eternal Gospel is proclaimed to all people. The living Word of God is brought to everyone. All people are called to fall before the Lord in repentance and worship. The creator of all things is declared as the one to fear and give glory. These verses are reminiscent of the book of Jonah. An evil and rebellious nation heard the prophetic Word and, by the power of the Holy Spirit, repented and experienced God's mercy. Jesus promised in Matthew 24:14, *"And this gospel of the kingdom will be preached in the whole world as a testimony to all nations, and then the end will come."*

We can be certain that when we get to heaven we won't say to God, "Uh, I think you made a big mistake. You forgot to share your message with millions of people!" No, we'll see His righteousness, His faithfulness, His grace, His justice, and His truth prevailing throughout heaven. We'll fall down in worship and give glory to God for putting everything together in just the right way. All creation will join in acknowledging the righteousness of God—His just condemnation of those who rightly receive eternal punishment and His gracious blessing of those given the gift of eternal life.

8And another angel, a second, followed saying, "It fell! It fell! Babylon the Great, which from the furious wine of her immorality gave all the nations drink."

The second angel brings more good news. Babylon is fallen, finished. Babylon represents captivity and exile. It stands for all who reject Jesus and attempt to crush His people. The words of verse eight echo Isaiah 21:9: *"Look, here comes a man in a chariot with a team of horses. And he gives back the answer: 'Babylon has fallen, has fallen! All the images of its gods lie shattered on the ground!'"* Evil never had a chance. God was in control the whole time. And now the last word of judgment is proclaimed by the second angel. Just as Isaiah declared in the Old Testament, the prophetic words were still true for those who suffered in the first century.

There are times when you feel as if evil, suffering, corruption, and heartbreak have the last word. Your heart grows heavy because sadness and hopelessness make any outlook for the future seem bleak. But a wonderful voice pierces the heavens to bring us hope. We may feel fallen, but it is Babylon that is fallen. Evil, sin, and death are fallen. Believers are not off track. If you trust Christ in the midst of the turmoil of this world, you are not crazy. The rebellious nations are the ones that drank the maddening wine of Babylon's corruption and adulteries. Jesus is alive and victorious. Trusting in Him makes sense. Having faith in the risen Lord is the right thing to do.

9And a third angel followed them saying in a loud voice: "If anyone worships the beast and his image and receives his mark on the forehead or on the hand, 10he, too, will drink from the wine of God's fury, which has been poured full strength into the cup of his wrath. He will be tormented with burning sulfur before the holy angels and the Lamb. 11And the smoke of their torment goes up for ever and ever, and the ones who worship the beast and his image, and anyone who receives the mark of his name, do not have rest day or night." 12Thus is the patient endurance of the saints, the ones keeping the commands of God and staying faithful to Jesus.

The third angel lets everyone know what is at stake. This is a matter of life and death. The price of forgetting the Eternal God, of walking away from Him, of making ourselves gods, of running with the crowd and delighting in the way of sinners, is eternal torment. If any question ever comes up about the existence of hell, these verses seal the deal. Yes, real torment awaits those who reject the true God.

This is not to be taken lightly by believers. It calls for patient endurance. One facet of patient endurance involves our witness. We're waiting for the Lord's return, but we do not wait without purpose. We have a serious and sacred calling. As Jesus articulated to the churches in the opening chapters of the book, God's people are here to be shining lights, lampstands for all to see. Lives are at stake. We cannot forget our purpose. The Church cannot become lazy, get distracted with infighting, or project a boring and meaningless image to the world. Believers in Jesus Christ have been commissioned to reach out with the Good News of Him as Savior. The Church brings genuine hope to the world. It brings life that is complete and full. God's people must patiently endure the long haul with the vitality of the Gospel.

Another facet of patient endurance involves our staying power. We are people who wait on the Lord. Our feelings may have their ups and downs. Our energy levels may fluctuate. Our desire to serve the Lord and follow Him may grow stronger or weaker. But regardless of how we feel, we are called to be faithful, to trust in God, to follow Him, to wait on Him.

What is the secret of waiting on God? It is His grace. God's living Word sustains us. It is the objective, Spirit-filled, living and active voice of God for our very subjective and erratic lives. We need God's say as the world rages around us and as our feelings rage within us. I remember reading a translation of Psalm 37:34 that said, *"Don't be impatient for the Lord to act; travel steadily along His path."* These living words have sustained me during difficult times. They've reminded me that small and gradual steps of faithfulness result in long-haul staying power. More than just a reminder, these words of God give gracious fuel for patient endurance.

We are also sustained by God's presence. When Jesus was getting ready for His crucifixion, He gave His disciples a precious gift. He took the bread and wine of the Passover and told them, "This is my body; this is my blood." The gift of Communion is the continued real presence of Jesus with us as we wait for His coming on Judgment Day. From walking in the garden with Adam and Eve, to the burning bush in Moses' presence, to the pillar of cloud and fire in the wilderness, to the birth of Jesus on earth, God has always been present with His people. God did not want to change that. As Jesus got ready to leave the earth physically, He gave His Church His forgiving and strengthening presence to sustain us until He comes again in glory. Receiving the gift of the Lord's Supper helps us wait faithfully on the Lord.

The gifts of fellowship with one another and prayer give us additional staying power. These blessings flow from God's Word and graciously keep us strengthened and on track. Remember, the book of Revelation was written to churches, to fellowships of believers. We are not meant to be alone in our journey through life. God supplies people who bring wisdom, encouragement, and accountability. These fellow believers may not be our best friends. They may not be people we socialize with on a regular basis. But they are godly people who show us God's love, who help us along the way, and who join us in prayer. Prayer allows us to have immediate access to God. It gives us a deep and abiding connection with Him. Prayer can be the ongoing conversation with our Savior that is always running in the background of our lives. Prayer gives power to endure. It is a tool that fills us with patient endurance as the world writhes in unfaithfulness and rebellion. It fuels our witness and our staying power. It helps us stand firm.

THE HARVEST

13And I heard a voice from heaven saying, "Write: Blessed are the dead who are dying in the Lord from now on." "Yes," says the Spirit, "they will rest from their labor, for their deeds will follow them." 14I looked, and behold, a brilliant cloud, and seated on the cloud was one "like a son of man" having on his head a crown of gold and in his hand a sharp sickle. 15And another angel came out of the temple crying out in a loud voice to the one sitting on the cloud, "Send your sickle and reap, because the hour to reap has come, because the harvest of the earth has ripened." 16And the one sitting on the cloud threw his sickle on the earth, and the earth was harvested. 17Another angel came out of the temple in heaven, also having a sharp sickle. 18Still another angel came from the altar, having authority over the fire, and he called out in a loud voice to the one having the sharp sickle, "Send your sharp sickle and gather the bunches from the grapevine of the earth, because its bunches are ripened." 19The angel threw his sickle to the earth and picked the grapevine of the earth, and he threw them into the great winepress of God's wrath. 20They were trampled in the winepress outside the city, and blood came up out of the winepress, up to the bridles of horses for a distance of 1,600 stadia.

We discussed the Parable of the Wheat and the Weeds in chapter 6. These verses from chapter 14 show that the harvest will come. The waiting will be over. What a relief to believers who wonder, "How long?"! What a comfort to know that, even in the face of scoffers and doubters, Jesus would truly return! Peter talks about scoffers in the last days who say, *"Where is this 'coming' he promised?" (2 Peter 3:4)* Revelation pulls back the curtain of heaven and shows Christians that Jesus is on His way.

Christians are also encouraged to keep running the race and fighting the good fight. Verse thirteen brings the good news that the life of every believer has lasting meaning. Even if you feel like what you do is meaningless and mundane, the voice from heaven says that your deeds will follow you. By the grace of God, you are making His important difference in the world.

Christians will also be given the gift of rest. Revelation 14:11 makes it clear that there is "no rest day or night" for those who unite themselves with unfaithfulness and evil. But 14:13 declares rest—beautiful, blessed and refreshing rest—for those who die in the Lord. This is good news for world-weary believers who may be tempted to give up hope. Rest is on its way!

It is telling that the harvest of chapter 14 comes so quickly after the evil aggression in chapter 13. The theme of Satan's power being short-lived is consistent in the book of Revelation. This theme will be reinforced in powerful and decisive ways in the chapters ahead.

It is also important to look carefully at the theme of justice in Revelation. Sin, evil, mistreatment, bullying, and persecution are not overlooked by God. The deep yearning in our hearts and souls for justice will be satisfied. God is just. He is fair and will make all things right. Those who wept and mourned over the persecution and death of their loved ones, those who were treated unfairly and harshly, would see God's justice prevail. The winepress of God's wrath would crush the unjust once and for all.

The reference in verse twenty to the winepress being outside the city points us to the crucifixion of Jesus. Outside the gates of Jerusalem, Jesus was "trampled." In Revelation 11:2 the church was trampled (the same verb is used in 14:20). Now there is justice as the Father and the Son direct the final harvest. The opposition is crushed. The flowing blood—perhaps a comment that brought to mind the destruction of the temple and the terrible slaughter of God's people—rose to heights of 1600 stadia (one stade was about 600 feet). This height was massive. The number 1600—40x40—may tell the story of the totality of the plan of God. The number 40 became a period of time that symbolized completion. Rooted in the flood, the wilderness wandering, the receiving of the Law from God, the temptation of Jesus, and His appearances before the Ascension, 40 showed a complete and whole work of God.

These harvest verses bring us back to the powerful and prophetic Word of God. God promised this righteous judgment. Joel 3:13 says, *"Swing the sickle, for the harvest is ripe. Come, trample the grapes, for the winepress is full and the vats overflow-- so great is their wickedness!"* Isaiah 63:3 tells us, *"I have trodden the winepress alone; from the nations no one was with me. I trampled them in my anger and trod them down in my wrath; their blood spattered my garments, and I stained all my clothing."* The God of the prophets, the true God who made a commitment to come through, has done so. It was reason to cheer. It is reason for us to praise Him.

FINISH WELL

The just and righteous work of God in chapter 14 brings refreshing answers and strong encouragement to believers. God is faithful and at work. He will come through. So every believer is urged to stay the course of faith. God calls people whose stamina levels are on empty to keep going, to finish well.

How can you finish well? I was watching the movie "Castaway" a while back. It's one of my favorites. The main character, Chuck, is played by Tom Hanks. At the end of the movie Chuck reflects on getting off the island, the reality of crushing heartbreak, and the challenge of

224

facing the pain life now held. His words capture the reality of life and how to finish well. He said:

> "I was never going to get off that island, terribly alone. I was going to get sick or injured or something...I had power over nothing.
>
> That's when this feeling came over me like a warm blanket. I knew, somehow, that I had to stay alive. Somehow. I had to keep breathing, even though I had no reason to hope, and all my logic said that I would never see [home] again. So that's what I did. I stayed alive. I kept breathing. And then one day that logic was proved all wrong because the tide came in and gave me a sail.
>
> And now, here I am. I'm back...And I know what I have to do now. I've got to keep breathing. Because tomorrow the sun will rise. Who knows what the tide could bring?"

Against all logic in your suffering, when you think you have no reason to hope, the message of Jesus' faithfulness and victory keeps you breathing. The cross of Jesus and His blood shed for you bring the tide in. It is the tide of grace and forgiveness and the tenacious determination of God to be with you through it all. In your days of suffering, you now have certainty that defies logic. With Jesus, you will make it. You might say that God gave you a sail. That's what the book of Revelation is. That's what this chapter underscores. And with that sail, you will make it home.

Study Guide for Revelation Chapter 14

1. Read Revelation 14:1-5. Why is news of a new song encouraging to you?

2. How do these verses give direction to your life now?

3. Read Revelation 14:6-7. What are we supposed to do as evangelists in the world?

4. What are our limitations?

5. Read Revelation 14:8-12. What helps keep you strong in your witness and staying power for Christ?

6. Read Revelation 14:13-20. What major themes in these verses are most compelling to you and why?

7. What will it mean for you to finish life well?

Revelation
Chapter Fifteen

✝

A few summers ago my family and I were in Harrods Department Store in London. We had already covered about eight floors of merchandise and we were taking a break for lunch. I was standing in line in the food court. Keep in mind that even though I can run ten miles and feel invigorated, my shopping endurance is that of a typical male. After fifteen minutes in a mall I'm looking for a bench so I can sit down and recover. So, as I stood in line at the Harrods food court, I was thirsty. The store had one of those self-serve soft drink dispensers—with ice. It was about one hundred degrees outside and I had just completed an Iron Man Triathlon's worth of shopping. It made sense to have a drink while I was waiting. After a few refreshing gulps, I refilled the cup and paid for our meals. When I was about half-way through my meal, I finished another glass of ice cold refreshment, so I went to fill the cup again. As I refilled my cold drink, took a few sips, and refilled it again, I noticed that the people behind the counter were staring at me. They were looking at me like I was a thief. Using my gift of astute perception, I approached them and asked, "Aren't there free refills?" They looked at me in their English way and said, "No." I offered to pay, but they just shooed me away. Another ugly American intrudes on Europe.

I've got news for you about life in this world: it offers no free refills. The empty promises of the world will drain you, wear you down, use you up, and push you relentlessly. Then, like a strict British department store, it will make you pay. The price of chasing what the world says is fulfilling will suddenly become evident. You may gain the world, but you'll lose your soul to fear, stress, illness, emptiness, difficulty, and death. There are no free refills in this journey of life.

But God breaks that destructive cycle. He does something new and revolutionary. He restores your soul. He's like good old American fast food establishments that give you all the refills you want. We hear God's invitation in Isaiah 55:1, *"Come, all you who are thirsty, come to the waters; and you who have no money, come, buy and eat!"* Jesus said in John 7:37, *"If anyone is thirsty, let him come to me and drink."* In the book of Revelation God was giving a free refill. Chapters 14 and 15 bring people from the darkness of evil to the glory of the saving God. They bring people from the confusion of idolatry to the clarity of truth in Jesus Christ. For parched and tired people, Revelation is a free refill.

CLOSER THAN YOU THINK

1I saw another sign in heaven, great and marvelous: seven angels having the seven last plagues, because with them God's wrath is completed. 2And I saw what looked like a sea of glass mixed with fire and, the ones overcoming the beast and his image and the number of his name, standing upon the sea of glass, having harps of

228

God.   3And they sing the song of Moses the servant of God and the song of the Lamb: "Great and marvelous are your deeds, Lord God Almighty. Righteous and true are your ways, King of the nations.   4Who will not fear you, O Lord, and will not glorify your name? For you alone are holy. All nations will come and worship before you, for your righteous deeds have been revealed."

While the book of Revelation has the reputation for being frightening, intimidating, and unpleasant, the reality is that nearly half of the book focuses on the victory of Jesus over all that is frightening, intimidating and unpleasant. Chapter 15 continues the excitement of God's final and relief-providing work to crush the enemy. Listeners are given the opportunity to see the end.

The mention of the fiery sea may be another reference to the Exodus Red Sea crossing.   Victors standing beside the sea singing the song of Moses bring us back to that great act of deliverance by God in Egypt. But God's miracles of rescue are not things of the past. The harps appear once again—celebration that exile is over. What is sung is not only the song of Moses; it is the song of the Lamb—miraculous rescue through Jesus is the new and wonderful celebration.

The themes of God's righteousness and justice fill the song in verses three and four.   The repetition of Revelation's themes reinforces God's encouraging message to His people. All nations will worship Him. As Paul said to believers in Philippians 2:10-11: *"At the name of Jesus every knee should bow, in heaven and on earth and under the earth, and every tongue confess that Jesus Christ is Lord, to the glory of God the Father."*

THE TEMPLE

5After these things I looked and the temple of the tabernacle of the Testimony was opened in heaven. 6And the seven angels having the seven plagues came out from the temple. They were dressed in clean, bright linen and wore golden sashes around their chests. 7And one of the four living things gave to the seven angels seven golden bowls filled with the wrath of God, who lives for ever and ever. 8And the temple was filled with smoke from the glory of God and from his power, and no one was able to come into the temple until the seven plagues of the seven angels were finished.

The phrase "tabernacle of the Testimony" is identical to the Old Testament phrase "tent of meeting." God's action in the Old Testament was identical to His action in Revelation. Exodus 40:34-35 tells us, *"Then the cloud covered the Tent of Meeting, and the glory of the LORD filled the tabernacle. Moses could not enter the Tent of Meeting because the cloud had settled upon it, and the glory of the LORD filled the tabernacle."*

The tabernacle was the portable temple that became the place of God's presence for the people of Israel. This reference in Revelation 15 brought listeners back to God's delivering presence and power during the time of the Exodus from Egypt. In this vision they were seeing the true God. This was not pagan trickery. This was the God of Abraham, Isaac, and Jacob. He was with His people to save and defend them. Plagues—reminiscent of the rescue from Egypt—would be the final step as God worked to bring people to repentance and as He brought judgment on stubborn evildoers.

The open tabernacle of the Testimony and the smoke that filled the temple showed that God had drawn near. He was close—so was the end of suffering. Those who trusted in Him were not alone. Judgment was closer than anyone realized.

WHY SUCH A COMPLICATED VISION?

Revelation chapter 15 is a good expression of what the whole book of Revelation is about. After travelling through fifteen chapters of this vision, you may ask yourself, "Why did God make it so complicated, so intricate, so mysterious, so scary?" Chapter 15 provides some answers.

First, **Revelation is very Biblical**—Scripture saturated, as I mentioned at the beginning of this book. It is thoroughly packed with Old and New Testament Scripture. We may never be able to find all the references or grasp the Scriptural depth of this vision. Believers in the first century with Jewish background were very well-versed in the Old Testament. They had large portions of the Scriptures memorized. They understood the history of God's work among His people. They could tell the stories. The images of the vision were easier for them to grasp and to connect with familiar Scriptural handles. One example from Revelation 14 is the cup of God's wrath in verse ten. Isaiah 51:17 shows that this cup is all about the message of judgment and deliverance (*"Awake, awake! Rise up, O Jerusalem, you who have drunk from the hand of the LORD the cup of his wrath..."*). One reason for the complex nature of Revelation is that it is filled with powerful messages from the Scriptures.

Second, **Revelation begs us to keep looking at the Word of God**. Jesus helped direct people to dig more deeply into the Word. In Luke 24:27 we hear what Jesus did as He visited with the travelers on the road to Emmaus: *"Beginning with Moses and all the Prophets, [Jesus] explained to them what was said in all the Scriptures concerning himself."* Jesus did the same with the rest of the disciples later in Luke 24:45, *"He opened their minds so they could understand the Scriptures."* Even Philip followed suit when he encountered the Ethiopian reading from Isaiah 53 in Acts 8:35, *"Philip began with that very passage of Scripture and told him the good news about Jesus."*

Revelation brings us back to God's Word in a powerful way. If anyone ever claims that the Bible is old news, worn out, completely understood, without mystery, or lacking compelling character, just open up to the book of Revelation! Reading this vision causes us to ask questions about the meaning of the Bible, its application, the work of God, and the deep truths of life. This book of the Bible puts the exclamation point on the Scriptures. It shows us there is still so much to learn, still so much to be discovered about our gracious and awesome Savior. Revelation fends off our attempts to make the Bible a dry academic exercise. Instead, it drives us to search the Scriptures with wonder, anticipation, need, and excitement.

Third, **Revelation reflects the character of God**. God is not easy. He is not the neighbor down the street or the buddy who goes to the movies with us. Yes, He is close. Yes, He draws near to us with loving kindness. But He is not ordinary. Chapter 15:3-4 brings us a song that lauds God's character:

> *"Great and marvelous are your deeds, Lord God Almighty. Just and true are your ways, King of the ages. Who will not fear you, O Lord, and bring glory to your name? For you alone are holy. All nations will come and worship before you, for your righteous acts have been revealed."*

Try to absorb those words. The word used for "holy" is a less frequently used Greek word that directs us to the unique holy perfection of God. This is a powerful song to God who has depth and breadth, who is wonderful and awesome.

One of my favorite authors, Helmut Thielicke, commented on the character of God and His Word in a book called The Trouble with the Church. He said,

> The men of God were never bold, brash pushers. For they were not like the false prophets— motivated by their will or their urge to power—but

were rather fully conscious of the darkness that covers the earth and the thick darkness that weighs upon the peoples. They suffered under the incomprehensibility of God. They felt the burden of contradiction between what their hearts demanded of God and what God was actually doing, and above all what He was. (107)

There is struggle and awe and incomprehensibility when you walk with the true God. Revelation shows God as merciful and faithful, but also powerful and unpredictable. In Revelation we see the "turbulence" of God in action as He works in every realm—spiritual and temporal.

Thielicke said that faithful proclaimers of the Word throughout the ages felt that speaking for God was too hard. He was too awesome. "And I fear," Thielicke went on to say, "that if they had not felt this inhibition, they would not have understood at all what it was all about, they would not have seen that the Tremendous was casting its shadow upon them" (108).

This is frightening—just like the book of Revelation. And it should be! It shows us that this remarkable work of reaching humanity for salvation is not about us. It is not casual. It is not a matter of simply getting our evangelism technique right or making sure we have pleasant surroundings and user-friendly ministries at church. Revelation shows us, as Thielicke said, "It would not be we, therefore, who would grasp his arm to liberate for him the territories over which that arm might then be

234

outstretched. It would rather be that his arm was already stretched over the earth and we need only to walk beneath the shadow of his hand" (108).

There is depth to God. He is bigger than us. The book of Revelation draws us into that fearsome and wonderful fact. We read Revelation and say, "I can't take it! The full dose of evil and the devil's work, the full blast justice and holiness of God, the battle in front of my eyes, the price of death and the reward of life—it's too much for me!" But when we want to flee, we must also say the words of Peter in John 6:68-69, *"Lord, to whom shall we go? You have the words of eternal life. We believe and know that you are the Holy One of God."*

Revelation pushes us away if we think we're the star players in the universe. It then brings us close to let us know that all the effort and action is truly for us because of God's lavish love.

Fourth, **Revelation opens our eyes to the mystery of God.** The book of Revelation reveals that life is not simply what you see and feel and can figure out. It places you in the midst of "the elemental confrontation between the kingdom of God and the kingdom of the world" (Thielicke, 109). It digs deeper and shows you that much is happening behind the scenes. God is not idle. Our plans and schedules are insignificant compared to the vast and unceasing work of God.

But Revelation also brings comfort as this massive universal battle rages. It shows that "God himself is on the battlefield...While you contend, Another will contend for you" (Thielicke, 109). Some servants of God in history understood this. David appealed in Psalm 35:1, *"Contend, O LORD, with those who contend with me; fight against those who fight against me."* Isaiah uttered God's wonderful promise in Isaiah 49:25, *"But this is what the LORD says: 'Yes, captives will be taken from warriors, and plunder retrieved from the fierce; I will contend with those who contend with you, and your children I will save.'"*

During my relatively short time on this earth, life has become more difficult to understand. You can't observe the goings on of this world for any period of time and really believe that life is a simple and carefree walk in the park. When our eyes are open we accumulate a heavy burden. It goes back to "the burden of contradiction between what [our] hearts [demand] of God and what God [is] actually doing, and above all what He [is]" articulated by Helmut Thielicke. 1 Corinthians 2:16 says, *"For who has known the mind of the Lord that he may instruct him?"* But before we descend into despair, we must look at the final words of this verse. What pulls it all together for us? Where does the book of Revelation lead us? Paul says, *"But we have the mind of Christ."* Revelation is all about Jesus. He speaks. He communicates. He reveals. He steps in to care for His Church. He shows that God is for us. The Mystery is on our side. Revelation shows us that He who alone can comfort us has come. And He will not leave our side.

Study Guide for Revelation Chapter 15

1. Read Revelation 15:1-4. Why is Exodus imagery so prominent in Revelation?

2. How do these verses speak to the assertion of our culture that "all gods are the same"?

3. Read Revelation 15:5-8. What was rekindled in the hearts and minds of first-century Christians when they encountered the tabernacle in this vision?

4. What helps to renew hope and determination in your walk of faith?

5. How does the book of Revelation keep people engaged with God and His Word?

6. In what ways is God "easy" and "very challenging"?

7. Why, in your opinion, is the book of Revelation an appropriate final book of the Bible?

Revelation
Chapter Sixteen

✝

The time for plagues has come. The seven angels from chapter 15 are waiting to pour out bowls of God's wrath on the earth. The people in the book of Exodus waited 430 years for deliverance. The exiles in Babylon waited 70 years for freedom. The suffering believers addressed by Revelation—you included—are still waiting. But Revelation 16 brings the good news that the God of deliverance and freedom is still at work.

Throughout the centuries many doubting voices have been raised, questioning the reality of God and His plan of deliverance. Peter quoted the scoffers: *"Where is this coming he promised? Ever since our fathers died, everything goes on as it has since the beginning of creation" (2 Peter 3:4).* The Psalmist cried out to God: *"Vindicate me, O God, and plead my cause against an ungodly nation; rescue me from deceitful and wicked men" (Psalm 43:1).* I ran across a comment on a Christian blog that said: "What's all this buzz about 'God' and 'Jesus'? They're just make-believe characters, sort of like Barney, the purple dinosaur."

Revelation 16 responds to each comment and outcry with the reality of God, the decisiveness of His justice, and the truth of His coming.

PLAGUES

1And I heard a loud voice from the temple saying to the seven angels, "Go and pour out the seven bowls of God's wrath on the earth." 2The first angel went and poured out his bowl on the earth, and bad and painful sores were upon the men who had the mark of the beast and worshiped his image. 3The second angel poured out his bowl on the sea, and it turned into blood like that of a dead man, and every living creature in the sea died. 4The third angel poured out his bowl on the rivers and springs of water, and they became blood. 5Then I heard the angel of the waters saying: "You are righteous, you who are and who were, the Holy One, that you judged these things; 6because they poured out the blood of the saints and prophets, and you have given them blood to drink as they deserve." 7And I heard the altar saying: "Yes, Lord God Almighty, true and just are your judgments."

The plagues of Revelation 16 bring us back to Exodus. It's really remarkable how many Exodus references there are in Revelation. Hearkening back to this miraculous and mighty act of deliverance through God's direct intervention is no accident. God was communicating a powerful message to believers. He hears the cries of His people. He is truly concerned about their suffering.

Exodus 9:9 is where boils break out on men, women, and animals in Egypt. It was all part of God's gracious deliverance. In Revelation 16 we see references to both the Exodus rescue and the ultimate rescue at the cross. This chapter compresses the history of salvation for God's people. In addition to these mighty acts of deliverance, chapter 16 also shows us the final act of salvation as the end finally comes.

After the sores, came the plague of water into blood. Exodus 7:17ff contains the parallel. Revelation 16:3-7 shows us God's deep and just reasoning. This blood is God's justice for the shed blood of the saints and prophets. We are reminded of the visionary nature of this book as we hear the altar speak in response to the angel. The place of sacrifices acknowledged that God's plans and ways are true and just. There is no arguing the fact. More than one witness concurs. Every hearer is being presented with clear and accurate testimony.

8The fourth angel poured out his bowl on the sun, and the sun was given power to scorch men with fire. 9And the men were scorched by the great heat and they blasphemed the name of God, who had authority over these plagues, and they did not repent to give him glory.

Those who worshipped the beast received a plague of sores. Those who killed the saints were cursed with water that became blood. Verses eight and nine bring another assault on the Roman god Apollo. It was said that Apollo drove his chariot of fiery horses across the sky each day to give people light. He was god of the sun. He was also the god of healing. Now he couldn't help. The sun was not in the hands of a pagan god. The true God was showing who was in command. But even under intense trial, the unbelievers blasphemed the true God. They would not repent.

It is important to notice God's goal as he dishes out suffering through these plagues. He is desperately trying to turn people's hearts to Himself. He is working hard to give a clear wake-up call to all who reject Him, to all who are trapped in evil and twisted belief. God desires all people to come to repentance (2 Peter 3:9). But we are stubborn and selfish creatures. Perhaps the frustration level of first-century believers was eased a bit as they saw that even God couldn't convince stubborn people to turn to Him.

10The fifth angel poured out his bowl on the throne of the beast, and his kingdom became darkened, and they gnawed their tongues from the pain 11and blasphemed the God of heaven because of their pains and their sores, but they did not repent from their deeds. 12The sixth angel poured out his bowl on the great river Euphrates, and its water was dried up to prepare the way for the kings from the East.

The fifth angel poured his bowl directly onto the throne of the beast! This is an all-out assault on the enemy. But instead of the desired result of repentance, blasphemy poured from the kingdom of darkness. God has a remarkable desire to reach His precious creation. As the bowls are poured, we witness the patience of God and give thanks that He gives His time and effort so that He can be known.

Verse twelve sets the stage for the final and great deliverance. The crossing of a dried up waterway makes us think of the Red Sea (Exodus 14:21-22). The Euphrates was a passage to Babylon. The kings from the East were the arch-enemy of God's people. Suddenly we see a convergence of the enemies of God's people.

THE GREAT DAY OF GOD ALMIGHTY

13And I saw from the mouth of the dragon, from the mouth of the beast and from the mouth of the false prophet, three unclean spirits like frogs. 14They are spirits of demons doing signs, which go out to the kings of the whole world, to gather them for the battle of the great day of God Almighty. 15 "Behold, I come like a thief! Blessed is the one staying awake and keeping his clothes, so that he may not walk naked and they will see his naked shame."

The only other frogs in the Bible are in the Exodus plagues (8:2-7). The interesting thing about the Old Testament plague of frogs was that the Egyptian magicians made even more frogs come into the land. They compounded the problem with their evil. In Revelation 16 frogs are also an evil-produced scourge. They come from the dragon and the two beasts. Verse thirteen is the first mention of the false prophet—revealing the true character of one of the fearsome animals. Though the "unholy trinity" was at work, the group was still under God's control. The ugly spirits croaking from their mouths were for the purpose of gathering all the evil leaders of the world for God's great day.

At this critical moment—a nervous moment for believers who feel like the kings of the world had the upper hand—Jesus speaks. Anyone who feels the book of Revelation is too frightening and strange can take heart at the timely comfort Jesus gives. This is central to understanding Revelation. During times of trouble, Jesus speaks. While John suffered in exile, Jesus spoke up. While the churches teetered on the brink of collapse or despair, Jesus intervened. Even now as we read the words of the vision, Jesus enters our troubled lives, reminds us of His coming, and encourages us to be faithful.

Jesus' words are reminiscent of His message to the church in Sardis in Revelation 3:3, *"Remember, therefore, what you have received and heard; obey it, and repent. But if you do not wake up, I will come like a thief, and you will not know at what time I will come to you."* They also bring us back to His message in Matthew 24:43-44:

> *But understand this: If the owner of the house had known at what time of night the thief was coming, he would have kept watch and would not have let his house be broken into. So you also must be ready, because the Son of Man will come at an hour when you do not expect him.*

Verse fifteen also directs us to Jesus' discussion of being prepared for the big wedding feast—His final coming (Matthew 22:1ff and Matthew 25:1ff). Without the necessary clothes or preparation, people will be left outside in misery.

Notice how Jesus underscores the fact that His coming will be a complete surprise. His return will be unpredictable and unexpected. This is the consistent message of the Son of God and the writers of the New Testament. Jesus let us know in Acts 1:7-8:

> *"It is not for you to know the times or dates the Father has set by his own authority. But you will receive power when the Holy Spirit comes on you; and you will be my witnesses in Jerusalem, and in all Judea and Samaria, and to the ends of the earth."*

This answer was in response to the disciples' question about whether Jesus was going to restore the kingdom now that He had risen from the dead. Jesus emphasized that we can't figure out when the final restoration will take place. We shouldn't waste our time trying to construct time and date scenarios. We have a specific calling and commission. These require urgency and no distraction. We are witnesses for Jesus on this earth.

The Apostles carried this message to the Christian Church:

> *"Now, brothers, about times and dates we do not need to write to you, for you know very well that the day of the Lord will come like a thief in the night"* (1 Thessalonians 5:1-2).

> *"The Lord is not slow in keeping his promise, as some understand slowness. He is patient with you,*

not wanting anyone to perish, but everyone to come to repentance. But the day of the Lord will come like a thief. The heavens will disappear with a roar; the elements will be destroyed by fire, and the earth and everything in it will be laid bare. Since everything will be destroyed in this way, what kind of people ought you to be? You ought to live holy and godly lives" (2 Peter 3:9-11).

The timing is up to God. We're not called to let our curiosity distract us from the mission God has given us. We are to be shining lights, bringing the Gospel of Christ to the world, always ready for Jesus' return.

ARMAGEDDON

16And they gathered them into the place called in Hebrew "Armageddon." 17The seventh angel poured out his bowl into the air, and out of the temple came a loud voice from the throne, saying, "It is done!" 18And lightning and noise and thunder happened, and a great earthquake happened, as has not happened since man has been on earth, so tremendous was this great earthquake.

Verse sixteen brings up one of the most intriguing references in the book of Revelation: Armageddon. We're told it is a Hebrew word. This underscores how Revelation is directing its listeners to the Scriptures—the Old Testament Scriptures written in the Hebrew language. God is revealing new depth and understanding as He shows how the Old Testament has brought the consistent and unchanging truth throughout the ages—even in these last days!

The Hebrew word "Armageddon" means "Mount Megiddo." Armageddon is a place. The significance of this place is twofold. First, the location is connected to paying the price of disobedience. King Josiah went to battle against Neco, King of Egypt, even though Neco warned Josiah that the Egyptian action was at God's bidding. Josiah was killed in the battle on the plain of Megiddo. Great weeping and mourning followed Josiah's death (see 2 Chronicles 35:20-26.) The prophet Zechariah connected the sadness of this event to the regret of those who put the Messiah to death:

> *"And I will pour out on the house of David and the inhabitants of Jerusalem a spirit of grace and supplication. They will look on me, the one they have pierced, and they will mourn for him as one mourns for an only child, and grieve bitterly for him as one grieves for a firstborn son. On that day the weeping in Jerusalem will be great, like the weeping of Hadad Rimmon in the plain of Megiddo"* (Zechariah 12:10-11).

Second, the fact that this is a Hebrew name gives a strong message to the faithful children of Israel who trust the Messiah, Jesus. Megiddo was a place of battle throughout history. It was contested because of its strategic location on an important trade and travel route. Revelation 16:16-17 shows that God's people will not lose this territory. They will prevail even though it appears that they are beyond help and hope.

Verse seventeen clinches this truth. The kings of the earth were gathered at Mount Megiddo—most likely at the base of the mountain, in the plain where battles took place. But no battle ever happens! As soon as all the enemy forces of the world are gathered together, the voice from the throne cries out, *"It is done!"*

There is no battle of Armageddon. Teachers who talk about a terrible war to end all wars at the end of the world are off target if they try to connect it to Armageddon. The destruction of the enemy comes with decisive swiftness. No believer is harmed. There is no suspense. It never appears that the true God will be overrun. In Greek, "It is done!" is one word. One word from the Almighty God destroys evil. Martin Luther said it well when he wrote the hymn "A Mighty Fortress is Our God":

> *Tho' devils all the world should fill, All eager to devour us,*
> *We tremble not, we fear no ill, They shall not overpower us.*
> *This world's prince may still Scowl fierce as he will,*
> *He can harm us none, He's judged; the deed is done;*
> **One little word can fell him.**
> *(The Lutheran Hymnal, 1941, #262 vs.3)*

This one word brings us to the cross on another "mountain," the hill called Golgotha. Jesus uttered, *"It is finished!"* when he died on the cross (John 19:30). This, too, is one word in the Greek language. One word completed the redemption of humanity as Jesus paid the price for our sins.

Verse eighteen continues the connection of Mount Megiddo's victory to the ultimate acts of God's salvation. Thunder, lightning and earthquakes showed the presence of God at Mount Sinai after God's people were freed from Egypt. A new life awaited them. Darkness and a strong earthquake accompanied the death of Jesus on the cross. Even the frightened centurion recognized the work of God when he cried out, *"Surely he was the Son of God!"* *(Matthew 27:54)*

Chapter 16 is a chapter of God's salvation. The Deliverer of Exodus, the Redeemer at the cross, and the Victor of the Last Day are one and the same. The true God prevails. He is alive, well, and working for His people. If any suffering believer doubts it, this vision brings back confidence in the active work of the Almighty God.

19The great city split into three parts, and the cities of the nations fell. God remembered Babylon the Great and gave her the cup filled with the wine of the fury of his wrath. 20Every island fled away and the mountains could not be found. 21And hail as large as a talent (90 pounds) fell from heaven upon men. And men blasphemed God because of the plague of hail, because her plague is exceedingly great.

Unfortunately, the unbelieving inhabitants of the earth did not respond like the centurion at the cross. As Babylon the Great received her cup filled with God's wrath and as giant hailstones pummeled the earth, the nations continued to blaspheme God. Verse twenty-one brings us back to the plagues of Exodus. Exodus 9:19ff describes the terrible plague of hail.

THIS IS REAL

God goes to great lengths to convince all people that the coming judgment is real. He gives fair and detailed warning. He shows His deep desire that all those for whom He gave His Son repent. He also shows the severity of life without Him.

Some have labeled Christianity as "boring and predictable." The blogger at the beginning of this chapter put Jesus in the same imaginary and harmless class as Barney the Dinosaur. I read about a high-profile executive who became a Thai Buddhist. In an article about his challenging business ventures he spoke about items he wore on his wrists. On one wrist he wore a woven bracelet blessed by a Thai monk. On the other he wore a single strand of string. The string reminded him of how little we really need in life. He said, "What's important in life isn't what you have, but how you live."

The business writers were happy to report this tidbit of Buddhist wisdom. They got all excited about the deep spirituality of this executive. That's how our culture behaves. It becomes enamored with philosophies, ideologies, and exotic religions. But Christianity? Even Christians buy into the "ordinary," "run-of-the-mill," "boring and predictable," reputation of Christianity. The One who stilled storms, repelled demons, and conquered death can become buried in mindless actions, meaningless rituals, Christian product lines, a social club mentality, and a "What else is new?" mindset. The roar of the Lion of Judah may be barely audible over the noise of ritualistic worship and apathetic teaching.

What happened? Why do believers wilt when confronted with arguments that the Bible and Jesus are thin imaginary myths? How have Christians forgotten the substantial evidence and eyewitness accounts that back the truth of the Scriptures? What happened to cause us to forget God's very real presence throughout history?

The book of Revelation is a wake-up call. This is all very real, God says. Christ is coming back. Justice will be done. He is the Savior, the only hope. It is time to repent.

If we have forgotten the mystery and power of the faith the true God has entrusted to us, it is time to wake up. If we have forgotten the awe and majesty of living in the presence of God, it's time to remember. If Christianity has become all about business and busyness, if faith in the Savior has become all about political influence or ecclesiastical power, it is time to repent with all our hearts. This is real.

Revelation

Are we as God's people reflecting who He really is? What happened to the simplicity, the selflessness, and the ethical leadership of God's people? What happened to the devotion of God's people to prayer and the reading of His Word? What happened to growth and maturity among God's people? Where is our dependence on the powerful and wise influence of the Holy Spirit? Where are the certainty and courage of living according to God's ways? Where is the boldness and excitement to testify to the One who has conquered death? Are believers in Christ living as bright lights in this dark and empty world?

The book of Revelation shouts, "Wake up!" We have been given a compelling, transcendent, life-transforming gift. It is real. It is meant for sharing.

Will we live it and bring it to the world? The time is short. The time is now.

Study Guide for Revelation Chapter 16

1. Read Revelation 16:1-7. The angels poured out plagues on those who poured out the blood of the saints and prophets. What in your opinion are the greatest injustices existing in the world today?

2. Read Revelation 16:8-12. Why do people refuse to listen to or follow the true God?

3. Read Revelation 16:13-15. How do Jesus' words affect your life?

4. Read Revelation 16:16-18. What typical teaching about Armageddon have you heard?

5. How does this chapter clarify what Armageddon is?

6. Read Revelation 16:19-21. The Bible indicates that there will be trial and suffering in these last days. How do you see that happening today? Is it changing people's hearts?

7. Reflect on and discuss the final section of this chapter ("This is Real"). What is your response to the questions raised?

Revelation
Chapter Seventeen

✝

Revelation chapter 17 continues the extended section of detailed judgment upon those who have rebelled against God and persecuted His people. It is also a chapter that reinforces the symbolic nature of this vision. As we are shown the mysterious images, an angel explains what each symbol means.

Unfortunately, the explanations can be just as confusing as the symbols themselves! God guides us and helps us to understand His message, but sometimes His message is too awesome for us to comprehend. Why does this vision have to be so cryptic? Why the mystery? The answer may surprise you.

DIGGING DEEPER INTO THE NATURE OF EVIL

1One of the seven angels having the seven bowls came and spoke with me saying, "Come, I will show you the punishment of the great prostitute, who sits on many waters. 2With her the kings of the earth committed adultery and the inhabitants of the earth were made drunk from the wine of her adulteries." 3And he carried me into the wilderness in the Spirit. And I saw a woman sitting on a scarlet beast that was covered with blasphemous names having seven heads and ten horns.

The seven-headed and ten-horned beast that came from the sea in chapter 13, and was called "the false prophet" in chapter 16, is now pictured with "the great harlot" or "prostitute" in chapter 17. This is not an unusual description for people who are unfaithful to God. Isaiah 1:21 says, *"See how the faithful city has become a harlot! She once was full of justice; righteousness used to dwell in her—but now murderers!"* Israel is described as an adulterer and prostitute when it goes after other gods. It is a familiar Biblical motif and identifies exact, unfaithful behavior. It is connected with the ritual prostitution involved in the pagan temples, both pre-Christ and in the first century.

The harlot had widespread influence. These verses serve as a stark warning about the lure and attraction of a sinful and destructive life.

The desert location of the great prostitute is intriguing. Comparing this to chapter 12, when the woman, who is the church, finds refuge in the desert, Louis Brighton said in his commentary on Revelation: "Does this harlot also station itself in the desert so that she can pretend that she is the true church and thus by her immoral deceptiveness wean people away from the church of Christ?" (Brighton, p.439)

The appearance of the woman and her evil steed bring us familiar symbols. The angel will help us understand what these are in detail.

4The woman was dressed in purple and scarlet, and was glittering with gold, precious stones and pearls. She had a golden cup in her hand, full of detestable things and the uncleanness of her adulteries. 5Upon her forehead was written a name: MYSTERY, BABYLON THE GREAT, THE MOTHER OF PROSTITUTES AND OF THE DETESTABLE THINGS OF THE EARTH. 6I saw the woman drunk from the blood of the saints and from the blood of the witnesses of Jesus. And seeing her, I was greatly amazed.

Revelation continues to tell the truth about the Roman oppressor. If anyone was tempted to join the ranks of Roman religion, God was making sure everyone knew the true character of that pagan practice. The woman's garb was the color of Roman royalty. She appeared to be wealthy and in control. But if there was any attraction to her, it is revealed as a fatal attraction. She is nothing but evil and detestable. Her title shows her true character. Her drunkenness shows what she has done and what she wants to do. The word for "greatly amazed" means "to marvel, to be in wonder." Evil is deceptive, shocking, and can even be attractive.

THE VISION OF THE WOMAN EXPLAINED

7And the angel said to me: "Why are you amazed? I will tell you the mystery of the woman and of the beast she rides, the one having seven heads and ten horns. 8The beast you saw, once was, now is not, and will come up out of the Abyss and go away to destruction. The inhabitants of the earth whose names have not been written in the book of life from the creation of the world will be amazed when they see the beast, because he once was, now is not, and yet will come. 9Thus the mind having wisdom. The seven heads are seven hills on which the woman sits. And they are seven kings. 10Five have fallen, one is, the other has not yet come; and when he comes, it is necessary for him to remain a little while. 11The beast who once was, and now is not, is an eighth king. He is from the seven and is going to his destruction. 12The ten horns you saw are ten kings who have not yet received a kingdom, nevertheless will receive authority as kings one hour with the beast. 13These have one purpose and will give their power and authority to the beast. 14These will make war against the Lamb, and the Lamb will overcome them because he is Lord of lords and King of kings--and with him will be his called, elect, and faithful ones." 15And the angel said to me, "The waters you saw, where the prostitute sits, are peoples, crowds, nations and tongues. 16The beast and the ten horns you saw will hate the prostitute, and will make her desolate and naked, and will consume her flesh, and will burn her with fire. 17For God gave into their hearts to do his purpose and to do one purpose, and to give their kingdoms to the beast until the words of God are fulfilled. 18The woman you saw is the great city that rules over the kings of the earth."

In verse seven the angel introduces his explanation of the woman on the animal. As I mentioned, this angelic episode in Revelation shows us how to understand and interpret the book. We're looking at symbols. The symbols of the vision point to important spiritual truths.

God uses symbols not to confuse us, but to come down to our level, to show us something we can understand. God pulls back the curtain on the complex and awesome heavenly plan and allows us to see a glimpse so we can have a greater understanding of the story behind the story. In His grace He gives us something to encourage us.

Verse eight tells us that the beast is from the Abyss, but will go to his destruction. This is good news! Unfortunately, he will deceive many people. The verses that follow bring some clarity to the web of Satan's deceit. The Roman Empire is singled out as an oppressor of Christ and His people. Verse nine says that the seven heads are the "seven hills" on which the woman sits. Rome has historically been known as "the city of seven hills." For the first-century listener, it was encouraging to hear God recognize Rome's persecution and paganism. Rome, however, is not the only culprit of these demonic deeds. Revelation chapter 17 shows us that the harlot and the beast represent every earthly kingdom and self-centered religion that rise up before Christ comes.

The seven heads are also kings. Scholars have tried to pinpoint which Roman emperors these might refer to. That may be the wrong interpretive strategy. Remember, numbers tell stories. Seven directs us to completion. This may be telling believers that all of these events are happening in the context of God's perfect plan.

The eighth king in verse eleven may also tell a number story. Eight is connected with sacrifice and circumcision. Everything comes back to God on the eighth

259

day. Because this chapter is detailing the ultimate destruction of evil, it may be that the eighth king who is destroyed shows us that all earthly might and power go back to God. He is Lord of all.

This symbolic story-telling with numbers may be what verse twelve is about. The ten coming kings who have authority for one hour may indicate God's control and precise completion of what He intends. Nothing will get out of hand as history unfolds. Verses thirteen and fourteen reinforce this point. While all evil has the same root and motive, the Lamb will overcome it. With the Lamb will be *"his called, chosen, and faithful followers."* You can't miss the strong encouragement of this message to believers. Evil will not win the day.

The explanation of the waters in verse fifteen may bring some clarity to the dragon's strategy in chapter 12. The waters are people. These rushing waters of demonic allies fight against the church. They're the armies of evil that make war against Jesus and His redeemed.

But evil implodes. Verse sixteen shows the demise of the enemies of God. This verse has been compared to Ezekiel chapter 23, a chapter that condemns the unfaithful and repulsive idolatrous behavior of God's people (*"This is what the Sovereign LORD says: Bring a mob against them and give them over to terror and plunder. The mob will stone them and cut them down with their swords..."* vss.46-47a). Unfaithfulness ends in an ugly and awful way.

Chapter 17 closes by identifying the woman. She is a combination of Rome and all the unfaithful powers of the earth. But verse seventeen shows God's mysterious and sovereign rule. God's will, purpose, and Word are running the show.

WHY SO CRYPTIC?

Yes, the angel explains the vision in chapter 17. But do we really understand it? We see the symbols. We grasp some of the connections. We get the gist of all this, but it's still challenging. It still leaves much to our imaginations. The debate about Revelation continues.

Part of the reason for the mysterious nature of Revelation is to keep us engaged with God's Word. But our question about its cryptic character may be flawed. When we ask the question, we may be forgetting that WE are the ones who may actually be the cryptic part of reality. Is it up to the natural world to clarify the supernatural or does the supernatural clarify what we experience in the so-called natural world?

Who's in the know here? Us or God?

When Job complained that the natural order of things was puzzling to him, God replied:

> *"Who is this that darkens my counsel with words without knowledge? Brace yourself like a man; I will question you, and you shall answer me. Where were you when I laid the earth's foundation? Tell me, if you understand" (Job 38:2-4).*

When Paul analyzed our current condition he said, *"Now we see but a poor reflection as in a mirror; then we shall see face to face. Now I know in part; then I shall know fully, even as I am fully known" (1 Corinthians 13:12).*

If we ask why God is so cryptic and hidden, we hear the answer of the Scriptures:

> *"Am I only a God nearby," declares the LORD, "and not a God far away? Can anyone hide in secret places so that I cannot see him?" declares the LORD. "Do not I fill heaven and earth?" declares the LORD. (Jeremiah 23:23-24)*

> *O LORD, you have searched me and you know me. You know when I sit and when I rise; you perceive my thoughts from afar. You discern my going out and my lying down; you are familiar with all my ways…Where can I go from your Spirit? Where can I flee from your presence? (Psalm 139:1-3, 7)*

Who says that God is cryptic and hidden? Perhaps we're the ones who miss Him and who stray into hidden places. If you ask whether or not God really understands you, sees you or hears you, He asks back:

> *Why do you say, O Jacob, and complain, O Israel, "My way is hidden from the LORD; my cause is disregarded by my God"? (Isaiah 40:27)*

Of course God understands, sees, and hears you. He is *"the everlasting God, the Creator of the ends of the earth. He will not grow tired or weary, and his understanding no one can fathom" (Isaiah 40:28).* But Jesus asks a bigger question. He told the parable of the widow and the unjust judge in Luke 18 to teach His disciples that *"they should always pray and not give up" (vs. 1).* They were wondering if God really paid attention, if He was really in touch with their lives, if the cryptic and hidden God was connected with the people He claimed were His own. The parable assured that God is paying attention. If an evil judge responds to a lowly widow, how much more does God respond to His children? But the parable ends with a surprise. Jesus asked in verse eight, *"When the Son of Man comes, will he find faith on the earth?"*

In other words, who is really cryptic, lost, hidden, and confused? We are. God is faithful and on track. The book of Revelation reveals God who has clear, concise, and dependable plans. Revelation shows God who has it all together. We're the ones who have it backwards. We're the ones who can't see clearly. We're the ones who live in a fog. He is the One who brings us out of confusion into the truth. Will we have faith in Him? Will we trust Him with His plans? Will we forge ahead through our fog and keep believing?

Over and over again, the Bible tells us that it is God who breaks through our foolishness and lack of understanding. His clear and complete message rescues us from our helpless confusion:

> *For since in the wisdom of God the world through its wisdom did not know him, God was pleased*

263

through the foolishness of what was preached to save those who believe. Jews demand miraculous signs and Greeks look for wisdom, but we preach Christ crucified: a stumbling block to Jews and foolishness to Gentiles, but to those whom God has called, both Jews and Greeks, Christ the power of God and the wisdom of God. (1 Corinthians 1:21-24)

We have not received the spirit of the world but the Spirit who is from God, that we may understand what God has freely given us. This is what we speak, not in words taught us by human wisdom but in words taught by the Spirit, expressing spiritual truths in spiritual words. The man without the Spirit does not accept the things that come from the Spirit of God, for they are foolishness to him, and he cannot understand them, because they are spiritually discerned. The spiritual man makes judgments about all things, but he himself is not subject to any man's judgment: "For who has known the mind of the Lord that he may instruct him?" But we have the mind of Christ. (1 Corinthians 2:12-16)

We know that we are children of God, and that the whole world is under the control of the evil one. We know also that the Son of God has come and has given us understanding, so that we may know him who is true. And we are in him who is true--

even in his Son Jesus Christ. He is the true God and eternal life. (1 John 5:19-21)

My purpose is that they may be encouraged in heart and united in love, so that they may have the full riches of complete understanding, in order that they may know the mystery of God, namely, Christ, in whom are hidden all the treasures of wisdom and knowledge. (Colossians 2:2-3)

The book of Revelation is visionary in nature. It contains symbols, allusions to the Scriptures, sights and sounds that boggle our minds. It is a glimpse of God's work behind the scenes of this broken world. But what is revealed and written isn't the problem. God isn't the one who needs remedial work in His communication abilities. The problem is that our minds are too dim. Our hearts and souls are too limited. We have trouble grasping the clear teaching of heaven. It's too much for us.

And praise God it is! His work, His understanding, His action, His love, and His plans surpass our knowledge. God transcends our ability to understand Him. He is able to do far more than all we ask for or imagine (Ephesians 3:20). Revelation shows us that fact. But it also shows us that God draws close so we can see Him. He speaks words we can understand. He brings messages for our level of comprehension. He tides us over with gracious truth. He is the incarnate God who cares enough to clue us in.

Study Guide for Revelation Chapter 17

1. Read Revelation 17:1-3. What "adultery" is present in people's relationships with God in our day and age?

2. Read Revelation 17:4-6. What developments in ungodly behavior have surprised you recently?

3. Read Revelation 17:7-18. What comfort did Christians receive from the obvious references to the Roman Empire in these verses?

4. Knowing what you do about the symbolism in Revelation, discuss how verse 12 gives hope to all who are oppressed.

5. What does verse 16 tell you about the nature of evil?

6. How does Revelation show us our weakness and lead us to humility?

7. Review the verses on pages 264-265. What do they tell you about our understanding and God's understanding?

Revelation
Chapter Eighteen

✝

Chapter 18 of Revelation brings us more echoes of the Old Testament. This chapter contains a lament. It resembles the lament for the city of Tyre in Ezekiel chapter 27. For hundreds of years Tyre was a dominant and wealthy force in the Middle East. Majestic harbors, beautiful architecture, brisk commerce, and mighty warriors were hallmarks of its power and reign. It seemed to have the wealth of the world. Ezekiel predicted its downfall. His prophetic lament showed that all the wealth in the world would not prevail against the will and work of God:

> *Your wealth, merchandise and wares, your mariners, seamen and shipwrights, your merchants and all your soldiers, and everyone else on board will sink into the heart of the sea on the day of your shipwreck. (vs.27)*

Many of the characteristics and themes of the lament are seen in chapter 18 of Revelation. The transient glory of the world and the fading egos of humankind are highlighted. As Tyre fell under Roman rule in 64 A.D., Rome and every other man-made kingdom would be sure to fall.

The lament of Revelation 18 also brought the significant reminder that the people of the first century were listening to a prophetic message. This was God's truth. It was real, unfailing, and soon to be fulfilled in history. The Apostle John was still alive, but he was an old man in exile. First century Christians may have felt that God was silent, that He needed to speak up again as they struggled with doubt and pressure from all sides. These prophecy-shaped words gave them the clear indication that God had truly spoken up. He was not silent. He gave a message with authority for their time.

That is a key purpose of the book of Revelation for you, too. If you ever think God is too silent, that He has backed away and is distant from our time, Revelation sounds the prophetic interruption of God's voice in our turbulent world. All of Scripture is meant to accomplish that, but Revelation makes us uncomfortable enough to listen. It is about hope and the future. It is packed with deliverance and help yet to be realized while directing us to help that has already come and still abides with us. It brings us God's reality.

As I drove onto the grounds of a conference center recently, I saw a sign that said, "You are now leaving the real world." I was entering a new reality—one of relaxation, tranquility, and refreshment. Revelation 18 clarifies reality for all who listen to the vision it communicates. What is really real? The advancement of evil? The victories of the world? The satisfaction of self-indulgence? NO! The real world is what Jesus reveals: His victory, His righteousness, His faithfulness, His rescue, His relief. Chapter 18 gives us a startling reality check.

Chapter Eighteen

A REALITY CHECK FOR THE WORLD

1After this I saw another angel coming down from heaven having great authority, and the earth was illuminated by his glory. 2He cried out in a strong voice: "It fell! It fell! Babylon the Great, and it has become a home for demons and a prison for every unclean spirit, and a prison for every unclean and despised bird. 3For all the nations have drunk the furious wine of her sexual immorality and the kings of the earth committed adultery with her, and the merchants of the earth have become rich from the power of her sensuality."

A bright and shining angel appears to remind every listener of the remarkable news: Babylon the Great has fallen. The angel recalls the prophecy in Isaiah 21:9, *"Look, here comes a man in a chariot with a team of horses. And he gives back the answer: 'Babylon has fallen, has fallen! All the images of its gods lie shattered on the ground!'"* The words of Jeremiah also come to mind: *"Babylon must fall because of Israel's slain, just as the slain in all the earth have fallen because of Babylon"* (51:49).

Remember, Babylon represents Rome and all the powers that try to crush the Kingdom of God. It also represents that which looks tantalizing and alluring, but is, in reality, deadly. Every sinful nation and person is connected with the demonic and evil haunt of Babylon. God is revealing the single source of corruption on the earth, the root of all that tries to lure us away from the truth of Jesus.

These days we can point to the lofty sounding theories of humanistic or naturalistic thought. Authoritative sounding voices tell us we're getting better and better. They tell us that everything has developed naturally and on its own. There is no God in the picture, they say. There is no grand plan. Because of that, we are told that there are no moral restraints, no "religious" limitations. The individual is meant to move forward, seeking his or her own pleasure and success. It's a personal right, after all.

This thinking calls those who believe in God ignorant, foolish, and wrong. He is too limiting, too primitive. And don't even mention Jesus! The atheistic experts call Him a myth. They cast the Bible aside as a man-made story book, ancient and irrelevant. They take the course of glorying in nothingness, making it up as they go along.

This is nothing new. An idol is an idol. Whether it is following ancient Roman religion, or vowing allegiance to Darwinian thought, or inventing the latest psycho-religious new age fad, or chasing the old-time lures of money, sex, and power, idolatry is rooted in one twisted and evil source. And the result is tragic.

DESTRUCTION

4And I heard another voice from heaven saying: "Come out of her, my people, so that you will not take part in her sins, so that you will not receive any of her plagues; 5for her sins are piled up to heaven, and God has remembered her crimes. 6Give back to her as she has given; and repay double according to her deeds. In the cup she mixed, mix her double. 7As she glorified herself and lived in luxury, so give to her torture and sorrow, because in her heart she says, 'I sit as queen; I am not a widow, and I will never see sorrow.' 8Therefore in one day her plagues will come: death, sorrow and famine. She will be consumed by fire, for mighty is the Lord God who judges her. 9When the kings of the earth who committed adultery with her and shared her luxury see the smoke of her fiery ordeal, they will weep and mourn over her, 10standing at a distance because of fear of her torture saying: 'Woe! Woe, the great city, Babylon, the strong city! In one hour your condemnation has come!'"

Verse four begins with a voice from heaven—the voice of God—calling His people out of Babylon. The fast action of final judgment has begun. God will not allow His people to be scathed because of the unfaithfulness of the world.

If troubled strugglers and sufferers ever need an encouraging word about where they stand in God's sight, here it is. He calls them out to safety. Sometimes it seems that followers of Christ are being overwhelmed by the godless force of the world. Revelation 18 shows the truth of Acts 16:31, *"Believe in the Lord Jesus Christ and you will be saved!"*

This chapter of Revelation redefines what the world has called true strength and true joy. The voices of the world and of our sinful flesh tell us to seek lasting happiness in what is created. The Bible tells us the truth:

"The grass withers and the flowers fall, but the word of our God stands forever" (Isaiah 40:8). Our existence and success are not about what we do or have. Who we are is not about our "might and power," but about the Spirit of God (Zechariah 4:6).

These verses of chapter 18 show that evil will be repaid and that justice will be done. Paul quoted Deuteronomy 32:35 when he said in Romans 12:19, *"Do not take revenge, my friends, but leave room for God's wrath, for it is written: 'It is mine to avenge; I will repay,' says the Lord."* God gives evil and wrongdoing double for its deeds. He leaves no hardened heart unpunished.

A COLLAPSING KINGDOM OF WEALTH

11The merchants of the earth will weep and mourn for her because no one buys their cargoes any longer--12cargoes of gold, silver, precious stones and pearls; fine linen, purple, silk and scarlet cloth; every sort of scented wood, and every object of ivory, precious wood, bronze, iron and marble; 13and cinnamon and spice, of incense, myrrh and frankincense, and wine and olive oil, and wheat flour and grain; cattle and sheep; horses and carriages; and bodies and souls of men. 14Your fruit of the desire of your soul went away from you, and all the costly and bright things are lost from you, and they will never find these things. 15The merchants of these things who grew rich from them, stand far off because of fear of her torture, weeping, and mourning 16saying: "Woe! Woe, the great city, dressed in fine linen, purple and scarlet, and adorned with gold, precious stones and pearls! 17In one hour such great *wealth has been made desolate!" Every sea captain, and everyone on a passenger ship, and sailors, and all who work the sea, will stand far off **18**and will cry out after seeing the smoke of her fiery ordeal saying, "What is like the great city?" **19**They will throw dust on their heads, and with weeping and mourning cry out: "Woe! Woe, the great city, where all who had ships on the sea became rich through her wealth, because in one hour she has been made desolate! **20**Rejoice over her, heaven and the saints and the apostles and the prophets! God has judged her for your punishment."*

The list of riches is extensive. The luxuries rival every culture, ancient and modern. The commerce and trade tell the story of a bustling society, busy and distracted by its own consumption. The description reminds me of the Best Buy of the first century! They've got everything.

Whenever I read the Sunday paper, I am overwhelmed with all the advertisements and flyers. About eighty percent of the Sunday paper is all about "stuff." There are clothes, shoes, home improvement items, tools, jewelry, and loads of high-tech gear. The Sunday paper serves as a litany of the best we can do, of what everyone wants and rejoices in. But if you were to hang onto the Sunday flyers for six months or so, nearly all of the items would be old news, obsolete. They would be replaced by newer and more stylish products, more of the latest "stuff."

It's so clear that what we do doesn't last. Revelation 18 shows that all of the reasons for the world's pride and joy disappear. The wealth and material things, the powerful connections in politics and commerce, the bragging rights of having it all, are gone in an instant. Verse eight said "in one day." Verses seventeen and nineteen say "in one hour" ruin has come. Verse fourteen says that the riches and splendor have vanished. Now the people who wanted to get close to power and luxury "stand far off" (vss. 15, 17). How sobering and how true.

I've spoken with person after person who has pursued pleasure and contentment in things—possessions, reputation, and personal indulgence. Each person reflected on their personal emptiness and pain. Each and every one has told me the same thing: "It's empty. It's not worth it. It's meaningless. It's destructive." Revelation 18 cries out above the deceiving voices that attempt to lure us into the same old path: "Stop! Don't go there. Trust the truth, not the lies."

Verse twenty brings the truth home. It calls heaven and all of God's people to rejoice. Justice has been accomplished. Finally, the deception of the devil has disappeared. The crooked has been made straight. The rough places have been made smooth. All is the way it should be. All are seeing the salvation and glory of God (Isaiah 40:4-5).

THE END OF EARTHLY TORMENT

21And a strong angel picked up a stone the size of a large millstone and threw it into the sea saying: "With such violence the great city of Babylon will be thrown down, and *it will never again be found. **22**And the noise of harpists and musicians, flute players and trumpeters, will not be heard in you any longer. Every craftsman of every trade will not be found in it any longer. The sound of a millstone will never be heard in you again. **23**The light of a lamp will never shine in you again. The voice of bridegroom and bride will never be heard in you again because your merchants were the greatest men of the earth, and by your witchcraft all the nations were led astray. **24**In her was found the blood of prophets and of the saints, and of all the ones slaughtered on the earth."*

The deceptive life of the dominating and destructive world will be put to an end. The persecutors who appear to thrive will be stopped in their tracks. The city of the world that seemed to run the show—including running God's people into the ground—would be thrown down.

Even the reference to music in verse twenty-two may refer to the musicians who signaled idolatrous worship (e.g. Daniel 3:5, *"As soon as you hear the sound of the horn, flute, zither, lyre, harp, pipes and all kinds of music, you must fall down and worship the image of gold that King Nebuchadnezzar has set up."*). God is thorough in His description of Babylon's destruction. It was important for persecuted believers to hear that every detail would be taken care of. Every injustice in business, in family, in faith, and in personal life would be addressed. God sees His people. He knows their hearts. He cares about every hurt—big or small. It all matters to Him. He takes it very personally. God's justice not only makes everything right. It also brings comfort, relief, and peace.

The question we're left with is similar to last chapter. Will God find faith on the earth? Will you trust Him for the long haul, even when life looks bleak and feels all wrong? Will you rely on His promise of hope and a future even when you can't see past the darkness that envelops you? Will you stick with Jesus no matter what?

The details of Revelation 18 show us that God is faithful. The extended and painstaking description of judgment emphasizes the fact that God doesn't miss anything. Even though it looks like He's overlooking something in this moment of time or in this season of life, He gives us the assurance that nothing escapes His faithful attention. This chapter demonstrates that although weeping may last for a while, the time for rejoicing will come (Psalm 30:5).

Will you seek refuge and consolation in this beautiful promise?

Study Guide for Revelation Chapter 18

1. Read Revelation 18:1-3. How do evil and disobedience eventually become a prison?

2. Read Revelation 18:4-10. Recall and discuss how God has called you out of difficult and hurtful situations.

3. Verse 10 shows the speedy demise of evil and wrongdoing. In what ways is this reality distorted by the world today?

4. Read Revelation 18:11-20. What from our time would be added to the list of products in these verses?

5. Why is materialism so enticing?

6. Talk about how materialism is ultimately disappointing.

7. Read Revelation 18:21-24. How do you find yourself needing to rely on God during this particular season of your life?

Revelation
Chapter Nineteen

✝

In Matthew chapter 22 Jesus told the parable of the wedding banquet:

> *The kingdom of heaven is like a king who prepared a wedding banquet for his son. He sent his servants to those who had been invited to the banquet to tell them to come, but they refused to come. Then he sent some more servants and said, "Tell those who have been invited that I have prepared my dinner: My oxen and fattened cattle have been butchered, and everything is ready. Come to the wedding banquet" (vss.2-4).*

You know what happened. The inviting king got a bit frustrated as people declined his invitation. They were too busy. They had other concerns. Other priorities got in the way. Finally, the king sent servants to the highways and byways, bringing in every guest he could find. He wanted to celebrate and he would celebrate!

Revelation 19 takes us to the actual celebration, the final wedding feast. The bridegroom, Christ, would be united with His bride, the Church. Every foe interfering with this romance was finally crushed. Now the rejoicing would begin.

But this wasn't simply a raucous party. Some key truths are revealed as the celebration begins in Revelation 19.

HALLELUJAH! YOU'RE NOT ALONE

1After these things I heard what sounded like a loud voice of a crowd of many in heaven saying: "Hallelujah! Salvation and glory and power belong to our God, 2for true and just are his judgments, because he judged the great prostitute who corrupted the earth by her adulteries, and he avenged the blood of his servants from her hand." 3And a second time they said: "Hallelujah! Her smoke rises for ever and ever." 4The twenty-four elders and the four living things fell and worshiped God, the one seated on the throne, saying: "Amen, Hallelujah!" 5And a voice came from the throne, saying: "Praise our God, all his servants and the ones fearing him, small and great!" 6And I heard what sounded like a voice of a crowd of many people, like the voice of many waters, and like the voice of strong thunders saying, "Hallelujah! Because our Lord God Almighty reigns."

The voice of a massive crowd fills heaven with celebration. "Hallelujah!" is the shout. This Hebrew word means "Praise Yahweh!" God's personal name from the Old Testament, "Yahweh," is translated as "LORD" in English language Bibles. The reason we have two spellings of "hallelujah" in the English language is because one uses the Hebrew letters and the other uses the Greek letters. The literal Hebrew spelling would be: "halleluyah." The literal Greek spelling would be: "allelouia." Regardless

280

of its spelling, this powerful declaration of praise has spanned the centuries and will be sung in eternity. A few years ago, as I listened to several languages being spoken in an African village, the two words I understood in every language were: "Hallelujah" and "Amen." All believers around the world are truly one body. This shout of praise echoes through the ages and will fill the heavens.

The Hebrew "hallel" was used for high festivals. Psalms 113-118 were the "Hallel of Egypt." Psalm 135 is the "Great Hallel." The weekday hallel was Psalms 145-150. These special songs of praise were reserved for celebrations like the night of Passover and the first day of the feast of unleavened bread.

Believe it or not, the only time the word is used in the New Testament is here in Revelation 19. A new hallelujah has taken hold. Eternal rejoicing has arrived!

This is a victory celebration. It's not just giddy happiness. It is the triumphal cry for the Savior God who has conquered evil, avenged wrongdoing, exercised justice, and righted all wrongs. These are significant and meaningful actions for so many who have suffered under the world's yoke of unfairness and cruelty.

It is interesting to see the recurring focus on the "adulteries" of the great prostitute. On one hand it refers to unfaithfulness to God, the heavenly groom. On the other hand it points out a vulnerability we have as humans. We can't overlook an obvious message of the Bible. Sexual sin is a big problem. Pornography is rampant. Marriage is under attack. Sexual intimacy has become a right for personal pleasure rather than a sacrificial gift for the lifetime commitment of marriage. The adultery of our culture will continue to bring destructive results. God takes sin very seriously. This continued emphasis in Revelation is another wake-up call to very specific sin.

The heavenly worship has intensified. Verse four is the first mention of the four living creatures falling down in worship. Chapters 4, 5, and 11 build up to this climactic scene of celebration. Verse six of chapter 19 mentions another large crowd singing hallelujah to the Lord God Almighty—the familiar title of praise, "Pantocrator."

Voices are dominant as this chapter opens. Verses 1, 3, 5, and 6 tell of voices—crowds and individuals. What a wonderful comfort for Christians to know that they are not alone! Hebrews 12:1 tells us of this reality:

> *Therefore, since we are surrounded by such a great cloud of witnesses, let us throw off everything that hinders and the sin that so easily entangles, and let us run with perseverance the race marked out for us.*

We are surrounded by the host of heaven. As the Apostles' Creed declares, we live in the "communion of saints." In Christ, we are joined together with all believers in heaven and on earth. For all believers feeling like they're strangers here on earth, the loud cheers of the saints and the voice of the Savior let us know we are not alone—never alone!

7*"Let us rejoice and be extremely joyful and give him glory! For the wedding of the Lamb has come, and his bride has prepared herself.* **8***And bright, shining, pure linen was given her to wear." (The linen is the righteous deeds of the saints.)* **9***And he said to me, "Write: 'Blessed are the ones called to the feast of the wedding of the Lamb!'" And he said to me, "These are the true words of God."*

Wedding celebration imagery shows the fulfillment of the Bible's deep and ongoing teaching about marriage. Marriage is an earthly reflection of God's relationship with us. Isaiah 54:5 says about God's people, *"For your Maker is your husband-- the LORD Almighty is his name-- the Holy One of Israel is your Redeemer; he is called the God of all the earth."* In Ephesians chapter 5 Paul articulates the sacred connection of God and His people to the sacred union of wife and husband *("Husbands, love your wives, just as Christ loved the church and gave himself up for her..." vs.25).* Jesus' parable comparison of the Kingdom of God to a wedding feast reaches its culmination in Revelation 19.

The bride, Christ's Church, is given what she needs to wear. In the Matthew 22 parable, the guest with improper clothes was thrown out into the darkness (vs.13). In Revelation, the assurance of God's grace is reinforced. We will have exactly what we need when the Bridegroom arrives. Our readiness for the end is by grace and by grace alone.

The garments of the bride in this vision are explained in the text—another example of the way Jesus helps us understand this vision. We will be adorned in the *"righteous acts of the saints."* In other words, the faithful life of a Christian matters. The way you glorify Jesus has lasting significance. You may wonder at times if there is any reason to live in obedience to God. You see people prosper even though they never follow Christ's ways. You know that true repentance—even at the end of a disobedient life—results in the gift of the forgiveness of sins. It may make you think that your obedience is insignificant. You may feel like all good and faithful works for Christ's glory are washed down the drain once Jesus returns. That's not true according to the Scriptures. Your works do not save you. But your works to the glory of God make a difference now and forever. Even if you can't see the difference, you can trust that your obedient and faithful life shines throughout the heavens. Your sanctified life has deep and lasting significance. In Christ, what you do matters. Believers need to hear this—especially as believers in the first century seemed to be spinning their wheels in their efforts to follow Christ. So the encouragement of Revelation comes to their ears and to ours: Stay faithful! Don't give up! Your Spirit-led obedience makes a difference in God's Kingdom.

Verse nine affirms the blessing of God's redeemed. God is at work in their lives. As Jesus declared in the beatitudes (Matthew 5), God's people are truly blessed. The word for "invited" in verse nine is the Greek word for "called." God calls us to be His own. As Martin Luther said in his explanation to the third article of the Apostles' Creed, God has "called us by the Gospel."

How is God calling you? Is it to renewed faith or purity? Is it to a new beginning? Is it to repentance? The voices of heaven urge you onward to the gracious call of Christ.

Years ago I had a chance to attend a Promise Keepers gathering. The conference was held in a 60,000 seat arena. As one of the final activities before the gathering closed, all the pastors were invited down to the stadium floor. I joined fellow pastors heading down the stairs. As we made our way to the field level, the speaker on stage asked everyone in attendance to shout their cheers as loud as they could. They wanted to encourage every pastor there. This was an amazing experience. I met a minister who was in tears because he had never been congratulated or encouraged in his thirty-year ministry career. To hear nearly 60,000 people cheering for my ministry blew me away. It lifted my heart.

Revelation 19 contains the cheers of the saints for all those who labor this side of heaven. The chapter brings voices of encouragement—even the voice of God. This celebration tells a wonderful story: you're not alone.

JESUS IS THE WAY

10And I fell before his feet to worship him. But he said to me, "Do not do it! I am your fellow servant and with your brothers who hold to the testimony of Jesus. Worship God! For the testimony of Jesus is the spirit of prophecy." 11I saw heaven opened and behold, a white horse and the one sitting on it called Faithful and True. With justice he

285

judges and makes war. 12His eyes are like a flame of fire, and on his head are many crowns. He has a name written on him that no one knows except himself, 13and he is clothed in a garment dipped in blood, and his name is the Word of God. 14The armies of heaven follow him on white horses and dressed in pure white linen. 15Out of his mouth comes a sharp sword with which to strike down the nations. "He will shepherd them with a staff made of iron." He tramples the winepress of the fury of the wrath of God Almighty. 16On his robe and on his thigh he has this name written: KING OF KINGS AND LORD OF LORDS.

The celebration in Revelation 19 also brings the important truth that Jesus is the only Savior, the only way to everlasting life. When the Apostle John fell at the feet of the messenger, he immediately made it clear that the true God is the only One to be worshipped. True prophecy is all about Jesus and Jesus alone. There is no other Savior. History has given leaders, philosophers, entertainers, teachers, counselors, and even quite a few people of religious standing and influence. But there has never been a Savior other than Jesus. Peter declared it in Acts 4:12, *"Salvation is found in no one else, for there is no other name under heaven given to men by which we must be saved."*

Verses eleven through sixteen bring us full circle. The Savior we saw in chapter 1 reappears in chapter 19. He is called *"Faithful and True."* He judges with justice. His crowns in verse twelve are diadems—the crowns of a true king. The beast in chapter 13 tried to mimic Jesus by wearing these kingly crowns, but to no avail. The truth prevails. The blazing eyes (compare 1:14) and transcendent name (like the promise in 2:17) show us that this is truly Jesus. The Scriptures come together as we see Jesus wearing a robe dipped in the blood of redemption and called "the Word of God" (John 1:1-14). The fine linen He wears recalls His promise of the same for those who follow Him (3:5). The sword of verse fifteen (2:27), along with the iron scepter (12:5), keep directing us to Jesus Christ as the central focus of this vision and our lives. The word for "rule" in verse fifteen means "to shepherd." Who are we seeing in these verses? Our Good Shepherd.

Jesus' title in verse sixteen stands in contrast to the title of the harlot in chapter 17. Jesus is "King of kings and Lord of lords." These ascriptions to the true God are found in the Old and New Testaments:

> *"For the LORD your God is God of gods and Lord of lords, the great God, mighty and awesome, who shows no partiality and accepts no bribes" (Deuteronomy 10:17).*

> *"Give thanks to the Lord of lords: His love endures forever" (Psalm 136:3).*

> *"God, the blessed and only Ruler, the King of kings and Lord of lords" (1 Timothy 6:15).*

If anyone doubted or questioned the divine nature of Jesus, these Scriptural titles gave a decisive answer.

A strong emphasis of Revelation is that Jesus is the only Savior. Religions, philosophies, and ideologies offer pathways to peace, harmony, and paradise. They offer systems of thought and behavior that are meant to make people one with the universe and in unity with God. All of these, however, are based on personal deeds and accomplishments. They are based on doing certain things to achieve certain goals. Unfortunately, all it takes is an honest look in the mirror to see that we don't cut it. We can't live perfectly. We can't get everything right. Our thoughts, words, and deeds are full of foul-ups. We are drowning in a sea of imperfection and brokenness. As we sink in the crashing waves of our imperfection, the world says to us, "Try harder!" Religions cry out, "Think good thoughts!" Human systems urge, "Follow the swimming rules more carefully or maybe you should hope to make it the next time around!" Jesus jumps in the water, pushes us to safety, and loses His life in our place. He is the only Savior. Ever. And He is the One we need.

THE VICTORY IS WON

17And I saw an angel standing in the sun, and he cried out in a loud voice saying: "All the birds flying in midair, come, be gathered for the great feast of God, 18so that you may eat the flesh of kings, generals, and mighty men, of horses and their riders, and the flesh of all people, free and slave, small and great." 19And I saw the beast and the kings of the earth and their armies gathered together to make war against the one sitting upon the horse and his army.

Chapter Nineteen

Just in case anyone listening to Revelation doubted the demise of the enemy, chapter 19 makes sure no one misses the point. Chapter 20 will show us the destruction of the spiritual enemy. Chapter 19 shows us the destruction of the earthly enemy.

But wait! Verse nineteen makes it sound like God is in jeopardy. Is there danger? Could evil win? Is a giant end-of-the-world battle about to break out? No. Just as there was no battle in chapter 16, there is no battle here. As in chapter 17 (vs.14), there is no battle. As we will see in chapter 20, there is no battle. The enemy is merely gathered for destruction.

20But the beast was seized, and with him the false prophet who had performed the miraculous signs on his behalf, with which he misled the ones receiving the mark of the beast and the ones worshipping his image. The two of them were thrown alive into the fiery lake of burning sulfur. 21The remaining were killed with the sword that came out of the mouth of the one sitting on the horse, and all the birds were satisfied with their flesh.

The beasts are seized. They are thrown into "the fiery lake of burning sulfur." The victory is won.

This is an important message of the book of Revelation. The difficult and intense battle against evil and unfaithfulness is not like a seven game heart-stopping NBA series. It's more like the Harlem Globetrotters. When you attend a Harlem Globetrotters game, the score may get close at times. The New Jersey Generals may seem to have exceptional basketball skills. They may appear very threatening during the course of the game. But one thing is certain. The New Jersey Generals will not win. No matter how the game goes, no matter how it appears, the Harlem Globetrotters will win. It is a fact.

If you're trailing right now or wondering about the outcome, if life seems shaky or disheartening, Revelation tells you that victory in Jesus Christ is certain. Trusting in Jesus through thick and through thin will have an assured result: singing loud hallelujahs with the heavenly hosts in a great victory celebration!

Study Guide for Revelation Chapter 19

1. Read Revelation 19:1-9. What is causing or has caused you to say "Hallelujah!" in your life?

2. Revelation shows that God is truly fair and just. How does this fact speak to the big questions you have in life?

3. How does the "communion of saints" affect your faith and life?

4. What clarity do these verses bring to the areas of marriage and sexuality—especially for the big issues we are facing today?

5. What makes you doubt the importance and significance of your life? How do these verses encourage you?

6. Read Revelation 19:10-16. Discuss what stands out to you about the specific characteristics and qualities of Jesus articulated in these verses.

7. Read Revelation 19:17-21. Today's culture claims that all religions are the same and that there are many paths to heaven. How does this chapter speak to those assertions? Discuss specific religious systems of thought as you study these verses.

Revelation
Chapter Twenty

✝

I saw an advertisement for a website that promised it would send post-rapture e-mails to friends, family, and other people close to you if you were whisked to heaven and they were left behind. For a small fee you could make final contacts through an unbeliever who was banking on being here on earth after a secret return of Christ.

This strategy was consistent with some end-time novels and some mainstream thought. The question is: how Scriptural is this?

Revelation chapter 20 is a key chapter in the discussion of what the millennium, the thousand year reign of Jesus, really means. The celebration that began in chapter 18 continues through chapter 20. In chapter 19 we saw the destruction of all earthly foes. Chapter 20 brings the destruction of spiritual foes.

In order to get some perspective about the events before the end of the world, take a look at 1 Thessalonians 4:13-18:

> *Brothers, we do not want you to be ignorant about those who fall asleep, or to grieve like the rest of men, who have no hope. We believe that Jesus*

died and rose again and so we believe that God will bring with Jesus those who have fallen asleep in him. According to the Lord's own word, we tell you that we who are still alive, who are left till the coming of the Lord, will certainly not precede those who have fallen asleep. For the Lord himself will come down from heaven, with a loud command, with the voice of the archangel and with the trumpet call of God, and the dead in Christ will rise first. After that, we who are still alive and are left will be caught up together with them in the clouds to meet the Lord in the air. And so we will be with the Lord forever. Therefore encourage each other with these words.

These verses describe the final coming of Jesus. Listeners were told that everything will happen in the proper order. The dead in Christ will rise first. They will appear with Jesus when the final trumpet sounds. The coming of Christ will be clearly visible and audible. There will be no question about His return—the Bible says nothing about a secret return of Jesus. All who believe in Him will be "caught up together with them in the clouds." This is the "rapture." It is the gathering of believers on earth into the presence of Jesus when He comes for the final judgment. His coming begins the eternal kingdom immediately. It is the promised new life we wait for. There are no secrets. Really, it's not very complicated. It is a teaching designed to encourage us as we wait for Him.

These are very important Biblical points. They are consistent with all the teaching of the end-times spoken by Jesus and revealed throughout the Scriptures. They are also consistent with the teaching in the book of Revelation—particularly in chapter 20. As we study this chapter, we'll look at some key points of curiosity and debate: the millennium, the first and second resurrections, the first and second deaths, the tribulation, Gog and Magog, and the great white throne judgment.

THE MILLENNIUM

1And I saw an angel coming down out of heaven, having the key to the Abyss and a big chain in his hand. 2He seized the dragon, that ancient serpent, who is the devil and Satan, and bound him for a thousand years. 3He threw him into the Abyss, and locked and sealed it over him, so that he would no longer lead the nations astray until the thousand years were ended. After these things it is necessary to loose him for short time. 4I saw thrones and the ones to whom judgment was given were seated on them. And I saw the souls of those who had been beheaded because of their testimony for Jesus and because of the word of God. They had not worshiped the beast or his image and had not received his mark on their foreheads or their hands. They came to life and reigned with Christ a thousand years.

"Millennium" means "thousand." It refers to the thousand years mentioned in Revelation chapter 20. Before jumping to conclusions about the thousand years, we must ask the same question we have asked about every number in the book of Revelation: What story does 1000 tell?

These days, popular literature and teaching talk about the thousand years of Revelation 20 as a literal number, years of Satan's bondage and of Christ's reign on earth after His visible coming. The Bible tells a different story.

We know that the number 10 is used to express completeness. It may be a combination of seven and three—seven tells the story of a perfect creation and three tells the story of the perfect God. The number 1000 is also used in the Bible to tell the story of God's complete Lordship this side of heaven. Psalm 50:10 says that God owns *"the cattle on a thousand hills."* This reference means that God owns everything. It's not a reference to a certain number of hills where God has His cattle. The number tells the story of His complete ownership and Lordship over all creation. Psalm 90:4 talks about *"a thousand years in [God's] sight being like a day"*—a reference to our current world and God's complete eternal plan for it (as also referenced in 2 Peter 3:8). Isaiah 7:23 uses the word "thousand" to show God's complete judgment against the enemy, *"In that day, in every place where there were a thousand vines worth a thousand silver shekels, there will be only briers and thorns."* The number 1000 refers to God's complete work for us this side of heaven, right now, while we fight the good fight of faith.

Revelation 20:2 tells us that an angel was sent to put the devil in chains for 1000 years. Just as the devil was thrown to the earth in chapter 12, these chains show us that the devil does not have free reign as we wait for the Lord's return. His time is short. He rages, but He is limited. Verse three lets us know that Satan will be released for a short time after the 1000 years is ended. In other words, when the wait for Christ is over and these "in-between" times come to an end, the devil will be released. The purpose for his release has been seen in chapters 17 and 19. God will allow him to gather together all those who are evil for their final destruction.

What does it mean that the devil is locked and sealed in the Abyss so he cannot deceive the nations? It seems like there is plenty of deception going on right now. It appears that the devil is on the loose. Peter even said that *"your enemy the devil prowls around like a roaring lion looking for someone to devour" (1 Peter 5:8).*

As we try to understand the Bible, we have to let the Bible speak for itself. Satan is prowling, but Satan is limited. God does not give him free reign. The devil operates a web of deceit, but God is still in control.

Satan is the deceiver, but he is not being allowed to deceive the nations until he is released for a short time. This is a reference to the way God is keeping Satan from gathering the nations together until it is time for the final judgment. As we've seen in previous chapters, it appears that the devil wants to gather together all the evil leadership on earth for an assault against God and His people. God will not allow him to accomplish this evil goal. Only when the Lord is ready to destroy evil once and for all will He release Satan to bring the wicked and rebellious together.

Verse four gives us more information about what is happening during the 1000 years. John saw the souls of the faithful martyrs living and reigning with Jesus during this period of time. As chapter 20 unfolds, we see that the 1000 years mentioned in all the verses is the same period of time. In includes God's complete Lordship right now, His rule during these last days. There is not a separate 1000 years for the devil and a separate 1000 years for believers who reign with Christ. These events are taking place during one span of time. Chapter 7 told us that the saints were reigning with Christ. Chapter 12 told us that the devil has been thrown down. Chapter 19 showed us the multitude in heaven. The 1000 years—the millennium—is now. It is the time between Jesus' first coming and His glorious return for the final judgment.

Jesus may have even referred to the in-between-times, last-days binding of Satan when He spoke in Matthew 12:27-29. In these verses Jesus discussed the accusation that He was driving out demons using the power of the prince of demons, Beelzebub. Jesus said:

> *And if I drive out demons by Beelzebub, by whom do your people drive them out? So then, they will be your judges. But if I drive out demons by the Spirit of God, then the kingdom of God has come upon you. Or again, how can anyone enter a strong man's house and carry off his possessions*

unless he first ties up the strong man? Then he can rob his house.

The verb for "ties up" is the same verb for Satan's binding used in Revelation. Jesus was explaining that He did not drive out demons with demonic power. Instead demonic power has been bound with the arrival and work of the Son of God and the Spirit of God.

MILLENNIALISM

Speculation about the coming of Christ and the descriptions of the end-times in the Bible has sparked much debate. People have always wondered when Jesus would return and what the end-times would be like. The disciples even asked Jesus, *"What will be the sign of your coming and of the end of the age?" (Matthew 24:3)*

Why is there such interest in trying to figure out when the end will come? One reason may be simple human curiosity. Inquiring minds want to know! Interpreting the mysteries and symbols of the Bible can be very intriguing. Another motivation for study of the end-times might be control. We do not like to be surprised. Trying to figure out the details may make us feel more secure.

But God has a different motivation when He discusses the end of the world. He wants us to study the Scripture passages that deal with the end-times so we can be prepared. Jesus said, *"Be on guard! Be alert! You do not know when that time will come" (Mark 13:33).* Paul said to believers, *"So then, let us not be like others, who are asleep, but let us be alert and self-controlled"* (1 Thessalonians 5:6).

God also wants us to be comforted. The Bible reveals facts about the last days in order to show us that God is faithful. He will destroy Satan, death and sin. He will save us from the destructive powers of this sinful world. That's why Paul could say in 1 Thessalonians 4:18, *"Therefore, encourage each other with these words."*

The Christian church has brought this Biblical message of preparation and comfort to believers throughout the centuries. Believers have proclaimed the Biblical message that we are called to wait for Jesus' second coming with hope and faithfulness. Judgment Day will come suddenly and clearly. At that point, Christ's eternal kingdom will be ushered in. This teaching is called "amillennialism." It means that there is not a literal 1000 year earthly reign of Jesus after He arrives on earth. By the 300's A.D. this Biblical understanding of the millennium was articulated by St. Augustine. He agreed with the teachings of Bible and early Christians that the 1000 years in Revelation 20 refers to the current time between Christ's first and second coming.

Jesus emphasized that His kingdom was not an earthly kingdom. He said in John 18:36, *"My kingdom is not of this world. If it were, my servants would fight to prevent my arrest by the Jews. But now my kingdom is from another place."* Jesus also made it very clear that we are in the last days—days that will culminate with His final, visible return (Matthew 24:7-13; 25:31ff). Hebrews 1:1-2 lets us know that we are in the "1000 years": *"In the past God spoke to our forefathers through the prophets at many times and in various ways, but **in these last days** he has spoken to us by his Son..."*

Early believers also confessed the Biblical teaching that Jesus will return visibly on the last day to gather all people together for the final judgment. There would be no waiting, no delay of 1000 years to tie up loose ends. Jesus said in John 14:3, *"If I go and prepare a place for you, I will come back and take you to be with me that you also may be where I am."* At His ascension recorded in Acts chapter 1, the angel told the disciples, *"Men of Galilee, why do you stand here looking into the sky? This same Jesus, who has been taken from you into heaven, will come back in the same way you have seen him go into heaven" (vs.11).* There would be no secret return—just one glorious return from heaven.

We looked at 1 Thessalonians 4:16 at the beginning of this chapter: *"For the Lord himself will come down from heaven, with a loud command, with the voice of the archangel and with the trumpet call of God, and the dead in Christ will rise first."* This is a very un-secret, once and for all, glorious return of Jesus. Even Jesus described his return this way, *"For as lightning that comes from the east is visible even in the west, so will be the coming of the Son of Man" (Matthew 24:27).* According to the Bible, there will be no secret return. Christ's second coming will be sudden, visible, and glorious.

The Bible also teaches that now is the time for urgent outreach to all unbelievers. Early Christians gave their lives for this mission. More believers trying to fulfill this calling were killed in the 20th century than in all of history! The view of the end-times called pre-millennialism—referring to a secret return of Jesus before a time of tribulation and His final return—states that unbelievers and the Jewish nation will have a chance to repent during the 1000 year reign of Christ on earth. The Bible, however, says that the time to believe is now! There will be no second chance after Christ returns.

Why believe this? Jesus commissioned us to make disciples of all nations in Matthew 28:18-20. Hebrews 9:27-28 reinforces the urgency of outreach: *"Just as man is destined to die once, and after that to face judgment, so Christ was sacrificed once to take away the sins of many people; and he will appear a second time, not to bear sin, but to bring salvation to those who are waiting for him."* Paul urges us to be ready for the day of Christ's coming because it will come like "a thief in the night" (1 Thessalonians 5:2). Even the devil knows that his time is short (Revelation 12:12). The call of the Scriptures is to trust in Christ today: *"Today, if you hear his voice, do not harden your hearts as you did in the rebellion" (Hebrews 3:15). "I tell you, now is the time of God's favor, now is the day of salvation" (2 Corinthians 6:2).*

The New Testament also demonstrated a new unity in the kingdom of God. Jews and Gentiles were now one in Christ. Jesus fulfilled perfectly what the people of Israel could not. Now all who trust in Christ are included as God's chosen people—a new "Israel of God" (Galatians 6:16). Romans 9:6-8 says:

> *It is not as though God's word had failed. For not all who are descended from Israel are Israel. Nor because they are his descendants are they all Abraham's children. On the contrary, "It is through Isaac that your offspring will be reckoned." In other words, it is not the natural children who are God's children, but it is the children of the promise who are regarded as Abraham's offspring.*

Romans 10:12-13 adds:

> *For there is no difference between Jew and Gentile—the same Lord is Lord of all and richly blesses all who call on him, for, "Everyone who calls on the name of the Lord will be saved."*

Some who adhere to the pre-millennialist view separate the people of Israel from the Christian Church. This turns God's plan backwards!

A key teaching of pre-millennialism is that there will be a secret "rapture" in which Jesus will return to whisk believers away from the world before intense tribulation happens. As I mentioned above, the word "rapture" refers to one of the events that will take place during Christ's final and visible return as recorded in 1 Thessalonians 4:17. Living believers will be "caught up together" with those who have died and are already with the Lord. This will be in preparation for the final judgment—the ushering in of the everlasting kingdom. The Bible never talks about a secret return of Christ that will spare us from the tribulation of the end-times. Instead, the Bible says that we will suffer in the last days. Hebrews 10:32-39 lets believers know that they will go through great trial, but that *"He who is coming will come and not delay" (vs.37).* The final, visible return of Christ is the answer for our suffering. Jesus said that we will experience difficulty: *"In this world you will have trouble" (John 16:33).* The final, visible return of Christ is the answer. The Apostle Paul encouraged believers with these facts about Jesus' visible and triumphant return in 1 Corinthians 15:51-58:

> *Listen, I tell you a mystery: We will not all sleep, but we will all be changed—in a flash, in the twinkling of an eye, at the last trumpet. For the trumpet will sound, the dead will be raised imperishable, and we will be changed. For the perishable must clothe itself with the imperishable, and the mortal with immortality. When the perishable has been clothed with the imperishable, and the mortal with immortality, then the saying that is written will come true: "Death has been swallowed up in victory." "Where, O death, is your victory? Where, O death, is your sting?" The sting of death is sin, and the power of sin is the law. But thanks be to God! He gives us the victory through our Lord Jesus Christ. Therefore, my dear brothers, stand firm. Let nothing move you. Always give yourselves fully to the work*

of the Lord, because you know that your labor in the Lord is not in vain.

While many wonderful and encouraging facts about the coming of Christ are detailed in the Bible, Jesus informed His followers that we will not know when it will happen. He said in Matthew 24:36, *"No one knows about that day or hour, not even the angels in heaven, nor the Son, but only the Father."* Paul urged believers not to be distracted by the times and dates of Christ's coming. Instead, we are to be ready: *"Now, brothers, about times and dates we do not need to write to you, for you know very well that the day of the Lord will come like a thief in the night" (1 Thessalonians 5:1).* Jesus emphasized the same approach to His second coming: *"Therefore keep watch, because you do not know on what day your Lord will come" (Matthew 24:42).*

Why is there such a debate about millennialism? A major departure from clear Biblical teaching and the consistent belief throughout centuries of Christianity was triggered by John Darby. Darby was an Englishman who, in the 1800's, started a dispensational pre-millennial view of Christ's coming. After he broke away from the Church of England, Darby, disillusioned by the church, rebelled against many Biblical and Christian traditions. He claimed that there were clear and identifiable time periods (dispensations) by which we could track the progression of God's work leading up to the return of Jesus.

This claim and view departed from all of historic Biblical Christianity. Darby lived during a time of religious revival. Many people were interested in understanding new spiritual "mysteries." There was talk that Christ's return was imminent. There was also a spirit of rebellion against church "traditions." Darby's view grew popular. Unraveling the mystery of Christ's return intrigued many people. The news that true believers would be spared from suffering in the last days was an attractive part of Darby's new interpretation.

A big question to ask, however, is: Why does any of this matter? Why quibble about confusing details? Why even talk about millennialism? There are some key reasons—some of the very reasons the book of Revelation was written:

- **So you won't get confused**. The Bible's teaching about the end-times is meant to bring us comfort and the spirit of readiness. The pre-millennial view may lead to confusion about our mission and preparation in these last days.

- **So you won't stray from the Bible's teaching**. The pre-millennial view is very intriguing, but it is not completely consistent with what the Bible says.

- **So you won't get distracted from the focus God wants**. God reveals information about the last days so we can be comforted and prepared for that time. The pre-millennial view may sidetrack us from the main point of the Bible and lead us to try to figure out schemes, structures, dates and times instead of focusing on the Gospel of Jesus and our calling to make disciples.

It's important to note that many who teach pre-millennialism are brothers and sisters in Christ who, generally, believe that the Bible is God's inspired and inerrant Word. They also believe in the visible return of Jesus, our Savior who died and rose again to forgive us. The goal in discussing the end times is to come away with the clear Biblical message, not to create divisions in the body of Christ. Together we move forward, searching the Scriptures, discussing the issues in a spirit of love, rejoicing in the grace of God through His Son.

FIRSTS AND SECONDS

5(The rest of the dead did not come to life until the thousand years were ended.) This is the first resurrection. 6Blessed and holy are the ones having a part in the first resurrection. The second death has no authority over them, on the contrary, they will be priests of God and of Christ and will reign with him for a thousand years.

Verse five gives us more information about what is happening now and what will happen when Christ comes. The first resurrection is the reign the saints have with Jesus until He comes again. It precedes the resurrection of all the dead and the final judgment. God's redeemed are risen with Christ, safe in His presence, and rejoicing in heaven as they await the final bodily resurrection of all people. This was comforting news for believers who were wondering about their loved ones martyred by the oppressive Roman rule. It is comforting news for us, too. We have the assurance that our loved ones who have died in faith are with Jesus and are okay.

Verse six mentions the second death. A sneak peak at verse fourteen lets us know what this means: *"Then death and Hades were thrown into the lake of fire. The lake of fire is the second death."* Those who reign with Christ by His grace need have no fear of eternal death, the second death. The first death, then, is physical death.

What is the second resurrection? It's what the book of Revelation and the Scriptures promise: the Judgment Day coming of Jesus, commencing the bodily resurrection of all the redeemed to eternal life. The way Revelation introduces these "firsts" and "seconds" gives clarity and comfort to believers. It also shows how serious and final our eternity is.

GOG AND MAGOG

7When the thousand years have been completed, Satan will be released from his prison 8and will go out to deceive the nations in the four corners of the earth--Gog and Magog--to gather them for battle. In number they are like the sand on the seashore.

Ezekiel chapters 38-39 contain the prophecy about Gog, the enemy of Israel, from the land of Magog. Gog would come from the north as judgment from the Lord. Even though Gog is used by God, he is an enemy of the Lord. Ezekiel 39 describes the destruction of Gog and

Magog—similar to the destruction of God's enemies in Revelation. Gog and Magog came to represent all evil forces against God. Louis Brighton commented in his writing on Revelation: "In rabbinic literature Gog and Magog frequently appear as types of nations who war against God's people and their Messiah" (Brighton, Revelation, p.573). First-century believers would be very familiar with this terminology. It would bring to mind the fact that God's enemies will be crushed and that even in the midst of struggle God is in control.

NO BATTLE AGAIN

9They went up across the breadth of the earth and surrounded the camp of the saints and the city he loves. But fire came down from heaven and devoured them. 10And the devil, who deceived them, was thrown into the lake of burning sulfur, also the beast and the false prophet, and they will be tormented day and night for ever and ever.

We see the massive number of God's enemies gathered together for battle. End-time teachers have forecasted World Wars and battles beyond all battles raging during the years before Jesus' return. They have painted a picture of Christians on the brink of extinction as evil gains the upper hand. They have used the term "Armageddon" to describe nuclear holocaust that would end the world. But the Bible doesn't teach that. Yes, there will be persecution and trouble. Yes, there will be wars and rumors of wars (Matthew 24:6). Yes, the suffering will be intense. But Revelation is communicating the fact that, when it comes to the massive forces of evil, there will be no battle. No battle! Just as God's people feel the pressure, just as they are surrounded and think all is lost, the enemy is devoured by fire from heaven.

The beast in chapter 13 used fire from heaven to impress people. He was a fake. Here in chapter 20 the real thing—God's true and complete power—destroys evil once and for all. Finally, the devil is thrown into the lake of burning sulfur. His torment will last forever.

THE GREAT WHITE THRONE JUDGMENT

11And I saw a great white throne and the one sitting on it, from whose face the earth and heaven fled, and there was no place for them. 12And I saw the dead, great and small, standing before the throne, and books were opened. Another book was opened, which is the book of life. The dead were judged from the things written in the books according to their deeds. 13The sea gave up the dead that were in it, and death and Hades gave up the dead that were in them, and each person was judged according to their deeds. 14And death and Hades were thrown into the lake of fire. The lake of fire is the second death. 15If anyone's name was not found written in the book of life, he was thrown into the lake of fire.

In the book of Revelation, the throne is occupied by God and the Lamb. The pure white throne that appears in Revelation 20:11 is the final judgment throne. The resurrection of the dead and the final judgment are commencing. This episode is the same as the sheep and goat judgment explained by Jesus in Matthew 25.

The book of life is mentioned throughout the Bible. Psalm 69:28 talks about evildoers: *"May they be blotted out of the book of life and not be listed with the righteous."* In Philippians 4:3 Paul refers to fellow believers as having their names written in the book of life. Several references to the book of life occur in Revelation: 3:5; 13:8; 17:8, here in chapter 20, and in 21:27. Daniel 12:1-3 summarizes the last day and includes a reference to the book:

> *At that time Michael, the great prince who protects your people, will arise. There will be a time of distress such as has not happened from the beginning of nations until then. But at that time your people--everyone whose name is found written in the book--will be delivered. Multitudes who sleep in the dust of the earth will awake: some to everlasting life, others to shame and everlasting contempt. Those who are wise will shine like the brightness of the heavens, and those who lead many to righteousness, like the stars for ever and ever.*

But what does Revelation 20:12-13 mean when it says people will be judged "according to what they had done"? Aren't we saved by grace, not works (Ephesians 2:8-9)? If anyone tries to use his or her own good deeds to claim worthiness for eternal life, they will be tragically mistaken. Our evil deeds are evil. Our good deeds are stained with sin. But the Bible tells us how even our deeds are cleansed from their sinful stain: *"For it is God who works in you to will and to act according to his good purpose"* (Philippians 2:13).   God is the One who works good works in us and through us. The only good works that can come out of our lives are works washed, cleansed, and given by the Holy Spirit. It is God who prepared works in advance for us to do (Ephesians 2:10). He gets all the credit and glory. But at the judgment, God gives us credit. He judges us as if we had no sin. He makes a ruling as if we were perfect. This is the result of being justified by grace through Jesus Christ.   Christ's perfect work is credited to us. Our deeds are made holy in God's sight. We live as forgiven people.

That's why the "sheep" didn't recognize their own service to Jesus in Matthew 25.   When told they had helped the hungry, thirsty, naked, stranger, sick and imprisoned, they replied, *"Lord, when did we see you hungry and feed you, or thirsty and give you something to drink? When did we see you a stranger and invite you in, or needing clothes and clothe you? When did we see you sick or in prison and go to visit you?" (vss.37-39)* These were works given by grace to God's redeemed people. It was Christ who was living in them (Galatians 2:20).

The "goats" never even saw Jesus in the needy and downtrodden. These unbelievers may have done very nice things, but nothing was done for Jesus. Nothing was done for His glory. None of their works were works of grace, cleansed and made pure by the Spirit of God. So the goats were judged by what they had done. Jesus was not in their deeds. It was all about them.

The lake of fire, therefore, became the place of torment for all those who rejected Jesus. That phrase, "the lake of fire," is mentioned three times in verses fourteen and fifteen. Whenever something is repeated in the Bible, the emphasis indicates that it is important. These verses underscore an important Biblical teaching: hell is real. Evil will be punished there. Justice will be done. Everything wrong will be made right. But be on guard! Stay the course of faith in Jesus Christ. The alternative is dreadful.

A SWIRL OF END-TIME ACTIVITY

Revelation chapter 20 is packed with news about what God is doing and what He intends to do. With rich symbolism and raw truth, the chapter tells the story of what is really happening behind the temporal curtain of life as we know it. More is happening than meets the eye—several things at once.

When my daughters were very young, I decided to construct a Barbie minivan for them. I took a cardboard box, cut windows in it, drew wheels and other details on it, made a dashboard and a front seat, and fashioned what I thought would be a memorable toy for my daughters. As I put the finishing touches on it, the razor knife I was using overshot its mark and went into my leg. This was not good. I clamped pressure on the wound, but I was helpless. After asking the girls to leave the room, my wife and I assessed the situation. She was too nervous to drive. I was unable to drive. We needed to call an ambulance. So, we called 911 and watched an amazing chain of events unfold.

Revelation

I was bleeding and immobilized. My wife was nervous. I was a little woozy. She was slightly panicked. But then the paramedics arrived. They sprang into action with their medical gear. I was loaded into the ambulance and a flurry of behind the scenes activity started to happen. While we drove to the hospital, the crew radioed all my information to the emergency room. When we arrived, I was brought immediately to a treatment room—no waiting, no forms, no delay. A doctor and staff members were ready to treat me. It was a beautiful thing—for being such an ugly and painful incident!

This is the message of Revelation 20. We see pain, temptation, death, and struggle in our lives. There is a lot of ugliness going on. What we don't see is the expertise of God, the preparation for our arrival, the victory of God's people and the reign of Christ behind the scenes. Something beautiful is going on even as pain and ugliness rage.

Before Christmas one year our family was reading through a daily devotional booklet from our church. The daily devotions were in the form of a story. A man named Bill was trying to share the news of Jesus with a co-worker named Chuck. The story had all kinds of ups and downs. There were disappointments and successes. Some days ended with a cliff-hanger. We didn't know what would take place.

One day, after we read the devotion, I commented, "I wonder what's going to happen to Chuck." Then I looked across the table at my daughter Abby. She had a knowing smile on her face. She said, "I know what's going to happen." I replied, "How do you know?" She answered, "I read the ending."

That was a smart thing to do. Knowing the ending helps ease the pressure, doesn't it? Revelation 20 is God's way of showing you the ending. When all looks lost in your life, when the battle seems like it will do you in, when you think God has abandoned you or isn't hearing you, you know the ending. And the ending is good. God wins. The devil and his troops lose. The Lord Jesus gives you the certain news that with Him, it's going to be okay. You will be okay.

Study Guide for Revelation Chapter 20

1. Read Revelation 20:1-6. List all the events taking place simultaneously during the 1000 years.

2. What have you heard and read about millennialism?

3. What clear information does the Bible give you about the coming of Christ?

4. What new dimension to life and death do the first and second deaths and resurrections give?

5. Read Revelation 20:7-15. What is the purpose of Satan's release from prison?

6. What characteristics of hell are communicated in these verses?

7. How does the judgment standard in these verses underscore the importance of Christ's work for you? Discuss the role of good works in a life of faith.

Revelation
Chapter Twenty-one

✝

Revelation chapter 21 is one of the most beautiful and comforting sections of Bible. Following the lake of fire destruction of the devil, death and Hades, a new heaven and new earth appear. For the Hebrew mind, a new heaven and new earth meant that everything would be brand new. The newness would be all-encompassing. God wasn't showing His people new and improved sky and land. He didn't redecorate the old earth so we could enjoy a pre-owned, but newly detailed, living quarters. God even declared what He was up to in verse five, *"I am making everything new!"* God is showing us a picture of heaven.

IT'S ALL NEW

Do you realize that heaven is one of the most dominant themes of the book of Revelation? If you think about it, it makes sense. The people suffering in the first century needed to hear that there was something more than this short and difficult life. God has eternal plans for His redeemed people, so Revelation is filled with heaven talk. In fact, did you notice that heaven was referenced in every message Jesus spoke to the churches in chapters 2 and 3? Heaven has also been mentioned in almost every chapter of Revelation. Visions of heaven happen in chapters 4, 5, 7, 11, 12, 14, 15, 19, 20, 21, and 22! As we arrive at the end of the book of Revelation—and may be a bit breathless and worn out, the temptation may be to breeze over the "easy" description of heaven in the final chapters. We wrestled with the meat of the vision. Why spend time deliberating about the heavenly home God is preparing? It's nice. It's golden and bright. Is there anything else we really need to know?

But God's dominant heavenly theme has a deep and important purpose. This vision ends not with a whimper, but with a bang! God truly saved the best for last. We need to take a close and careful look.

HEAVEN MEANS COMFORT

1And I saw a new heaven and a new earth, for the first heaven and the first earth went away, and there was no longer any sea. 2I saw the Holy City, the new Jerusalem, coming down out of heaven from God, prepared as a bride adorned for her husband. 3And I heard a loud voice from the throne saying, "Behold, the dwelling (tent) of God is with men, and he will dwell with them. These people will be his, and God himself will be with them and be their God. 4He will wipe every tear from their eyes. There will be no more death or mourning or crying or pain, for the earlier things have gone." 5The one sitting on the throne said, "Behold, I am making everything new!" Then he said, "Write this down, for these words are faithful and true."

Heaven is an amazing source of comfort. If you've experienced the death of a precious fellow believer, someone you love, you know what I mean. As you read this book, you may read it with a heavy heart. Your wife or your husband may be waiting for you in heaven. You may have a son or a daughter who reigns with Jesus, and you can't wait to be reunited. You may have a friend whom you look forward to being with again. What better comfort could there be than to know that the joyous reunion will certainly take place?

When my wife and I were dating we spent long stretches apart from each other. It would be months before we could see each other. I wish I could describe how wonderful it felt to see her again after we had been apart for so long. She was away on a trip a few years ago and it happened again when she returned—a mix of happiness, exhilaration, and tears, a new and wonderful reunion. Heaven brings that promise and comfort.

Revelation 21 is one of the greatest chapters of heavenly comfort in the Bible. The voice of God in verses three and four, and the assurance of verse five are precious gifts of hope:

> *"Now the dwelling of God is with men, and he will live with them. They will be his people, and God himself will be with them and be their God. He will wipe every tear from their eyes. There will be no more death or mourning or crying or pain, for the old order of things has passed away." He who was seated on the throne said, "I am making everything new!" Then he said, "Write this down, for these words are trustworthy and true."*

The Greek word for "dwelling" is "skeinei," or "tent." It's the same root word used in John 1:14: *"The Word became flesh and made his dwelling among us."* God comes to us with gracious rescue! The promises of no more tears along with the solid truth of new life from God hearken back to the beautiful description of heaven in Isaiah 25:7-9:

> *On this mountain he will destroy the shroud that enfolds all peoples, the sheet that covers all nations; he will swallow up death forever. The Sovereign LORD will wipe away the tears from all faces; he will remove the disgrace of his people from all the earth. The LORD has spoken. In that day they will say, "Surely this is our God; we trusted in him, and he saved us. This is the LORD, we trusted in him; let us rejoice and be glad in his salvation."*

Revelation 21 uses the future tense. These things haven't happened yet, but they will. As sure as Jesus gave His life on the cross and rose from the dead, this heavenly new creation is certain. The phrase "trustworthy and true" in verse five is the same Greek phrase used to describe Jesus in Revelation 19:11. This is all about the comfort of the Savior.

Your dear ones who trusted in Jesus are with Him. It's true! The blood of Christ brought them the gift of forgiveness and eternal life. Through Christ's work, having faith in Him, you will see them and join them again. Heaven means comfort.

HEAVEN MEANS CARE

6He said to me: "It is done. I am the Alpha and the Omega, the Beginning and the End. I give to the one who is thirsty from the spring of living water without cost. 7The one who overcomes will inherit all this, and I will be his God and he will be my son. 8But the cowardly, the unbelieving, the detestable, the murderers, the sexually immoral, the sorcerers, the idolaters and all liars--their place will be in the fiery lake of burning sulfur, which is the second death."

In addition to the comfort of a reunion with loved ones, heaven brings relief from suffering. Heaven means care from the Savior.

During one of my pastorates, I broke my arm during a church softball game. Christians play rough! Ever since that happened I've had painful arthritis in my wrist. Sometimes the pain is worse, sometimes it's better, but it is constant pain. During a mission trip to Africa, however, I had no pain at all. I don't know why, but for two weeks I had no pain. It was amazing! It was a welcome relief!

Heaven is an important blessing because it brings relief. It brings God's face to face care. When you're experiencing pain—the pain of loneliness, the pain of heartbreak, the pain of illness, the pain of conflict, the pain of addiction, or the pain of guilt, you need relief. If you have pain in your life, God declares, *"It is done. I am the Alpha and the Omega, the Beginning and the End. To him who is thirsty I will give to drink without cost from the spring of the water of life."*

The message of Heaven is important because God lets you know that your pain is temporary. There will be a final end to sin, suffering and pain. Verse eight reminds us what the second death is. The fiery lake of burning sulfur is mentioned again. God wants His care to prevail. Walking with Him is of utmost importance. Every lure of the world, no matter how attractive it seems, is empty, worthless, and destructive. God's will is that you receive His inheritance. His heart's desire is that you are cared for as His precious child.

HEAVEN MEANS COMPLETENESS

9One of the seven angels who had the seven bowls full of the seven last plagues came and said to me, "Come, I will show you the bride, the wife of the Lamb." 10And he carried me away in the Spirit to a mountain great and high, and showed me the Holy City, Jerusalem, coming down out of heaven from God, 11having the glory of God, her light was like a precious stone, a crystallized jasper stone. 12It had a great, high wall with twelve gates, and with twelve angels at the gates. On the gates were written the names of the twelve tribes of the sons of Israel. 13There were three gates on the east, three on the north, three on the south and three on the west. 14The wall of the city had twelve foundations, and on them were the twelve names of the twelve apostles of the Lamb. 15The one speaking with me had a measuring rod of gold to measure the city, her gates and her walls. 16The city was laid out like a square, as long as it was wide. He measured the city with the rod at 12,000 stadia, her length and width and *height are equal. **17**He measured her wall as 144 cubits thick, by man's measurement, which the angel was using. **18**The wall was made of jasper, and the city of pure gold, like pure glass. **19**The foundations of the city walls were adorned with every kind of precious stone. The first foundation was jasper, the second sapphire, the third chalcedony, the fourth emerald, **20**the fifth sardonyx, the sixth carnelian, the seventh chrysolite, the eighth beryl, the ninth topaz, the tenth chrysoprase, the eleventh jacinth, and the twelfth amethyst. **21**The twelve gates were twelve pearls, each and every one of the gates was from one pearl. The wide street of the city was of pure gold, like transparent glass.*

The beautiful description in these verses is not an architectural plan. Remember, this is a vision. This is a picture of the beauty of God's restored bride, the church. The beautiful precious stones recall the priestly garments and show that this place is truly of God. The numbers, once again, tell the story of God's action of salvation through the ages. The number 12, used over and over again, shows us the glory of God's church. The tribes of Israel and the names of the apostles show us that all of God's redeemed are part of this beautiful place. The majesty and wonder of heaven—including the massive dimensions—show us that we are in store for blessing beyond all we can ask for or imagine. Everything will be made right. We are truly loved by our gracious Savior. This is a place of total completeness.

A couple of years ago I met an 80-year-old woman who was a newlywed. She had never been married. But about a year earlier she met a man in his early eighties who was THE guy for her. They fell in love and, voila! Wedding bells. Who would have thunk it? They were on a new adventure.

God has an adventure in store for you. Heaven will be the perfect and complete place. It will be a place where relationships are perfect—more fulfilling and complete than any relationship you have now. It will be a place where your gifts and talents are used fully. It will be a place where each moment is exciting and compelling. If you are too busy to do the things you really want to do here on earth, if you are overwhelmed and can't keep up, if you have an unexplored talent that you would like to try out, or a list of things that is always undone, heaven will tie up all the loose ends. There will be no frustration. Heaven will make you complete. It will shape you into the person God created you to be. The resurrection of Jesus means that your life will not be stuck in incompleteness. By grace, you are on a journey of being completely fulfilled and thrilled with the new adventures God brings in eternity.

HEAVEN IS THE CLINCHER

22I did not see a temple in her, because the Lord God Almighty and the Lamb are her temple. 23The city does not need the sun or the moon to shine on her, for the glory of God gives her light, and her lamp is the Lamb. 24The nations will walk by her light, and the kings of the earth will bring their glory into her. 25On no day will her gates ever *be closed, for there will be no night there. **26**The glory and honor of the nations will be brought into her. **27**Nothing unclean will ever enter her, nor will anyone who does what is detestable and false, but only those whose names are written in the Lamb's book of life.*

Comfort, care, and completeness. Heaven puts it all together, doesn't it? But there's another reason heaven is important in your life. It is important because it's the CLINCHER, the clincher of God's immense and everlasting love for you. There is no need for a church, for any representation of God in heaven. The Lord God Almighty and the Lamb are present. Even the sun and moon are mere reflections of the true source of light—God Himself. Everything that appeared to be glorious in the world will be completely possessed by heaven. The truth will be seen. Everything will be right and good. There will be nothing impure. You can finally rest.

This is God's gift of love to His people. His plans are mind boggling. His presence changes everything. The suffering, death, and resurrection of Jesus earned us a future beyond all we could ever imagine. This message is of utmost importance to share with the world. There is a much better ending possible than the lake of fire. Heaven is ready and waiting.

The news of heaven is not just harps, clouds, and streets paved with gold. It is fuel for the soul, fuel for this journey of life. My pastor told me that The Lord's Supper is a taste of heaven. At first I didn't get it. But now I do. In Communion, Jesus boldly steps into your life and says to you, "Let's go. I've got plans for you. With me, you'll make it."

I'll never forget a quote about the presence of Jesus in communion by Frank Capra. He directed movies like "It's a Wonderful Life" and "Mr. Smith Goes to Washington." In his autobiography, Capra commented on Holy Communion:

> I sneaked into...church to kneel; ...hear the angels sing, and be lifted out of my shoes by the passion and resurrection of Christ...You walk back from Communion with the [bread] on your tongue—a nobody...Slowly the wonder of it fills you with joy— the dissolving [bread] in your mouth is the living Christ!...And out of its glory a word infuses your spirit: "Courage!" You have glimpsed the Eternal!...You leave filled with the urge to shout it to the whole world—"Courage! Courage!" (p. 130, Frank Capra, <u>The Name Above the Title</u>.)

That is what the first listeners to the book of Revelation needed. It's what we need too. We need a taste of heaven. We need it over and over again as we trudge through this challenging and broken world. The Lord's Supper brings us this blessing. So does Revelation chapter 21. We desperately need it because heaven makes all the difference in the world.

Chapter Twenty-one

Study Guide for Revelation Chapter 21

1. Read Revelation 21:1-5. What comfort do these verses give you?

2. Read Revelation 21:6-8. How have you experienced God's pain relief in your life?

3. From what pain do you need relief these days?

4. Read Revelation 21:9-21. What frustrates you most about life this side of heaven?

5. How might heaven specifically address those issues?

6. What thoughts and feelings do you have when you read about the beauty and vastness of heaven?

7. Read Revelation 21:22-27. Talk about how you can make practical use of the Bible's teaching of heaven as you face earthly challenges.

Revelation
Chapter Twenty-two

The angelic tour continues in Revelation chapter 22. It is the final chapter of this book of the Bible and your final stop as you travel through this vision. Like Picasso's Guernica on the cover of this book, you have examined the variety of images in the book of Revelation. You looked and listened, not to put together a schematic diagram of the end times, but to discover the important messages God had for His people—messages that He still communicates to us today as we await His return.

What have you seen in this beautiful mural of God's Word?

- God cares – He stepped in to speak personally

- God reigns – the Lamb, the Pantocrator, the throne

- Clarity about false teachers in the church

- Clarity about false gods outside the church

- Clarity about the devil behind evil and deception

- Clarity about persecution now, but eternal glory

- God's effort to bring about repentance

- God's desire for us to bring the prophetic Word

- God's plan to destroy death, the devil, and evil

- Jesus as one with the Father

- Jesus as the only Savior

- The living nature of God's Word

- We are not alone

Of course, there's much, much more. This meaningful, relevant, and important book of the Bible is the living Word, reaching deep into your heart and soul. It is a message that brings you refreshing truth and perspective. It is a Word from God that sustains and directs you. It brings you spiritual facts that impact temporal events. This is exactly what we need as we run the race and fight the good fight of faith.

Chapter 22 brings us back into the current moment, restored and ready to serve.

THERAPY

1And he showed me the river of the water of life, as bright as crystal, coming out of the throne of God and of the Lamb 2down the middle of the wide street of the city. On each side of the river stood the tree of life, making twelve crops of fruit, giving its fruit every month. And the leaves of the tree are for the healing of the nations. 3And nothing will any longer be under God's curse. The throne of God and of the Lamb will be in her, and his servants will serve him. 4They will see his face, and his name will be on their foreheads. 5There will be no more night. They will not need the light of a lamp or the light of the sun, for the Lord God shines upon them. And they will reign for ever and ever.

This final chapter brings us back to God's purpose in the Garden of Eden. The tree of life appears. The curse is gone because of Jesus' work. Now it is time to live. The leaves of the tree are for the healing of the nations. The Greek word for "healing" is the root of our word for "therapy." After the fall into sin, the long struggle, and the fulfillment of God's plan, the time for healing therapy had come. Heaven will be a place of restoration.

As we saw in chapter 7, heaven will also be a place of service. We will not be bored in heaven. No floating on clouds for hours on end! God will allow us to use the gifts He has given us. We will be engaged in stimulating and important service to God and His people.

These verses reinforce what we encountered in chapter 21. God wanted listeners to be completely assured of the victory and peace in store for them. Suffering, battered, and hope-drained people heard the life-giving news that they would reign!

SOON AND VERY SOON

6He said to me, "These words are faithful and true. The Lord, the God of the spirits of the prophets, sent his angel

to show his servants the things that must soon take place."
7"Behold, I am coming soon! Blessed is the one keeping the words of the prophecy in this book." 8I, John, am the one who heard and saw these things. And when I had heard and seen them, I fell down to worship at the feet of the angel who showed me these things. 9But he said to me, "Do not do it! I am your fellow servant and of your brothers the prophets and of all who keep the words of this book. Worship God!" 10And he said to me, "Do not seal up the words of the prophecy of this book, because the time is near. 11Let him who does wrong continue to do wrong; and the one impure still be impure; and the righteous one still be righteous; and let him who is holy continue to be holy." 12"Behold, I am coming soon! My reward is with me, to give each according to his deeds."

For the third time in three chapters the Greek phrase "trustworthy (faithful) and true" is used. As the vision comes to an end, God wants listeners to know that this is the truth—His genuine Word. Verse six references the prophets. This was a Scriptural message. This is God's Word. Jesus speaks and the Apostle John bears witness to His Savior.

Jesus tells Christians that He is coming soon. It is a message of urgency and encouragement. If anyone was tempted to worship other gods, verse nine brings clarity. Don't do it! Worship God! If anyone feels like worshipping the vision of Revelation or getting preoccupied with its miraculous nature and delivery, God says pointedly: don't do it! Worship God. Revelation brings us to God and the

Lamb. Its point is to deliver Jesus. If we get caught up in letting our imaginations run wild with messages that depart from the text and from the rest of the Bible, we're on the wrong track.

Verse ten reinforces the fact that this message has the clarity of Jesus Christ and is meant to be shared with all people. Verse eleven gives us the reality of who is listening. Some people are following Jesus. Others are rebelling against Him. For all who walk the earth this side of heaven, the urgency of the coming Christ is lifted up. The Gospel needs to be shared. Jesus repeats His cry of arrival in verse twelve. The call is urgent. Who will hear?

THE INVITATION

13"I am the Alpha and the Omega, the First and the Last, the Beginning and the End. 14Blessed are those who wash their robes, that they may have their authority to the tree of life and may go through the gates into the city. 15Outside are the dogs, the sorcerers, the sexually immoral, the murderers, the idolaters and everyone loving and doing falsehood. 16I, Jesus, have sent my angel to testify to you all these things for the churches. I am the Root and the Offspring of David, and the bright Morning Star." 17The Spirit and the bride say, "Come!" And let him who hears say, "Come!" Whoever is thirsty, let him come; and whoever wishes, let him receive living water as a free gift.

Verses twelve through sixteen are the words of Jesus. It is a stirring thing to have Jesus speak up during a time of dire suffering and need. Jesus' words assure us of His authority and His grace. They tell us of His justice and His eternal work. They give us certainty that the prophecies are true. He is the Root and the Offspring of David. They show us who to worship and follow. He is the bright Morning Star.

For every person slogging through hopelessness and heartache in this world, the whole church—the bride—and the Spirit call us to come. They call us to join in extending this invitation to others. We have seen the truth. We have been shown what is happening behind the scenes. We know the ending. It is time to join in a chorus of invitation instead of a chorus of groaning. It is time to join in a chorus of grace rather than a chorus of grumbling. It is time to invite people to receive the free gift of the water of life instead of believing we live in a parched land of suffering with a drought of God's presence.

The spiritual bond between those in heaven and those on earth is strong. Our voices are joined together by the Spirit of God. Jesus has stepped in. Life is different. This refreshing gift is for all people. We all cry out, "Come!"

MULTIPLICATION ONLY

18I testify to everyone who hears the words of the prophecy of this book: If anyone adds anything to them, God will add to him the plagues described in this book. 19And if anyone takes away from the words of this book of prophecy, God will take away from him his share in the tree of life and in the holy city, which are written in this book. 20The one testifying to these things says, "Yes, I am coming soon." Amen. Come, Lord Jesus. 21The grace of the Lord Jesus be with you all.

The book of Revelation was given as a sacred prophetic trust. The Apostle John was well aware that this vision could be twisted and misinterpreted. The Gospel of Jesus Christ was at stake. This vision, after all, is from Him and all about His work. There could be no tampering. No addition, no subtraction. The only "math" allowed would be multiplication—multiplication of the message of Jesus to others. Increase in comfort. Increase in grace. Increase in hope, for Jesus is coming soon.

THE END

I remember when I ran my first triathlon. I struggled more than I thought I would during the swim. I found out I didn't have very good gear once I got on the bike. Still wearing my wet swimsuit, and peddling an old road bike, I lost ground. Then came the run. My legs felt heavy and slow. I pushed through the course with plenty of pain. Finally, I came to the finish line. It's hard to describe the feeling. I was overjoyed. I felt refreshed. It was worth it. I had run long races before. I had biked long distances. But this race was somehow refreshing and fulfilling. The end was good. I let out a sigh of relief: "Ahhhh!"

The book of Revelation brought first-century believers, and has now brought you the reader, through a unique "race." This prophetic message urged God's people to be faithful. It revealed the real story behind evil's thin veneer of allure. It showed that Jesus and His heavenly armies are never idle—they are fighting for us. It let us know that our labor is not in vain. It allows us to let out a sigh of relief: "Ahhh!" The end is good.

Revelation is a very practical and relevant book of the Bible. It's exactly what we need as we wait for Christ's return. It contains mystery and depth that apply to every era in history and to every situation for ones living through history. It strips away falsehood and allows us to engage fully in life as ones very much aware of the raging spiritual battle. It gives us strong warnings and calls us to major course corrections of conduct in the church and in the world. It shows us why we are here and where we are headed.

This book of the Bible was not given to send you running away from the Scriptures or to fill you with unreasonable fear. It was given to shape you into a person of truth. This vision was given to fill listeners to overflowing with the living Word of God. Revelation moved life from hopelessness to promise, from helplessness to the power of God. This remarkable book of the Bible, Jesus' final Word, was given so that your life could be all about what Revelation 22:21 expresses so wonderfully: *"The grace of the Lord Jesus be with you all."*

May you live in and live out that grace until you see Jesus face to face.

Chapter Twenty-two

Study Guide for Revelation Chapter 22

1. Read Revelation 22:1-5. Verse 2 mentions the "nations." How does this final chapter articulate God's eager desire for the salvation of all?

2. The book of Revelation gives us comfort as individuals, but it was written to churches. In what ways do these verses direct and encourage local churches?

3. Read Revelation 22:6-12. Jesus took time to speak to John and the Church in the late first century. What does that tell you about Jesus' attention and care for you?

4. What was God's hope and purpose for the book of Revelation?

5. How is that being interfered with during our time in history?

6. Read Revelation 22:13-17. How does the book of Revelation motivate you to reach out with the Good News of Jesus?

7. Read Revelation 22:18-21. What major impressions, perspective changes, and lessons, did you come away with from these verses and from the entire book of Revelation?

Acknowledgements

It is my hope and prayer that this book helps people understand the practical blessing of the book of Revelation. The encouragement I've received to teach and write about Revelation has been very heartening. Writing this book also required a great deal of encouragement and support.

I would like to thank my wife for her loving and kind support for my writing. It is more precious than words can describe. I am deeply grateful to my daughter Hannah, as well. She is one of the best editors and proofreaders you'll ever find.

My colleagues in ministry are consecrated servants of the Lord with hearts dedicated to outreach. They are all-around great people. Their support for my teaching and writing is invaluable.

I owe a deep debt of thanks to all who have enthusiastically received my books, spread the news to their friends, studied my writings in small groups and Bible classes, and have given these tools a chance in God's great Kingdom work. Thank you for including me in your faith journey.

And, of course, to you who have taken time to read, to study, and to reach out with the saving news of Jesus: Thank you. You make this all worthwhile!

Michael W. Newman

About the Author

Michael Newman has been a pastor, teacher, author, and speaker for over 20 years. He has served churches in Texas, Minnesota, and in the Chicago area. His current ministry is all about expanding God's Kingdom by helping healthy churches plant new churches and ministries. He also continues to be active in writing, preaching, and teaching. Married to his wife Cindy since 1983, they have been blessed with two wonderful daughters. When not immersed in ministry opportunities, you might catch him hanging out with his family, running a few miles on the Texas roads, strumming a tune on the guitar, or enjoying a good book.

Check out these books written by Michael W. Newman:

SATAN'S LIES
Overcoming the Devil's Attempts to Stunt Your Spiritual Growth

STEPS FORWARD
The New Adventures of Ernest Thorpe

HARRISON TOWN
Discovering God's Grace in Bears, Prayers and County Fairs

If you'd like to purchase books, download free resources, find out where Michael Newman is speaking, or contact the author, go to **www.ABCPassages.com.**

Books are also available at Amazon.com

Made in the USA
Lexington, KY
16 April 2010